A Unified Theory
of Global
Development

A Unified Theory of Global Development

VAN B. WEIGEL

PRAEGER

New York
Westport, Connecticut
London

Library of Congress Cataloging-in-Publication Data

Weigel, Van B., 1954–
    A unified theory of global development / Van B. Weigel.
      p.　cm.
    Bibliography: p.
    Includes index.
    ISBN 0-275-93134-X (alk. paper)
    1. Basic needs.　2. Economic development.　I. Title.
HC79.B38W45　1989
338.9—dc19　　　88–25211

Library of Congress Catalog Card Number: 88–25211
ISBN: 0–275–93134–X

First published in 1989

Praeger Publishers, One Madison Avenue, New York, NY　10010
A division of Greenwood Press, Inc.

Printed in the United States of America

∞

The paper used in this book complies with the Permanent
Paper Standard issued by the National Information Standards
Organization (Z39.48-1984).

10　9　8　7　6　5　4　3　2　1

For my parents, Rev. Robert and
Mrs. Donna Weigel, and
my sister Miriam

Contents

Figures and Tables

FIGURES

TABLES

Abbreviations

ASEAN	Association of South East Asian Nations
ASNCP	Alternative Submarine National Command Posts
ASW	antisubmarine warfare
BN	basic needs
BNA	Basic Needs Approach
BNI	Basic Needs Imperative
BNM	Basic Needs Mandate
C^3I	command, control, communications, and intelligence
EEC	European Economic Community
ELF	extremely low frequency
ELL	equivalent length of life
ESS	evolutionarily stable strategy
FAO	Food and Agriculture Organization
GDP	gross domestic product
GNP	gross national product
ICBM	intercontinental ballistic missile
IGO	intergovernmental organization
IMF	International Monetary Fund
INGO	international nongovernmental organization
LDC	less developed country
MAD	mutual assured destruction
MDC	more developed country

NATO	North Atlantic Treaty Organization
NCA	National Command Authority
NEACP	National Emergency Airborne Command Post
NIEO	New International Economic Order
ODA	official development assistance
OECD	Organization for Economic Cooperation and Development
PGC	Principle of Generic Consistency
PQLI	Physical Quality of Life Index
SAC	Strategic Air Command
SIOP	Single Integrated Operations Plan
SLBM	submarine-launched ballistic missile
SLCSAT	submarine laser communications satellite
STOP	Strategic Triad Operational Phasing
TNC	transnational corporation

Preface

Perhaps there is no subject as awesome and troubling as the topic of global development. Not only do we lack a unified framework for understanding individual and national moral obligations in cross-cultural contexts, but also we experience an overwhelming sense of powerlessness in seeking global reforms, owing to the sheer complexity of the issues and their intimidating magnitude.

Typically the subject of development has been construed in fairly narrow terms. Of necessity, the topic has been compartmentalized into a variety of fields and subfields, such as economic development, rural development, urban development, international relations, human development, and social/cultural development. While such compartmentalization is certainly understandable, it has led to an unfortunate lack of perspective in comprehending and responding to the planetary problems facing humanity.

Of particular concern is the traditional association between development studies and the discipline of economics. Because the subject of development is often confined to *economic* development and assumed to be the private preserve of economists, our collective reflections on the topic are frequently constrained by the limited scope and conceptual weaknesses of economic methodologies. This is unfortunate. Clearly the debate over development must be expanded to include philosophers, theologians, biologists, anthropologists, political scientists, sociologists, and others as full partners in the dialogue.

I have set out in this book to map the rudiments of a unified theory of global development. Admittedly this task is so ambitious that many will deem it impossible, if not absurd. After all, how is it possible to formulate anything like a global theory of development in a world brimming with ideological and cultural diversity?

Prudence would have dictated a book of more modest proportions. Not a few readers will chide that I am trying to solve all of the world's problems at once. It is my conviction, though, that unless we begin to conceptualize planetary problems within a unified framework, we will lack both the insight and moral resolve to formulate an effective, long-term response to the immense challenges that lie ahead.

I have constructed the theory on what I call the ''open genetic program of human life.'' Building on a synthesis of three independent developments of the 1970s (which have received significant elaboration in the 1980s), I argue that it is possible to deduce and justify logically a universal development norm called the ''Basic Needs Mandate'' and a universal moral principle called the ''Basic Needs Imperative'' on the basis of the human evolutionary experience. I contend that these principles retain their credibility in both cross-cultural and transhistorical applications; and, when linked to a well-articulated theory of basic human needs, they provide us with a meaningful guide to public policy dilemmas in both domestic and international contexts.

Literature from a number of fields has been utilized in developing the theory, including economics, ethology, sociobiology, neurobiology, anthropology, sociology, game theory, political theory, moral philosophy, international relations, and international law. While I do not and cannot claim expertise in these divergent fields, I have tried my best to weave a synthesis that respects the integrity of the distinctive methodologies, vocabularies, and perspectives of these disciplines.

Common sense presumes that a project of this scope will necessarily have conceptual weaknesses and blind spots that await clarification by others more capable than myself. Additionally, by its very nature, the theory invites the participation of academics and policy makers in applying aspects of the theory to the real world. The applications that I outline in the latter half of the book are only a suggestive beginning in this regard.

I look forward to a day when a common paradigm, in a Kuhnian sense, is shared by philosophers, social scientists, and biologists alike, enabling the academic community to enjoy a measure of cooperation and specialization in the study of human behavior and development, without constantly having to reformulate and defend a set of first principles. Perhaps it is fantasy to think that such a common development paradigm is possible. If so, then attempts like this one will be rightly deemed as misguided expenditures of energy. But if there is even a remote chance that such common paradigms lie within the realm of the possible, then disciplinary fragmentation must no longer be sanctioned by gnostic appeals to specialized vocabularies and methodologies, and academics from across the disciplines should join in the fray to debate and clarify the structure and boundaries of such a common paradigm.

In a real sense, this book would not have been possible apart from the work and brilliance of three individuals: Paul Streeten, Edward Wilson, and Alan Gewirth (under whom I had the privilege of studying while at the University of Chicago). I am also indebted to Franklin Gamwell and Robin Lovin for their assistance in formulating many of the ideas contained herein during my dissertation work.

Moreover, I owe a great debt of gratitude to Timothy Penner, my research assistant and respected colleague, and to Elizabeth Morgan, who offered penetrating editorial assistance throughout the project. Additionally, special thanks are due to my dean, Jean Kim, who provided me with a substantial block of time for writing the manuscript; to Eleanor MacDonald, who assisted in preparing the figures and tables; to Ellen Hargreaves, who patiently endured countless interlibrary loan requests; and to Alberta Kirk, who expended great energy in typing and proofing the manuscript. Also I would be remiss not to recognize those of my friends and associates who provided much assistance and insight during the course of the project: Clayton Barnes, Jeffrey Baxter, Carmen Beals, Carolyn Beck, Patricia Boehne, John Dobson, Audrey Ferrante, William French, W. L. Gaines, Linwood Geiger, Peter Genco, Anne Gray, Gilbert Heebner, William Innes, Christina Jackson, Robert Kinscherff, Ronald Kirstein, Thomas McDaniel, Ann Montaney, Culbert Rutenber, Marty Saalbach, Sally Sedgwick, Earlene Smith, Augusta Tsie, David Wilcox, and Zheng Yile.

Finally, the nurture and inspiration of Linda Thomasson as well as the support and friendship of Victor and Valerie Dalosto and Ram Subramanian have meant more to me than words can convey. Moreover I am deeply appreciative of the love and unwavering support of my parents and my sister Miriam, to whom this book is dedicated.

A Unified Theory
of Global
Development

1

On the Brink of a
Copernican Revolution

1.1. THE CRISIS OF IMAGINATION

Imagination, insight, and daring have perhaps never been more pivotal for the human quest than in our day. Not since our ancestors stood on the wooded fringe of the African savanna, poised to explore an unfamiliar and threatening environment, have the welfare and survival of our species been so dependent upon the vicissitudes of human imagination. At a time when many members of our species enjoy unparalleled material wealth and prosperity, nearly 1 billion human beings (most of them children) live in conditions that we would not deem acceptable for animals. At a time when human technological genius has birthed an era of unprecedented discovery and invention, the power of the atom has cast a long shadow of doubt on the very survival of our species. At a time when humans have perfected extravagant means of dominating the environment, we run the risk of dominating ourselves through the proliferation of our own species, exceeding the marginally comfortable carrying capacity of earth by the end of the 21st century. In short, we are confronting the social and technological demands of the Industrial Revolution and the Nuclear Age with the genetic baggage of the Pleistocene.

The march of technological development has given the human race incredible opportunities for doing good and awesome potentialities for destruction. Tragically man's technological achievements have far outstripped his meager accomplishments in moral and social progress. Morally speaking, humanity is just ahead of the discovery of fire. Not only is the world's current repertoire of institutional machinery ill-equipped to respond decisively and creatively to the planetary problems facing the human community, but also our extant stock of moral, economic, and political ideas is deficient in many respects.

It is an unfortunate accident of history that we are so ill-prepared to comprehend, much less to respond to, the challenges of global development in the 21st century. Moral theory has only recently occupied itself with the formulation and defense of universal, substantive moral concepts, having emerged from a sterile preoccupation with formal linguistic analysis. Moreover, economic theory has failed thus far to comprehend adequately the human dimensions of resource allocation, production, and distribution, preferring instead to rely on arid methodological abstractions bearing on the nature of efficiency and the behavior of firms and markets. Finally, much of the theory of international relations (and international law) remains captive to an outmoded and indefensible notion of state sovereignty that reifies the nation-state and imbues it with attributes normally reserved for persons.

Obviously it will take far more than good theory for the human community to negotiate the dangerous shoals of the 21st century successfully. Good theory is no substitute for action. Yet it seems clear that a sustained and intelligent response to the problems of planetary development will necessarily require some theoretical foundation. An integrated response requires an integrated theory; a global response requires a global theory.

As a foundation for an integrated, planetary response to the critical problems of the 21st century and beyond, we need a unified theory of global development. In light of the youth of development studies in general (e.g., development economics received its disciplinary identity only after World War II) and the disciplinary fragmentation that has characterized much of the work in this field to date, there is a clear need for some type of unifying paradigm that maps present development realities and charts a course for the future. One would expect that, as with the quest for a unified field theory in physics, the pursuit of a unified theory of global development will open up new horizons of exploration and research, raising at least as many questions as it purports to answer.

What would be the defining characteristics of such a unified theory of global development? First, the theory would have to be multidisciplinary in content. Second, it must identify and justify a universal and categorical norm of development. Third, the theory would need to be consistent with available descriptive accounts of human capabilities and behaviors. Fourth, the theory should be sufficiently dynamic in structure in order to accommodate changes that may take place in the course of human cultural evolution. Fifth, the theory would need to provide some account as to how its foundational norm of development could be actualized in the real world.

This book represents an attempt to sketch a basic structure for such a unified theory of global development. It is only a beginning. I certainly do not presume to have constructed a fully articulated theory of development. The scope of the book and the tyranny of space necessarily preclude an extended discussion on the implications of the theory for public policy. Considerably more research and reflection remain to be done by representatives of numerous academic disciplines and subfields, particularly related to the strategic problems involved in applying the theory to the real world.

The theory of global development presented herein builds on a synthesis of three conceptual advances of the 1970s that have received considerable elaboration during the 1980s. I contend that it is possible to construct a universal development norm and a universal moral principle that find their ground and justification in what I call the "open genetic program of human life." The universal development norm, called the "Basic Needs Mandate" (BNM), holds that *all human beings have the right to meet their basic needs*. The universal moral principle, which I refer to as the "Basic Needs Imperative" (BNI), is simply a reformulation of the BNM, addressed to individuals as a moral imperative: *Act in accord with the basic needs of other human beings as well as yourself*. I have fashioned both of these principles after Alan Gewirth's (1978) "Principle of Generic Consistency." It is argued that these principles, when linked to a theory of basic human needs, provide an adequate conceptual foundation for a unified theory of global development.

There is little doubt in my mind that if the BNM and the BNI, or principles like them, became guiding norms for the global human community, historians of the 25th century would liken their impact on human affairs to the way that the invention of agriculture redefined human groupings some 10,000 years ago. For millenia hominids have relied upon strong family and tribal loyalties and a modicum of xenophobia for their evolutionary survival. It is only within this century—a mere speck in the sands of time—that humans are challenged with a paradigm shift of profound proportions: We must learn to see the stranger as brother or sister and the human species as the human family. It is likely that the future of our kind (as well as many of the earth's plant and animal species) depends upon this expanding movement of human identity from individual to family to tribe to nation to the global human community.

The motif of the expanding circle may well become one of the most powerful images of human culture.[1] If zoologist Richard Dawkins (1976, 1982) is correct in his assessment concerning the incredible impact of idea-replicators (which he calls "memes") in shaping the course of human cultural evolution, future generations may look upon the meme of the expanding circle as the watershed ideological mutation that opened the way for the flowering of our species across the planet.

1.2. THE CHALLENGE OF ABSOLUTE POVERTY

Approximately 1 billion people on planet Earth are trapped in the vortex of absolute poverty.[2] Absolute poverty is characterized by persistent undernutrition, illiteracy, unsafe drinking water, inadequate or nonexistent sewerage, parasitic disease, severely limited access to health care, and bleak prospects for productive employment. It is a form of poverty so acute that it is virtually nonexistent in North America, Europe, Japan, Australia, and the Soviet Union. Approximately three-fourths of the absolute poor live in Asia; almost two-thirds of this number reside in only four countries: India, Indonesia, Bangladesh, and Pakistan (World Bank, 1975a).

One in every three children born today faces the tragic reality of absolute poverty. These children can anticipate a future filled with deprivation. Their life expectancy at birth ranges from 35 to 45 years (compared to 73 years in the United States). Before they can be aware of the odds against their own survival, they face a 30% chance that they will never see their fifth birthday. Those unlucky enough to sustain severe calorie deficits in infancy and early childhood may suffer from permanent learning disabilities for the rest of their lives (Winick, 1976).

As these children progress through adolescence, they may be able to attend some school, but their educational career will be short-lived—probably only through the second grade. Their teachers are poorly trained, and their textbooks (if they have any) are of low quality. (In Mali, West Africa, 90% of the population is illiterate.)

The health problems faced by these children as they grow into adulthood are legion. The nearest medical facility is either miles away or beyond the economic means of the poor. Sickness is a way of life, and medicine is scarce. (In Ethiopia there is an average of one physician per 76,000 people.) The water is foul, and proper sanitation facilities simply do not exist. (In Indonesia only 12% of the population has access to a safe water source.)

Unfortunately the tragedy of absolute poverty is bound to get worse. By the year 2000, 92% of the world's population growth will take place in less developed countries (LDCs). Much of this new population growth will be absorbed in squalid slums and unplanned squatter settlements. Rapid, unplanned urbanization will swell Calcutta's population of 8.1 million in 1975 to 19.7 million by the year'2000. Jakarta's 5.6 million inhabitants in 1975 will increase to 16.9 million by the year 2000. Similar ominous projections apply to Mexico City, Greater Bombay, Greater Cairo, Manila, Karachi, Dehli, and Lagos (U.S. Council on Environmental Quality and the Department of State, 1980).

1.3.   THE TRAGEDY OF PUBLIC IGNORANCE

A major obstacle in the struggle against world poverty is the appalling degree of misinformation and public ignorance about it. For instance, polls conducted in 1979 by the U.S. Presidential Commission on World Hunger (1980) revealed that the American public seriously underestimates the magnitude of global undernutrition and consistently overestimates the amount of U.S. aid devoted to this problem. Moreover, the study found that many Americans have "very little understanding" of the meaning of the term "development assistance." The commission goes on to note that educating the public is an important precondition for a sustained national response; however, the resources of private relief and development agencies are spread so thin that "they can allocate little to educational efforts not connected with fund-raising."

To make matters worse, it has long been part of the conventional wisdom of many relief and development agencies that people more readily contribute money in response to emotional, short-term appeals for famine relief than to appeals based on long-term development efforts that will prevent future famine-related mortality. Consequently many well-intentioned agencies have unwittingly contributed to the misinformation surrounding global poverty by depicting a *chronic* problem as a series of intermittent famines that are remedied by private donations and emergency relief measures by nation-states. While such intermittent famines may receive a wave of press attention for a short period of time, once the most critical phases of the crisis have passed, the issue of global poverty soon recedes into the background of other international and domestic concerns. Therefore the public has been conditioned to think in terms of ad hoc, short-term, Band-Aid responses to a problem that requires nothing less than a consistent, long-term, informed commitment to global development. Ultimately development issues must be construed as matters of national responsibility and global justice, instead of individual charity. Furthermore, the public dialogue on development must not be limited to the industrialized countries, but must also extend to the publics of the developing countries as well.

1.4. THE POVERTY OF POSITIVISM

It is unfortunate that widespread public ignorance about global underdevelopment has coincided with the underdevelopment of two academic disciplines that hold great potential for making significant contributions toward the resolution of the problem: political science and economics. Historically these disciplines have been closely related (e.g., until the 20th century economics was known as ''political economy''). Traditionally both the economist and the political theorist have viewed the promotion of human well-being through the development of more just political and economic institutions as being a central, if not preeminent, aspect of their work. It is significant that the great economic thinkers were often good political and moral philosophers in their own right, such as Adam Smith and John Stuart Mill. Moreover, political theorists since Plato have been occupied with attempting to resolve the central normative question of political life: How do we assure the flourishing of the human individual while preserving the integrity of the social whole?

In the 20th century a marked shift took place in the way that professionals within both disciplines conceived of their work. Representatives from both fields became preeminently concerned with winning scientific credibility for their respective disciplines—an objective that was thought to be attainable by employing rigorous mathematical methodologies in the analysis of political and economic behavior. Unfortunately, though, the development of increasingly sophisticated quantitative techniques and specialized jargon was accompanied by a disturbing limitation of vision that tended to insulate both communities from socially relevant questions that could not be easily incorporated into their scientific paradigm of the real world (see Kuhn, 1970, p. 37). Their quest for scientific legitimacy was construed as a mandate to purge both disciplines from all considerations that required fundamental ethical commitments, instead of seeking scientific credibility by advancing the breadth and relevance of their methodologies. This bias can be traced directly to a philosophical movement known as logical positivism that originated in Vienna during the 1920s and 1930s.

Logical positivists aspired to extend the realm of science to all fields of knowledge by claiming that all forms of true knowledge must be capable of empirical verification (except logic and mathematics). Consequently all propositions that could not be empirically verified (e.g., ethical or metaphysical propositions) were deemed, *ipso facto*, meaningless and nonsensical. While the movement held great appeal until World War II, this extremely narrow understanding of human knowledge was soon rejected by the philosophical community and logical positivism died as a distinctive movement in philosophy.

Yet, curiously, the ethos of this defunct philosophical movement currently exercises considerable influence on both the behavioral movement in political science[3] and the neoclassical school in economics.[4] Both of these schools of thought have upheld the guiding presumption of the positivist movement: True science is concerned only with the systemic description of facts and must necessarily exclude from its purview all normative considerations, as these are not empirically verifiable.

In political science this narrow, positivist definition of knowledge has led to the triumph of method over theory. In the words of Sheldon Wolin (1969, p. 1071), professionals within the discipline have been encouraged to believe that when one has "offered statements rigorous, precise, and quantifiable, he is in the presence of truth," confusing the difference "between truth which is economical, replicable, and easily packaged, and truth which is not." Since the discipline has been reticent to enter the realm of normative discourse, political science has been condemned to the realm of "small conversations" (Ricci, 1984, pp. 296–304), and practitioners tend to "treat politics and morals in a way that avoids fundamental criticism as well as fundamental commitment" (Wolin, 1969, p. 1068).

For economics, the preoccupation with positivism has entailed a methodological disregard for historical, institutional, and cultural factors that shape economic realities, with the attendant conviction that it is possible to formulate economic theory without resorting to any ethical valuations (Deane, 1978, pp. 216–218). As a consequence, one often detects a disturbing gap between economic theory and economic realities (Helleiner, 1981) and "there is a perpetual game of hide and seek in economics" consisting of "hiding the norm in the concept" (Myrdal, 1953, p. 192).

The studied avoidance of value-oriented considerations in political science and economics is perhaps most evident in the history of welfare economics. Prior to the so-called ordinalist revolution of the 1930s, economists generally believed that it was possible to make interpersonal comparisons of welfare based on an observable concept of utility (Cooter and Rappoport, 1984). Generally speaking, they understood utility in relation to economic goods that promoted an individual's physical well-being in some sense. This empirical, cardinal notion of utility implied, in conjunction with the principle of diminishing marginal utility, that a relatively equal distribution of economic resources would be necessary if a society was to maximize its aggregate level of utility.

During the 1930s this need-oriented notion of utility came under severe attack, most notably by the British economist Lionel Robbins (1932). Robbins and others within the academic community were strongly influenced by positivist ideas that were being formulated in Vienna, and he dismissed the cardinal notion of utility on the basis that it was not empirically verifiable. Moreover, he defined utility strictly in terms of subjective preferences and correctly noted the impossibility of making interpersonal comparisons on this basis. Such an association of utility with subjective preferences diverged sharply from the notion of utility employed by economists from the material welfare school.[5] The former notion of cardinal utility was replaced by a subjective, ordinal notion of utility that held that one could identify whether an individual's relative level of utility had increased or decreased only by measuring additions or losses to an individual's economic goods. By narrowing the definition of utility to the ordinal concept, Robbins was able to forge a persuasive straw-man argument against the plausibility of interpersonal comparisons, but like his positivist counterparts in philosophy, scientific objectivity was confused with a decision to see narrowly.

Unfortunately the "ordinalist revolution" and the development of "the new welfare economics" have confined much of economic theory to the optimization of preferences, reducing the meaning of allocative efficiency to the vacuous affirmation that "more is better." Instead of defining allocative efficiency with reference to some need-oriented concept of welfare, most economists define efficient resource allocations in terms of Pareto optimality (i.e., you cannot make one person better off without making another person worse off). The implication of Pareto optimality is that the satisfaction of anyone's preferences takes priority over the satisfaction of everyone's basic needs.

Accordingly, most contemporary notions of allocative efficiency are composition-blind and fail to account for the tremendous social costs associated with the external diseconomies of consumption that accompany highly unequal distributions of real income and wealth (Di Quattro, 1980; Little, 1957, p. 64; Self, 1975). The fact that the Pareto criterion told us nothing about the actual composition of an economic distribution mattered little, because it told us all that we can know, according to the professed agnosticism of logical positivism. In short, the poverty of positivism obscured the tremendous social costs of material poverty, and the quest for scientific objectivity became a foil for the poverty of thought.

1.5. THREE SIGNIFICANT BREAKTHROUGHS

During the 1970s three notable developments opened up the possibility of constructing a unified theory of global development: (1) the formulation of the

Basic Needs Approach to economic development; (2) Alan Gewirth's unique synthesis of the naturalistic and Kantian traditions in ethical theory; and (3) the development of the multidisciplinary fields of sociobiology and neurobiology.

1.5.a.   The Basic Needs Approach

The first of these three developments was the formulation of the Basic Needs Approach (BNA) to economic development by the International Labor Office (1977), in conjunction with the World Employment Conference of 1976. The fundamental tenet of the BNA is that development policies must be formulated with primary attention given to the alleviation of absolute poverty, or, put positively, the satisfaction of basic human needs. Properly speaking, the BNA is not a unique development strategy per se, but instead promotes a distinctively ordered set of policy objectives.[6]

From its inception, the basic needs concept gained much popularity among the international community of development economists and planners. By the end of the 1970s it was apparent that "basic human needs" was becoming a catchword for a number of development programs and strategies, including the World Bank's "new style" projects (particularly after McNamara's Nairobi speech of 1973) (Burki and ul Haq, 1981; Hurni, 1980), the 1973 "New Directions" congressional mandate for the U.S. Agency for International Development (USAID, 1976, 1980), the "basic services approach" of UNICEF (Carter, 1977), human capital formation (Quibria, 1982), participatory strategies of development from below (J. Friedman, 1979; Healey, 1979; Nagamine, 1981; Wijemanne and Wanigasekera, 1980), social cost-benefit analysis (Harberger, 1984), and integrated rural development (Coombs, 1980).

Two distinctive features of the BNA distinguished it from alternate approaches to development: (1) it examined *actual* consumption from a disaggregated, microlevel perspective; and (2) it gave primary attention to the role of public goods in national development. Both features help explain the sudden popularity of the BNA.

First, the BNA emerged within an international environment that was becoming increasingly skeptical of development strategies that focused on aggregate levels of consumption to the exclusion of distributional considerations. For example, Brazil sustained high rates of growth in the 1960s, but the lower half of the population experienced less than a 1% increase in real income, whereas the incomes of the richer half grew by over 30% (Streeten and Burki, 1978). Even though the average daily per capita food consumption for Brazil in the early 1960s was 2,566 calories (116 calories over the Food and Agriculture Organization [FAO] requirements), an analysis of food consumption by income groups found that 44% of the population experienced calorie deficits (Reutlinger and Selowsky, 1976, pp. 10–11). The case of Brazil is by no means unique. The extent of inequality in LDCs, reflected in available data, is characteristically very high. Unweighted, aggregate indicators that reflect overall levels of consumption usually mask these extreme distributional inequalities. Hence proponents of the BNA emphasized the need for a disaggregated, microlevel analysis of actual consumption patterns at the household level (and often within the household).

Second, the BNA highlighted the importance of targeted public goods in national development. Public goods are forms of collective investment that generate external economies of consumption. Basic needs theorists emphasized that crucial social objectives (e.g., health care, education, safe water, and sanitation) could be met only by government investment in public goods that were targeted for poor populations. The rationale behind the public goods approach is that the poor do not have sufficient effective demand to stimulate the supply of these goods through the market system.

The genius of the BNA is that it did not insist upon any one type of production scheme to support basic needs policies. This created the widespread impression that the BNA spans the ideological spectrum, being at home with free-market, mixed, and socialist economies (Green, 1979). This does not mean, though, that supply-side considerations are unimportant for the BNA. It is clear that effective basic needs policies must be complemented with judicious macroeconomic and supply-management policies that create a favorable environment for basic needs programs in terms of capital formation, economic growth, inflation, balance of payments, and employment (Streeten et al., 1981, pp. 42–45, 58–60).

Finally, it is most significant that the BNA represented a truly normative approach to the task of global development. The BNA introduced a new vocabulary that made cross-country interpersonal comparisons of welfare comprehensible. In so doing, the BNA challenged the concept of Homo oeconomicus in neoclassical economic theory, which conceives a man as a utility-maximizing preference machine who possesses only insatiable wants (and, by implication, needs nothing) (Weigel, 1986). The fact that the BNA introduced several conceptual difficulties (e.g., are basic needs culture-specific or universal?) in relation to the received paradigm of neoclassical economic thought led to its premature dismissal by many economists, including those among the staff of the World Bank.[7] Yet these conceptual problems reflected far more about the inadequacy of our current stock of interpretative paradigms of reality than about the structural deficiencies of the BNA.

1.5.b. Gewirth's Moral Theory

It is significant that at a time when development economists and planners were exploring the basic needs (BN) concept and its implications for long-range strategic planning, moral philosophers were making striking progress in the field of distributive justice. With the publication of John Rawls' monumental work, *A Theory of Justice* in 1971, moral philosophy emerged from the seductive embrace of erudite yet arid formal linguistic analysis. Unfortunately the postwar preoccupation with the logic of the *language* of moral judgments (instead of logic of the judgments themselves) had the effect of trivializing ethical considerations in relation to the immensely important public policy issues of the modern age.

The significance of Rawls' theory of justice was that it liberated moral philosophy from small conversations and it became both fashionable and cogent to speak about substantive, universal moral concepts. Rawls' guiding aim was to work out a theory of justice that transcends the variability of intuitionist moral theories (which lack criteria for ordering first-order duties) and yet avoids the aggregative pitfalls of utilitarianism (which is pervaded by a fundamental confusion of the relation between the right and the good). He argues that a refurbished social contract theory, carried to "a higher order of abstraction," offers the best possibility of grounding a theory of justice. The novel aspect of Rawls' reformulation of the social contract is his initial situation—the original position—which is the analogue of the state of nature in traditional contract theory.

While Rawls' theory located the traditional concerns of moral and political philosophy within a powerful scheme of justification or metaethical framework, there are numerous problems associated with his theory, especially relating to the following considerations: (1) his strong lexical ordering between political freedom and economic resources; (2) the lack of criteria for constructing internal and external weighted orderings of primary goods; (3) difficulties related to the "maximin" decision rule of the original position and the "difference principle"; and (4) the lack of integration between Rawls' derivation and ordering of primary goods and the rest of his system. Fortuitously it was only seven years before Alan Gewirth of the University of Chicago presented an ethical theory that would largely resolve several of these and other problems.

With the publication of Alan Gewirth's *Reason and Morality* in 1978, two seemingly disparate ethical traditions were united in a trenchant synthesis: ethical naturalism and Kantianism. As with other thinkers in the naturalistic tradition, Gewirth is convinced that the very structure of human existence yields certain morally significant data that form the basis of substantive moral concepts. Yet, in a tack that diverges sharply from ethical naturalism, Gewirth claims that factual data about human life alone are not a sufficient basis for categorical moral concepts. Instead our immediate perceptions of the nature of reality must be mediated by rational reflection (the Kantian aspect of his theory) in order for our moral judgments to attain a categorical status. Hence Gewirth classifies his theory as a "modified naturalism" (p. 363).

While Gewirth's Kantianism is evidenced by his strong appreciation of logical consistency and his conviction that moral discourse must necessarily have a categorical status, he attempts to hurdle two notable weaknesses of the Kantian tradition: (1) its predilection to define categoricalness in terms of universal moral *conduct*; and (2) its attempt to derive substantive moral notions from the nature of rationality itself.

Gewirth begins by suggesting that the appropriate point of departure for moral reflection is action or, more precisely, human agency. He claims that action is to moral philosophy what empirical data are to the natural sciences. Gewirth defines action in a morally neutral way, and observes that all morally relevant action must have two invariant or "generic" features: (1) voluntariness (referring to an agent's ability to control their behavior); and (2) purposiveness or intentionality (referring to any goal or end of an agent). These generic features of action mean that freedom and well-being (or generic purposiveness) are necessary goods for any agent. The well-being of an agent is understood as "the general abilities and conditions required for attaining any of his purposes" (p. 61). By approaching the subject of morality from the standpoint of morally neutral action, Gewirth sets up the major challenge of his book: Does morally neutral action logically necessitate normative moral conclusions? He argues the affirmative by establishing what he calls the "normative structure of action." Gewirth maintains that his defense of the normative structure of action effectively bridges Hume's venerable gap between fact and value, is and ought.

Gewirth contends that the structure of all forms of human action logically requires all agents to accept the truth of a supreme moral principle, which he calls the Principle of Generic Consistency (PGC): "Act in accord with the generic rights of your recipients as well as yourself" (p. 135). Using a well-defined and limited concept of rationality (i.e., agents are able to trace logical entailments and value logical consistency), Gewirth constructs an impressive logical proof designed to establish the validity of the PGC through what he calls a "dialectically necessary method." This (Socratic) dialectical method attempts to translate an agent's informal, practical judgments into equivalent formal, linguistic expressions, enabling one to enter the agent's perspective without sacrificing the precision of a logical argument. Gewirth claims that his dialectically necessary method reveals that any agent who values logical consistency and has the capacity to trace logical entailments will affirm the validity of a universal, substantive, categorical moral principle, namely the PGC. The function of this supreme moral principle is to provide "the justification of all correct moral judgments and rules" (p. 7).

Gewirth's remarkably productive synthesis of the naturalistic and Kantian traditions represented a major advance in the theory of distributive justice in three respects. First, his "dialectically necessary method" provided a conceptual framework through which the naturalistic tradition in ethics could be rehabilitated after its abrupt demise at the hands of G. E. Moore's (1903) "Naturalistic Fallacy." Second, Gewirth's concept of generic goods (those goods necessary for human agency) offered a more precise theory of the good than had been found in the utilitarian tradition (which regards the good as a commensurable quality inherent in objects or subject-object relations) and the libertarian tradition (which narrowly defines the good in terms of the unhindered expression of individual preferences). Third, Gewirth's theory of the good was effectively integrated into his system of justification, such that his method of deriving and ordering generic goods was logically related to the founding postulates of his system, instead of proceeding from considerations external to his system (as in Rawls' theory of primary goods).

The specific structures and criticisms of Gewirth's theory will be discussed at length in Chapter 3, sections 3.2 and 3.3. I conclude that discussion with the claim that all of the problems facing Gewirth's system relate directly to his initial decision to select human agency as the only morally relevant common denominator of human life. I argue that his foundational postulate introduces needless abstraction to his conceptualization of generic goods, as well as biasing the determination of certain critical questions by giving agency priority over being. The upshot of this criticism is that I believe that Gewirth's rigorous method of justification can be effectively integrated with a more adequate theory of the good that lies somewhere between his instrumentalist theory of the good (which attempts to derive the invariant means of variable ends from the facts of human existence) and the facile assumption of the naturalistic tradition that the *specific* moral ends of human life can be readily distilled from the constitution of human life or the common threads running through human cultures.

How would one go about constructing a defensible, universal theory of the good that overcame the problems attending Gewirth's moral theory and provided the Basic Needs Approach with a firm conceptual foundation? The answer, I suggest, lies in formulating a well-articulated theory of basic needs, which is founded on what I call the "open genetic program of human life." This brings us to a third breakthrough of the 1970s: the development of sociobiology and neurobiology as distinct academic disciplines.

1.5.c.   Sociobiology and Neurobiology

During the same decade that saw economists become increasingly concerned with cross-country comparisons of human welfare and moral philosophers launching bold attempts to construct global theories of justice, two new fields of biology were carving out their disciplinary identities: sociobiology and neurobiology. Both disciplines were strongly multidisciplinary in character and sought to unearth the universal biological determinants of animal behavior, freely appropriating insights from the fields of ethology, behavioral ecology, evolutionary biology, comparative psychology, population biology, neurophysiology, genetics, and cellular and molecular biology.

Within the confines of this discussion, the appearance of these two disciplines was extremely significant in this respect: they provided a biological foundation for an elaborate, global conception of Homo sapiens that is grounded in the neurological structures and genetic history of the species. The immediate impact of this development was a robust rekindling of the nature/nurture debate, but its ultimate impact will be to refurbish the Aristotelian notion of the "proper function of man,"[8] rescuing that notion from the ruins of Aristotelian metaphysics and the demise of the natural law tradition, placing it on a firm biological foundation.

Unfortunately the importance of this development has been obscured somewhat by the polemical excesses and uneven generalizations that have been associated with the field of sociobiology. There has been a tendency within the discipline to impose an oversimplified genetic teleology upon complex animal behaviors, often involving the subtle imputation of rational motivations on lower species and the corresponding neglect of the behavioral significance of cognition for our species. This somewhat deterministic outlook on human behavior, combined with the casual acceptance of ethical naturalism, has drawn strong, and sometimes vociferous, criticism from many quarters (see Baldwin and Baldwin, 1981; Bateson, 1982; Breuer, 1981; Campbell, 1979; Etkin, 1981; Ruse, 1985; Sahlins, 1977, P. Singer, 1981; and Trigg, 1983). Moreover, the brand of disciplinary imperialism practiced by some sociobiologists has not helped matters. Nonetheless, the field has much to contribute toward a fuller understanding of the nature and significance of the human species.

Any attempt to map the distinctive dimensions of human behavior must begin with a fundamental distinction between genetic evolution and cultural evolution, according the latter a large role in recent hominid development (Dawkins, 1976; Dubos, 1968; Huxley, 1948; Medawar, 1959). Figure 1.1 presents a suggestive interpretation of the relative influence of these two evolutionary processes in shaping hominid behavior during the past 12 million years.[9] It should be emphasized that it is not the capacity for humans to *transmit* culture that is unique to the species (as cultural transfer occurs with many animals),[10] but instead it is the ability of humans to *accumulate* (and hence evolve) culture that has no known precedent within the animal kingdom (Tinbergen, 1973, p. 201). This phenomenon of cultural evolution was made possible by the development of a uniquely human kind of intelligence and sociality—the by-products of a long process of genetic evolution that began about 12 million years ago on the wooded fringe of the African savanna.

Certainly the most striking feature of the evolutionary history of hominids is the significant growth in the size of the human brain. Extant fossil evidence provides eloquent testimony of this remarkable development. Whereas the mean value of the cranial capacity of extant Australiopithecine skulls is only 464 cm^3 (compared to a range of 300 to 480 cm^3 for chimpanzees), extant Homo habilis skulls have a mean size of 657 cm^3 and Homo erectus averages 978 cm^3. The mean brain size of Homo sapiens is 1,300 cm^3 with a range of 1,000–2,000 cm^3 (Crook, 1980, pp. 128–129). Of particular significance was the visible expansion of the frontal lobes of the brain (which include the Broca's area, a primary language center)—a development that required the formation of the unusually high forehead that characterizes human craniums (Leakey and Lewin, 1977, pp. 192, 205).

While increased brain size has certainly made some contribution to the distinctively human brand of intelligence that has evolved over the past 3 million years or so, the enhanced circuitry that developed *within* the cerebral cortex was of far greater consequence. Recent studies in neurobiology have revealed that the significance of any cortical region is related to the internal organization of the synaptic circuits, as well as its connection to other regions of the brain, both cortical and subcortical. In both invertebrates and vertebrates the organization

**Figure 1.1
Schematic Interpretation of the Relative Impact of Genetic and Cultural
Evolution on the Human Evolutionary Experience**

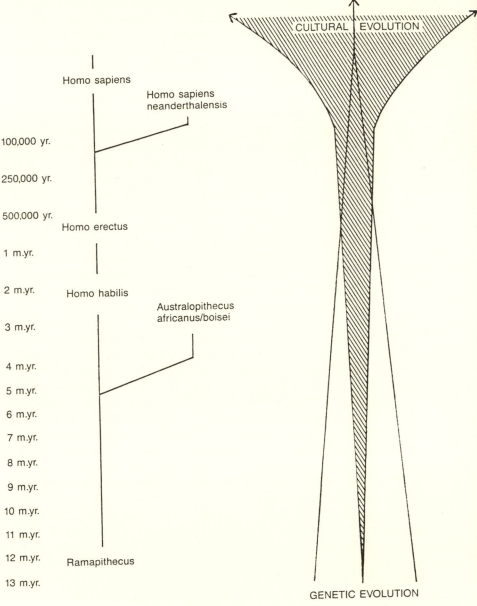

of these synaptic circuits typically follows a kind of polarized, two-dimensional, input-output format. With the extraordinary expansion of the neocortex in humans (the gray matter, which spans the surface of the brain and more than doubled in the brief transition from Homo habilis to Homo sapiens), a quantum leap in neurological circuitry took place (Lumsden and Wilson, 1983, p. 107). Because the human neocortex is a layered structure doubled back on itself, a truly three-dimensional array of circuits was possible, allowing neurons in every layer of the neocortex to be accessible to the inputs and outputs of contiguous layers. This exceptionally complex and versatile circuitry, combined with the fact that the neocortex is accessible to every major sensory input of the brain, permitted a vast number of ways in which information could be integrated, stored, and recombined. The enhanced flexibility that this multifaceted, three-dimensional circuitry allows is especially important in view of the fact that brain functions do not tend to be localized in certain regions (as was previously thought), but instead are organized in terms of distributed systems involving both hemispheres of the brain, as well as subcortical systems (Shepherd, 1983, pp. 575–577, 583–585).

It is not possible to identify with any precision the conditions that triggered the phenomenal growth of the human neocortex. The process could have been triggered by any one (or combination) of several distinctive innovations, including the use of tools and weapons, the advent of hunting and gathering, or the adoption of a socioreproductive system that involved food sharing and central place foraging (Isaac, 1983). Moreover, it should be emphasized that all of these more recent technical and social innovations were made possible by the physiological adaptations associated with bipedalism and the refinement of the prehensile hand.

With increased brain size and cortical sophistication, hominids developed markedly enhanced capabilities, in comparison to their primate counterparts, to conceive and execute courses of intelligent behavior (i.e., "behavior that is adaptively variable within the lifetime of the individual") (Stenhouse, 1974, p. 31). This enhanced capacity to behave intelligently reflected the maturation of four primary factors that contribute to the occurrence of intelligent behavior: (1) the P factor—an ability to pause before automatically responding to a situation; (2) the C factor—a memory store for the long-term storage of information; (3) the A factor—the capacity to abstract, to generalize, to compare and contrast events; and (4) the D factor—the sensorimotor capability to execute a patterned response (pp. 74–128). Sapientization or the maturation of this four-factored cognitive organization permitted the development of two notable hominid capacities that formed the basis of a distinctive brand of human sociality: (1) the capacity of self-representation; and (2) the remarkable facility of humans to engage in symbolic communication.

The ability to represent oneself to oneself as a self is a key feature of human cognitive organization that has enabled hominids to perceive themselves as individual agents and to empathize with conspecifics (Crook, 1980, p. 243). While this capacity is not uniquely human, as self-awareness has been evidenced among chimpanzees and orangutans (Gallop, 1983), the self-other dichotomy is a pivotal construct of human cultural evolution (perhaps the foundational "binary opposition") and probably has a basis in actual neurological structures (Laughlin and d'Aquili, 1974, p. 115).

Moreover, the remarkable facility of humans to engage regularly in symbolic communication (which is predicated upon the development of a long-term memory store) has enabled humans to accumulate, modify, and transmit culture. While some fascinating experiments with chimpanzees and gorillas have demonstrated their capability to communicate with symbols (Gardner and Gardner, 1969; Patterson, 1978; Premack and Premack, 1972), the human child "instinctively" acquires language and almost immediately outdistances the linguistic competence of the mature ape (Lumsden and Wilson, 1983, p. 107; Meulders, 1983, pp. 604–605). Moreover the presence of an innate or "deep structure" human grammar (Chomsky, 1968, 1976) is probably linked to specific neurological structures (e.g., the Broca's area and the Wernicke's area) (Crook, 1980, pp. 138–139; Marshall, 1980). Additionally the anatomical capacity to vocalize a wide variety of phonemes is uniquely human (E. O. Wilson, 1975, p. 556), though evidence suggests that the extensive use of vocalization was a rather late arrival in the communication repertoire of hominids (Kimura, 1979).

Of course, humans had to pay a price for the remarkable intellectual capacities that developed during their evolutionary journey through time. With the evolution of bipedalism, anatomical difficulties developed in the birthing process, which placed obvious restrictions on the size of the human cranium, making it necessary for the hominid baby to be born in a relatively underdeveloped state. As a result, approximately two-thirds of the growth of the human brain occurs after birth, and humans require parental attention for basic survival for a period of six to eight years (compared to about three years for chimpanzees) (Leakey and Lewin, 1977, pp. 149–150).

Consequently, considerable effort must be expended in child-rearing by human parents. Given the division of labor characteristic of hunting and gathering societies, this responsibility has fallen to the mother (Crook, 1980, pp. 104, 117). In view of the mother's substantial investment in raising her children and the affirming responsiveness of the human infant (e.g., smiling behavior appears to be genetically programmed), an extremely strong bond has evolved between the mother and her child (Lumsden and Wilson, 1981, pp. 79–82). In most instances the father has participated in child-rearing by defending his offspring.

Clearly the evolution of human sexuality has also played a critical role in the development of human sociality. With the nearly total suppression of estrus, the hairlessness of the human body[11] (which enhanced the sensitivity of the skin), and the development of sensitive erogenous zones, the stability of the family unit was enhanced by the development of long-term sexual bonds (Crook, 1980, pp. 104–104). Moreover, the potentially destructive aspects of this increased sexual activity for the family unit have been countered by the development of strong, near-universal taboos prohibiting incest (Lumsden and Wilson, 1981, pp. 147ff.)

Many of the traits that have been associated with human sociality proceeded from a revolutionary new cultural development known as the hunting and gathering way of life. The basic structure of this new form of social organization emerged perhaps as early as 5 million years ago, but the phenomenon of large-scale, big-game hunting (and the high level of social cooperation/communication it required) was a far more recent phenomenon, developing within the past 2 million years (Leakey and Lewin, 1977, p. 148). The hunting and gathering way of life was typified by central-place food sharing, a division of labor between males and females, extensive geographic mobility, the increased use of tools, and a high degree of intragroup coordination (Crook, 1980, pp. 127–134). Obviously the discovery of fire and the innovation of cooking food (which certainly was widely practiced 500,000 years ago, but may be as ancient as 2.5 million years ago) markedly enhanced the sociality of hominids by extending the day and providing a central place for social interaction (Leakey and Lewin, 1977, p. 131).

In short, the distinctive features of human intelligence and human sociality were brought about by the gene mutations and selection pressures associated with increased brain size and cortical sophistication, as well as various anatomical adaptations, including the underdeveloped birth and prolonged maturation of the human child, the near total suppression of estrus, and the capacity to vocalize a diverse repertoire of phonemes. These evolutionary developments, in conjunction with the advent of the hunting and gathering way of life, enabled humans to generate distinctively social forms of culture—characterized by the extensive display of symbolic communication, altruism, empathy, reciprocity, long-term contractual relationships, and social cooperation (Lumsden and Wilson, 1983, pp. 35–36).

Therefore the unique phenomenon of human cultural evolution has been made possible by two pivotal evolutionary adaptations—intelligence and sociality—which themselves were products of the selection process. As such, natural selection followed certain evolutionary pathways that evolved the nexus of adaptations we conveniently subsume under the headings of intelligence and sociality. In essence, these adaptations constitute what Ernst Mayr (1970, pp. 402–404; 1976, pp. 22–25, 694–701; 1988, pp. 48–51) has called an "open program," enabling humans to gather information not contained in the DNA and to store, recombine, and transmit that data through human cultural evolution. The very existence of an open genetic program suggests, in the words of Konrad Lorenz (1981, p. 258), that the organism is in a "state of adaptedness," in spite of various changes associated with the instability of its environment. Hence the human capabilities of intelligence and sociality were phylogenetically written into the nature of our species existence, exponentially increasing our adaptive capabilities and enabling humans to populate nearly every latitudinal zone of the earth's surface, as well as to live outside the earth's atmosphere and beneath its oceans.

It is readily apparent that the concept of an open genetic program provides us with an exceptionally strong standpoint from which to evaluate developments in human cultural evolution. The species capabilities of intelligence and sociality have offered humans a finite yet extremely broad array of cultural forms. What is termed social progress, cultural advancement, or human development essentially represents developments in cultural evolution that have increasingly promoted and refined the human species capabilities of intelligence and sociality in relation to previous cultural forms. In short, we may now have a biological basis for Aristotle's concept of the ''proper function of man,'' founded not on the basis of metaphysical teleology but upon the open genetic program of human life.

In summary, the aforementioned independent developments in biology, moral theory, and economic theory have given us a new way to think about the distinctive structure of human existence (via neurobiology and sociobiology), to utilize this scientific account of human life as the basis for a well-integrated, global theory of distributive justice (via Gewirth's moral theory), and to work out the real-world implications of this for international public policy, as well as for contemporary economic and political theory (via the Basic Needs Approach).

1.6. A MAGNA CHARTA FOR THE 21ST CENTURY?

The past three centuries have been marked by remarkable signposts of social progress. The notion of individual human rights was born in the 18th century, and the 19th century saw the abolition of institutionalized slavery. During the past two centuries we have witnessed the proliferation of constitutional democracies and democratic ideologies. Moreover, the appearance of international governmental organizations (IGOs), whose mandates transcend simple security alliances, is one of the singular accomplishments of the 20th century. Since the mid–20th century we have witnessed the repudiation of colonialism and racism, the inclusion of the individual within the sphere of international law (e.g., the Nuremberg trials, the 1948 U.N. Convention on Genocide, the 1949 Geneva Conventions on Prisoners of War), and the development of international public opinion as a restraint upon the actions of sovereign states.

In spite of these extraordinary achievements, we are still in a Kuhnian ''preparadigm period'' with respect to our conceptualization of universal moral concepts, particularly as this concerns the relation between political and economic human rights (see Kuhn, 1970, pp. 160–164). As a consequence, the slow but significant progress in our understanding of distributive justice is obscured by the prevalence of competing versions of moral obligation, which create the impression that moral theory is unable to transcend the particular standpoints of individuals or cultures. Yet one might expect that one day, in the not too distant future, moral theory will emerge from its pre-paradigm stage, as the natural sciences did only a few generations ago. Just as common scientific paradigms freed natural scientists to achieve a division of labor, instead of having to return constantly to scrutinize their first principles, a common moral paradigm may one day permit ethicists, social scientists, and biologists to articulate a theory of distributive justice with a precision thought heretofore impossible to attain.

Could it be that future generations will view the BNA, or something like it, as a kind of Magna Charta for an emergent concept of human rights that fully integrates fundamental political rights with basic economic rights? Could it be that observers in the 21st century will view the global maldistribution of resources with the same disdain that we presently hold for the institution of slavery?

There is no reason why mothers must forever sob over the corpses of their malnourished children. There is no reason why preventable diseases must continue to ravage human communities. There is no reason why children must grow up imprisoned in ignorance. There is no reason why people must be cheated out of 30 to 40 years of life by poverty's angel of death. Indeed the world is waiting for another Copernican Revolution.

NOTES

1. For an interesting discussion of this idea in the context of the sociobiology literature, see Peter Singer (1981).

2. The absolute poverty line is the World Bank's nutritionally defined poverty line—the per capita income needed to purchase sufficient calorie intake for a subsistent diet.

3. See Nelson (1978); Ricci (1984, pp. 144–149, 238–242, 296–304); Spragens (1973, pp. 4, 137–139, 165–168); and Wolin (1969).

4. See Balogh (1982); Deane (1978, pp. 109–111, 143–149, 216–218); Hirsh (1976, pp. 137–151); Katouzian (1980, pp. 45ff.); Neill (1978); Sen (1977); and Thurow (1984).

5. It should be noted, though, that some economists prior to Robbins understood utility in a more subjective sense, such as Stanley Jevons (1911).

6. Throughout the discussion I make a distinction between the terms "strategy" and "objective." BN objectives or policies can be achieved by a number of development strategies (e.g., autarkic development, import substitution, export promotion, agricultural development, etc.); hence there is no one particular BN strategy (see Leipziger, 1981b; Stewart, 1985, p. 2).

7. After Robert McNamara resigned as president of the World Bank in 1981, there was a widespread perception throughout the bank that the BNA was "dead." Many on the staff, including the bank's new president, felt that it was time to get back to business as usual (i.e., focusing on the infrastructure projects which the bank has traditionally pursued instead of basic needs projects). This rapid reorientation of the bank's focus after the McNamara presidency must be understood in the context of two factors operative in the bank's institutional structure: (1) the tendency for the projects staff to be less willing to adopt innovations than the programs staff; and (2) the ideological division between neoclassical and structuralist schools of economics within the bank (i.e., Chicago versus Sussex). Support for the BNA was primarily centered among those of a structuralist bent in the program divisions of the bank. While it is true that some reorientation in the bank's

policy actually took place during the McNamara years, it would be unrealistic to assume that the poverty-oriented new style approach was embraced widely throughout the bank. (See Ascher, 1983.)

8. See Aristotle, *Nichomachean Ethics*, Bk. 1, cp. 7.

9. The time line is adapted from Leakey and Lewin (1977, pp. 84–85).

10. For some interesting examples of cultural transfer among animals, see E. O. Wilson (1975, pp. 168–172).

11. The loss of body hair among humans was probably related to the development of an extraordinarily efficient cooling system in the form of more than 5 million pores for their sweat glands. See Leakey and Lewin (1977, p. 137).

2
Toward a Theory of Basic Human Needs

2.1. THE CENTRALITY OF A THEORY OF THE GOOD

Since William Galston's (1980) incisive analysis of the importance of a theory of the good for any theory of justice, there can be little doubt that the definition, justification, and operationalization of a universal theory of the good is one of the central issues facing contemporary moral and political philosophy. No cogent theory of justice can escape the task of defining and justifying a theory of the good. Moreover, no theory of justice can have strong relevance for public policy decisions unless it is able to operationalize its particular theory of the good by the construction or appropriation of relevant and measurable indexes.

One of the major weaknesses evidenced throughout the history of moral and political philosophy has been that theories of the human good have consisted of (1) an expansive account of the *specific* ends of human life (distilled from claims about human nature or commonalities among human cultures), which is largely coterminous with a set of moral directives (as in the natural law tradition); (2) an ill-defined, commensurable quality thought to be inherent in objects or subject-object relations (as in the utilitarian tradition); or (3) an assumed and largely undefended aspect of a comprehensive theoretical structure (as in the libertarian tradition). Because of the notable lack of precision in definition and justification of a theory of the human good, there has been a great deal of distortion in the formulation and justification of moral rules.

In this chapter I wish to outline a theory of the good based on the three species universals that emerged from our discussion of sociobiology and neurobiology in Chapter 1, section 1.5.c. (i.e., biological existence, human intelligence, and human sociality). In essence, the task of charting a universal, operationalized theory of the human good (based on the open genetic program of human life) represents the functional equivalent of attempting to construct a universal theory of BN. Once this conceptual framework is established, we will be in a position to examine the derivation and justification of the Basic Needs Mandate and the Basic Needs Imperative in Chapter 3.

2.2. DIFFICULTIES WITH EXISTING NEED HIERARCHIES

There have been several recent attempts to establish a cross-cultural classification of human needs and, in some cases, to identify a hierarchy among these needs (Braybrooke, 1987; Galston, 1980; Gewirth, 1978; Goulet, 1978; Maslow, 1970; McHale and McHale, 1978; Rawls, 1971; Shue, 1980). Without describing these frameworks and their respective strengths and weaknesses, it will suffice to note a few difficulties that often surface in attempts to classify human need.

First, there has been a tendency to confuse needs with preferences, thereby creating an overly expansive range of human needs. Clearly all human needs are a subset of the universal set of human wants (such that every human need could be properly labeled a human want); however not all human wants are human needs. Unfortunately the linguistic convention of distinguishing between real needs and felt needs has contributed to this confusion, as felt needs are typically better categorized as strong human wants.

Second, the hierarchical distinction between material and nonmaterial needs is often overdrawn, the effect being that the importance of nonmaterial goods is underrated at low levels of need satisfaction and overrated at higher levels of development, a criticism especially apropos for Maslow's famous typology (Czudnowski, 1982; Leiss, 1976, pp. 56–58).

Third, nearly all of the proposed need hierarchies suffer from too much generality. While all hierarchies rank-order particular *classes* of human needs, most do not set forth precise principles for intraclass rankings, where most of the significant policy issues emerge.

Fourth, many of the proposed need hierarchies treat security as a threshold concept and assign it a high priority relative to other human needs and preferences. The problem with this is that the perception of security (i.e., low levels of insecurity) is functionally related to several complex variables: (1) *perceived* past instabilities in need-satisfaction, (2) *perceived* prospective instabilities in need-satisfaction, (3) an individual's propensity to accept risk, and (4) an individual's ideological resources (e.g., religious beliefs). Clearly all of these factors are extremely subjective, giving the concept limited applicability in a theory of universal human needs. Moreover, any attempt to define a security threshold in cross-cultural contexts would have to (1) identify a universally valid propensity for humans to accept risk and (2) determine universally valid, age-specific, threshold probabilities that indicate acceptable degrees of failure in the continuation of individual longevity (clearly no earthly society can promise its citizens immortality, perfect health, complete protection from accidents, etc.). Consequently it is inadvisable to regard security as a threshold concept in any universal BN hierarchy.

2.3. A FORMAL DEFINITION OF NEED

A major factor that contributes to the difficulty of defining a theory of basic human needs is the semantic ambiguities surrounding the use of the term "need." Unfortunately the concept of need is often confused with the notion of "want." However, need-statements, unlike all uses of the term "want," require some kind of implicit justification. For example, the statement—"I want a new Mercedes"—is intelligible in its own right, that is, if one is aware that a Mercedes is a desirable automobile. However the statement—"I need a new Mercedes"—requires some further explanation for it to be comprehensible (e.g., "in order to project a successful image to my business clients"). Therefore, as Brian Barry (1965, pp. 47–49) has emphasized, all need-claims are derivative, being correctly interpreted as instrumental means to some end, whether implicit or explicit.[1]

Given the fact that need-claims attempt to relate specific, variant means to attain certain invariant ends (deriving their persuasive force from the latter), it is possible to define the concept of need formally in the following manner:

I need X if and only if X(1) is a *weak or strong condition*(2) for *acquiring, keeping or actualizing*(3) Y(4), which I am *voluntarily disposed or required*(5) to acquire, keep or actualize (where Y is a commodity, a biopsychosocial attribute or a moral/religious/social ideal).

On the basis of this formal definition, it is apparent that the concept of need is a construct of five components: (1) a first-order good (X), (2) a probabilistic judgment, (3) a mode of possession, (4) a second-order good (Y), and (5) either a pro-attitude toward the possession of Y (e.g., "I need a loan in order to finance my education") or the perception that the possession of Y is a basic requirement, irrespective of whether or not a pro-attitude toward Y exists (e.g., "I need oxygen in order to breathe"). Hence the persuasive force of any need-claim will directly relate to two factors: (1) the goodness, urgency, or desirability of the particular second-order good (Y) in question; and (2) the probable strength of a particular means (X) for attaining the desired end (Y).

The significance of this formal analysis is that it demonstrates that any need-claim presupposes (implicitly or explicitly) some type of good. Hence any concept of objective human need must lay claim to some theory of the good that can be justified as a *universal* theory of the good. Without such a universal theory of the good, the basic needs concept will never be able to transcend the labyrinth of individual relativity (i.e., a subjective concept of human need) or cultural relativity (i.e., a socially constructed concept of human need).

2.4. ELABORATING THE BASIC NEEDS CONCEPT

A logical springboard for reflection in clarifying the basic needs concept would be to examine the meaning of basic as a limiting condition for a universal set of human needs. At least three different interpretations of the term are possible.

First, the set of human needs labeled "basic needs" may be basic because they are *deficiency* needs. In this case needs are identified in terms of the pathologies associated with the deprivation of particular goods. The problem with this approach to the derivation of needs is that it presumes a normative concept of health that either remains undefined or undefended. Obviously the task of defining and justifying such a cross-cultural norm of human health (beyond simply physiological traits) would be extremely difficult. Moreover, it is easy to see how some norms of health would generate an overly expansive range of BN (e.g., Maslow regards belongingness/love needs and esteem needs as deficiency needs).

Second, the term "basic" could be used as a synonym for "urgent." Urgent needs are immediate needs that dominate the attention of a human subject and receive the highest priority at that moment. Hence the criterion of urgency would identify and rank-order a set of BN according to perceived priorities within a discrete time frame. An obvious difficulty with this criterion is that it is highly subjective (totally unsuited for any attempt to define a universal set of BN) and is strongly weighted in favor of a short-term time preference. For example, a person who becomes acutely aware of some relative deprivation in social status (with an attendant loss of self-respect), would probably view status-enhancing forms of luxury consumption as being more urgent than gaining access to some basic goods (e.g., health care), even though the latter is in his or her long-term interests.

Third, the notion of BN could be interpreted as being basic in the sense of *essential* needs. The criterion of essentiality presumes that there is a logical, hierarchical structure of need satisfaction that conforms to a universal, descriptive account of human behavior. Hence what is essential to human life is a basic good because without it one's capacity to function as a human being would be severely diminished.

It is readily apparent that this third interpretation of the term "basic" in the phrase "basic needs" is the preferred alternative. By treating "basic human needs" as a synonym for "essential human needs" we are able to surmount the serious conceptual difficulties attending the first two options. Furthermore, a cursory examination of the nature of human life would suggest that there exists something like a hierarchy of human needs, at some level of generality, such that some needs are perceived as more essential than others (e.g., food and water are more necessary for human existence than access to education). If we opt for this third interpretation of basic needs, then we are faced with a key question: What is essential to human life?

In the discussion on sociobiology and neurobiology in Chapter 1, section 1.5.c., it was found that the unique species capabilities of human intelligence and sociality have given humans an exceptional degree of environmental adaptability and developmental plasticity (via cultural evolution). These species capabilities, conveniently subsumed under the headings of intelligence and sociality, emerged from a constellation of adaptations that took place during the course of natural selection. In essence, these adaptations constituted a kind of "open program," phylogenetically written into the biological structure of human existence, which enabled humans to gather information not contained in the genes and to store, recombine, and transmit that data through human cultural evolution. Of course, neither intelligence (Homo intelligens) nor sociality (Homo civilis) can exist in a biological vacuum. Like all animal and plant species, humans have certain biological requirements that must be satisfied in order for life to be sustained (Homo corporeus). (See Pugh [1977] for a similar tripartite analysis.)

Do these three dimensions of human life (biological existence, human intelligence, and human sociality) describe the essence of what it means to be human? What about the human capacity to love and other noteworthy human goods such as self-respect, hope, spirituality, and security?

Clearly all of these are important aspects of human life. In a real and meaningful sense, life would cease to be authentically human if it were not possible to achieve and enjoy a modicum of love, hope, self-respect, and spirituality/ transcendence. Furthermore it would be difficult to craft a meaningful life plan without some degree of security.

I would argue, though, that these other human goods are either derivative ideals or constructs of the three core dimensions of the open genetic program of human life (i.e., biological existence, intelligence, and sociality). Specifically, love is an ideal of sociality; self-respect is an ideal of intelligence (influenced but not determined by social status); hope and spirituality are constructs of intelligence and sociality; and security is a construct of all three categories. The intent here is not to diminish the worth of these prominent human goods by reducing them to their least common denominator. Instead the intent is to map the relationship between these important human goods in relation to the three core attributes of human life, emphasizing the logical priority of the latter. Figure 2.1 summarizes the relationship between these derivative goods and their parent capabilities.

Expressions of love (including friendship and conjugal/parental love) represent sociality in its highest and most noble form. The ability of humans to devote themselves to others, demonstrating protracted care and loyal concern for another's well-being, often at great costs to themselves, is a truly remarkable achievement.

Although one can only speculate as to the origin of love emotions, it is likely that they first surfaced in the relationship between a mother and her children. Given the social structure of the hunting and gathering way of life, the substantial investment of time and energy required by human offspring, and the affirming responsiveness of the human infant (e.g., smiling behavior), the mother had an opportunity to develop the nurturing qualities of caring and sensitivity (traits that have been attributed to the maternal instinct or characterized as feminine qualities in the popular imagination). With the father's investment in protecting his offspring and the development of the distinctive features of human sexuality

Figure 2.1
The Core Capabilities of Human Life and Their Derivative Goods

IDEALS

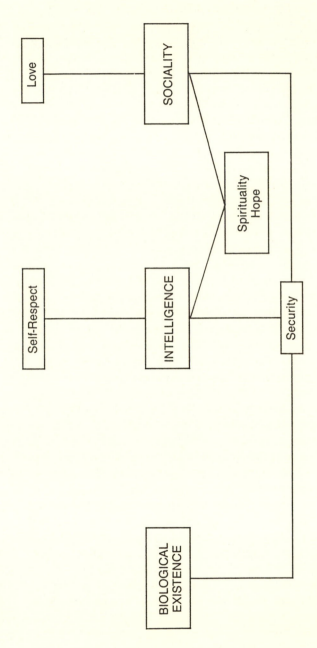

CONSTRUCTS

(e.g., the nearly total suppression of estrus, the hairlessness of the body and enhanced sensitivity of the skin, the development of sensitive erogenous zones), durable bonds evolved between males and females, and the love emotions shared by the mother and child were generalized across the family unit.

Through thousands of years of cultural evolution, love emotions were made sacred in storytelling and religious rituals and were further elaborated across the social structure, so that these emotions extended to clan and tribal allegiances. Eventually the concept of friendship evolved, which took love emotions beyond limits of genetic relatedness or geographic proximity and transformed transient alliances into durable relationships. In this regard, Aristotle was probably correct in viewing friendship as the pinnacle of love emotions (see *Nicomachean Ethics*, bks. 8 and 9). Even in our contemporary culture, authentic forms of love between men and women are often validated in terms of the concept of friendship (e.g., "my wife is my best friend").

Self-respect is a complex human good. It seems to be weakly dependent on inequalities in income, wealth, and political power, and strongly dependent upon social status, an individual's propensity for envy, and personal ideological resources (e.g., religious beliefs). Clearly a certain modicum of self-worth and confidence is an important aspect of human development.

I suggest that self-respect is best interpreted as an ideal of the core attribute of intelligence. For most individuals, self-respect is a durable personality attribute that is not necessarily linked to transient forms of prestige or power. Human beings are routinely able to develop self-respect at all levels of material well-being. Although the incidence of self-respect is probably strongly correlated with an individual's perceived social status (which may or may not reflect particular endowments of income/wealth or political power), a renewed sense of self-respect is often the by-product of status-depriving experiences. In such "critical situations" (see Giddens, 1979, pp. 123–128) people often reassess their values and reflect upon the grounds of their own self-worth. Hence self-respect is properly interpreted as an ideal of intelligence, as the recovery of self-worth in status-depriving experiences is rooted in an enlightened self-awareness and the appreciation of human individuality (perhaps mediated by an affirming friendship, a religious experience, etc.).

Like love and self-respect, hope is an important facet of human life. Hope seems to be linked to one's degree of personal investment in the future. That investment or personal stake in the future may take a number of forms, ranging from the simple anticipation that the future will bring about some improvement in the current state of affairs to the expectation that certain aspirations or goals will be achieved during the course of time. I suggest that hope can be interpreted as a construct of the core attributes of intelligence and sociality. Certainly the religious and technical dimensions of human intelligence provide the immediate inspiration for much of human hope, as they provide grounds for believing that one's material and nonmaterial environment can be improved in some respect. However, human sociality (and particularly the experience of child rearing) is also a very important source of human hope, as individuals fully engaged in the social system are forced to make substantial investments in the future.

Spirituality is clearly an important human good, despite the fact that many contemporary observers may wish to downplay its significance. Throughout history human beings have used sacred symbols, rituals, and beliefs to map their environment, to sanction their moral obligations, and to interpret the meaning of their existence. If human spirituality is understood broadly as the capacity to relate religious symbols to everyday life, and if religion is defined with appropriate breadth (see Geertz, 1973), the phenomenon of human spirituality is a near universal trait of human behavior.

Obviously religious beliefs and practices can be analyzed from a variety of perspectives (e.g., philosophy, sociology, psychology, theology, ethnography). For the purpose of this discussion, human spirituality will be treated simply as a social fact and interpreted as a construct of the core attributes of intelligence and sociality. Insofar as religion is a resource for resolving problems of meaning (Geertz, 1968; Levi-Strauss, 1955; Ricoeur, 1967; Weber, 1946, 1963) or re-creating the world through sacred symbols and rituals (Eliade, 1954, 1959, 1961; Gill, 1982; B. Wilson, 1973; Worsley, 1957), it is a complex, multidimensional manifestation of human intelligence (irrespective of the metaphysical realities that may underlie the religious consciousness). Moreover, inasmuch as religion is an important cohesive force that helps unify and regulate human communities through shared symbols and rituals, it is a facet of human sociality (Durkheim, 1915).

Of all the human goods mentioned thus far, security is probably the most complex. As previously emphasized, security is a highly relative concept, representing a function of perceived past instabilities in need-satisfaction, perceived prospective instabilities, one's individual propensity to accept risk, and one's ideological resources. Therefore one cannot treat security as a simple threshold in a hierarchical schema of human needs that is passed on the way to higher needs, because security is an aspect of need-satisfaction at every level for both basic and nonbasic needs. For example, a businessman may develop an ulcer over his financial security, even though the worst-case scenario of bankruptcy would not interrupt the fulfillment of his BN. Truly security is in the eye of the beholder; one person's security is another's insecurity.

Despite the inherent subjectivity of the notion of security, it certainly cannot be dismissed as an unimportant human good. Most of us operate best when we feel reasonably secure with our immediate circumstances, as some degree of security enables us to make plans for the future and permits us to direct our energies away from worrying about tomorrow. Additionally, it should be emphasized that a great deal of security (which most of us take for granted) comes from the confidence that we will be able to meet our BN. Hence some sense of security is an important by-product of stable BN programs.

Are the derivative goods of love, hope, self-respect, spirituality, and security essential goods for human life? It remains a moot question whether all of the derivative goods are essential for human life in a strict sense of the term. For example, the ability to receive and give love is certainly a very important facet of human existence. However, is love really essential for human life? People often feel inadequately loved (or unable to give love) but otherwise continue to function reasonably normally, perhaps suffering some psychological disorder or exhibiting antisocial behavior at the worst.[2] To note an extreme example, Turnbull (1972) found the Ik society in northern Uganda completely void of emotions or behaviors that could be described as loving, even though the Iks demonstrated much creative intelligence and some degree of sociality. However, irrespective of whether these derivative goods are essential for human life, it cannot be disputed that human life would be less than fully human apart from the possibility of enjoying such goods.

Are these derivative goods capable of being packaged in BN bundles and distributed across a society? Obviously the answer is no. The goods of love, hope, self-respect, spirituality, and security cannot be treated as commodities in any sense of the term. Instead the ability to attain these goods depends on whether or not the three core attributes/capabilities of human life remain intact.

According to the formal definition of need set forth in section 2.3, it was shown that all need claims try to relate a specific variant means (X) to a certain invariant end (Y) and can be placed in the following form:

I need X if and only if X(MEANS) is a weak or strong condition for acquiring, keeping or actualizing Y(END), which I am voluntarily disposed or required to acquire, keep or actualize (where Y is a commodity, a biopsychosocial attribute or a moral/religious/social ideal).

Consequently any need-claim presumes (implicitly or explicitly) that the possession of a certain first-order good (X) will lead to the acquisition, preservation, or actualization of a second-order good (Y).

Any attempt to construct a universal set of basic needs must justify the universality of some second-order goods $(Y$s) and determine which set of first-order goods $(X$s) will lead to the development or preservation of the second order goods in question. Assuming that our three second-order goods (biological existence, human intelligence, and human sociality) constitute the core attributes of human life, it is possible to generate a universal set of first-order basic human needs based on these species universals.

In order to establish an interclass ranking of these first-order goods $(X$s) once they have been identified, it is necessary to rank-order the second-order goods $(Y$s) according to some logical criterion. The obvious choice would be to assign priority to those second-order goods that are essential prerequisites for the development of other second-order goods.

In the case of our three species universals, clearly biological existence would rank first, as the distinctive attributes of human intelligence and sociality would not be possible apart from biological subsistence. In terms of the priority between intelligence and sociality, it seems fairly clear that intelligence should be ranked second with sociality third. While it is impossible to conceive of human sociality apart from human intelligence, the distinctive features of human intelligence (including the capacity for symbolic communication) remain fundamentally intact when isolated from social interaction. Even if sapientization (i.e., increased brain size and enhanced neural organization) was stimulated by the need for social sophistication in hunting and gathering groups (required for apprehending big game or perhaps for communal defense against other humans), this would lend confirmation to the priority of intelligence over sociality (as increased brain size and cortical sophistication would have been selected as adaptive traits and sociological sophistication would have been built upon an evolutionary substratum of increased neurological complexity).

2.5. TWO SETS OF FIRST-ORDER GOODS

Once these second-order goods have been rank-ordered, it is possible to generate two sets of first-order goods: (1) an objective universal set of basic needs, and (2) an objective, time-relative basic needs bundle. The first category conceives of basic needs at a higher level of generality than the second. It posits universal (i.e., transcultural, transhistorical) conditions for developing and maintaining the essential attributes of human life. The second category consists of generic goods that are time-relative but defined according to objective criteria (which are equally valid from one culture to the next).

Obviously it is impossible to construct a credible basic needs bundle that is not time-relative, due to the impact of technical change on the satisfaction of human needs. For example, prior to Salk's discovery of a vaccine for poliomyelitis, it could not be said that a vaccination against polio was a basic need. Similar advances in medicine, agriculture, education, and sanitation have dramatically increased both the quantity and quality of life for individuals who have benefited from these developments. Hence it would be inappropriate to construct a basic needs bundle for the late 20th century on the basis of 19th-century technology.

The chronological/technological constraints on the contents of any BN bundle reflect an important difference between BN claims and need-claims in ordinary language. That distinction is this: BN claims require that the first-order good (X) is an existing, definite good (instead of simply a term that refers to a good that remains unidentifiable at this time, e.g., "We need a *cure* for cancer").

It should be noted, though, that in addition to technological constraints on the contents of a specific BN bundle, there are also economic constraints. Ought implies can, and it is readily apparent that not all accessible technologies are economically feasible. For example, access to kidney dialysis cannot be considered a BN at this time. Moreover, it is not feasible for LDCs to replicate the curative, physician-dominated health care systems found in more developed countries (MDCs). Instead some form of "primary health care," which utilizes nurses and paraprofessionals (e.g., community health workers/barefoot doctors, midwives) represents the appropriate choice of technology (i.e., economically feasible for global implementation). Hence the above distinction between BN claims and need-claims in ordinary language should be expanded to the following: BN claims require that the first-order good (X) is an existing, definite good that is technologically/economically capable of global coverage.

These aforementioned considerations can be summarized in terms of the interaction between two principles: (1) the Principle of Optimal Coverage, and (2) the Principle of Technological Adaptation. The Principle of Optimal Coverage simply holds that "economic, social, and political entitlements should be arranged so that a maximum number of the reference group population can meet their BN."[3] The Principle of Technological Adaptation requires that "available technologies should be adapted to as wide a range of socioeconomic contexts as possible."

The interaction between these two principles is shown graphically in Figure 2.2. The vertical axis depicts a hypothetical scale of needs/wants satisfaction (reflecting assorted levels of economic/social/political entitlements) ranging from 0 to 120, and the horizontal axis represents various population deciles, ranging from 0 to 100. A hypothetical basic needs threshold has been established at level 30 on the needs/wants satisfaction scale.

The concave-to-origin curves A, B, and C depict three different technology curves (the term is used very broadly to include available economic and social/institutional resources within a particular time frame). The concavity of these curves reflects the increased costs that are necessary to achieve the upper bounds of either high degrees of needs/wants satisfaction on the vertical axis or high magnitudes of population coverage on the horizontal axis. The flatter slopes of technology curves B and C represent instances where the Principle of Technological Adaptation has been realized; whereas, the steeper slope of technology curve A depicts a restricted technological range that is biased in the direction of higher levels of needs/wants satisfaction for fewer numbers. One would expect that steeper technology curves would reflect research and development (R&D) expenditures that are skewed in favor of select groups (e.g., about 98% of the world's R&D expenditures are concentrated within MDCs [H. Singer, 1977, p. 12]), as well as a deficiency of mechanisms for technology transfer, human capital formation, and small-scale enterprise development (e.g., there seems to be an inverse relationship between the size of a firm and its willingness to employ appropriate technologies [World Bank, 1978, pp. 19–21]).

Lines X, Y, and Z depict the coverage trajectories for technology curves A, B, and C, respectively. These coverage trajectories represent three different instances of the Principle of Optimal Coverage. In order for a particular coverage trajectory to conform to the Principle of Optimal Coverage, it must intersect the technology curve at a point that optimizes the population coverage on or above the BN threshold. In the case of coverage trajectory X, only 80% of the reference group population will have their BN met. By contrast, the coverage trajectories

Figure 2.2
Graphic Depiction of the Principle of Optimal Coverage and the Principle of Technological Adaptation

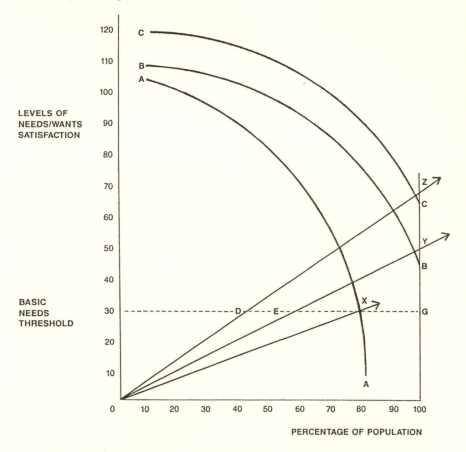

Y and *Z* intersect their respective technology curves well above the BN threshold and insure the near complete coverage of the population. The increased magnitude of BN satisfaction and coverage brought about by trajectory *Y* simply represents the impact of the Principle of Technological Adaptation in moving from technology curve *A* to technology curve *B*, yielding a BN surplus of *EGY*. However, the outward movement from technology curve *B* to technology curve *C* illustrates the impact of overall technological development (as distinguished from enhanced technological adaptation), yielding a large BN surplus of *DGZ*.

Understandably, technological development over several time periods may not only increase the satisfaction of BN within the reference group population, but also it may have some effect upon the definition of the BN threshold itself. For example, Figure 2.3 depicts three different BN thresholds (BNT), each of which corresponds to three different time periods (t_1, t_2, and t_3). Technology curves *A*,

Figure 2.3
**The Interaction Between Basic Needs Thresholds and the Principles of Optimal
Coverage and Technological Adaptation**

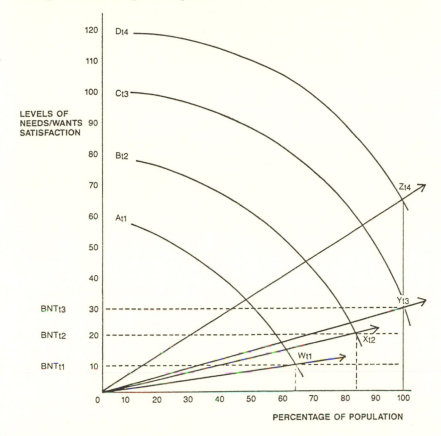

B, C, and D represent the available range of technological/economic resources
for each of four time periods (t_1, t_2, t_3, and t_4). The coverage trajectory W_{t1}
intersects the severely restricted technology curve A_{t1} at the lowest BN threshold
(BNT_{t1}), enabling only about 65% of the reference group population to meet
their BN during t_1. With the enhanced technological capabilities represented by
technology curve B_{t2}, it becomes feasible to raise the BN threshold from level
10 to level 20, and the coverage trajectory for this time period (X_{t2}) indicates
that it would be possible to insure that about 85% of the reference group population had their BN satisfied. Similarly the technological advances achieved
during the third time period (depicted by technology curve C_{t3}) warrant new
additions to the BN threshold, bringing that threshold up to level 30 (BNT_{t3}).
The corresponding coverage trajectory for this time period (Y_{t3}) intersects the
technology curve right at the BN threshold, indicating that it is feasible for 100%

Figure 2.4
Transformation of a Universal Set of Basic Needs into a Time-Relative Basic Needs Bundle

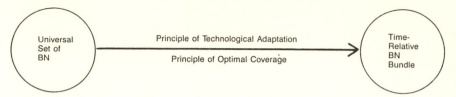

of the reference group population to have sufficient resources in order to meet their BN.

The expanding constitution of the BN bundle from time periods t_1 through t_3 would understandably lead a skeptic to assume that the concept of BN is simply another way of stating the theory of relative deprivation, since in each case the BN threshold expands at a rate in proportion to the structure and magnitude of the technology shelf of that time period. Yet it is instructive to note that the movement from technology curve C_{t3} to D_{t4} highlights the difference between the BN needs concept and the concept of relative deprivation. During t_4 the corresponding coverage trajectory (Z_{t4}) intersects the technology curve at a point well above the BN threshold (BNT$_{t3}$), indicating 100% of the reference group population could have their BN met, while still retaining a considerable BN surplus. Since the present state of global technological/economic resources suggests that our current situation is far more like technology curve D_{t4} than any of the lower technology curves (and probably lies considerably above D_{t4}), the reasonably fixed benchmark provided by the BN threshold becomes quite significant in comparison to relativistic definitions of poverty lines or minimum endowment thresholds. This distinction between BN thresholds and relative poverty lines becomes especially important in mapping intrastate and interstate moral obligations to provide BN assistance (see Chapter 5).

It is important to emphasize that although the *generic* contents of a BN bundle should not be culture-relative, the *specific* BN packages will vary from one culture to the next, depending on cultural or individual factors (e.g., required calorie intake will vary with age, sex, height, climate, activity level, pregnancy/lactation; sanitation schemes will vary with local customs; formal or nonformal educational programs will take a variety of forms, including distance teaching by radio and the use of folk singers/entertainers).

Figure 2.4 illustrates the relation between the Principle of Technological Adaptation and the Principle of Optimal Coverage in relation to the two sets of BN. It is readily apparent that only the broad parameters of the time-relative BN bundle can be described, given the difficulties involved in determining the precise location and slope of the current global technology curve in relation to the coverage trajectory that intersects it. In other words, it is necessary to make an educated *judgment* as to which of the possible candidates for a BN bundle can feasibly conform to the Principle of Optimal Coverage within the broad range of technological options mandated by the Principle of Technological Adaptation. Establishing the parameters of a BN bundle will become more difficult the higher we proceed in a needs hierarchy (i.e., at the X_2 and X_3 levels), given the strong temptation to expand those classes of human needs beyond what our estimated technology curve and coverage trajectory would permit. Moreover, we can assume that the parameters of a BN bundle may be adjusted from time to time as a result of alterations in the global technology shelf, as well as changes in the magnitude and distribution of the world's population. For example, the discovery of of Oral Rehydration Therapy by the World Health Organization and UNICEF in Bangladesh during the early 1970s is an extremely simple technological achievement that may one day be placed on a par with the discovery of penicillin in terms of its potential for saving human life. It is clear that provisions for the dissemination of this new technology would definitely be part of a time-relative BN bundle.

Table 2.1 presents a heuristic outline of both a universal set of basic needs and a time-relative basic needs bundle in relation to our three species universals (Y-values). The universal set of BN listed in the table is self-explanatory and does not require further elaboration. However the time-relative BN bundle is considerably more complex because of its greater degree of specificity and, accordingly, will be discussed at some length.

2.6.   NEEDS RELATING TO PHYSICAL EXISTENCE

The X_1 variables for the time-relative BN bundle are: minimum nutrition intake, safe water/sanitation, primary health care, shelter/clothing/energy/transportation, and municipal protection/national defense.

2.6.a.   Minimum Nutrition

First, let us examine minimum nutrition as a BN. Current estimates of the number of seriously undernourished people in the world range from 500 million to 1 billion. As previously mentioned, individual nutritional requirements vary with age, sex, height, climate, level of activity, and whether females are pregnant or lactating. This variability, along with the fact that nutritional requirements refer not only to energy (calories) but also to protein, vitamins, and minerals, makes food intake approaches to nutrition assessment difficult.

Fortunately we have two shortcuts available. With respect to children, undernutrition can be quickly detected by regular anthropometric measurements of height and weight (i.e., growth monitoring), as nutrition is a far stronger factor in accounting for growth differences than genetic endowments (Austin, 1980, pp. 43–45; Caliendo, 1979, pp. 80–86). For adults, calorie intake is an effective (but not completely reliable) indicator of deficiencies in protein and vitamins.

Table 2.1
A Typology of Basic Human Needs

CORE ATTRIBUTES OF HUMAN LIFE	UNIVERSAL SET OF BN	TIME-RELATIVE BN BUNDLE
(Y1) existence	(X1) food, water, air, retention of body heat, sleep, mechanisms for communal protection	(X1) minimum nutrition, safe water/sanitation, primary health care, shelter/clothing/energy/transportation, municipal protection/national defense
(Y2) intelligence	(X2) communication, informal education (e.g., rites of passage)	(X2) basic education/literacy; access to uncensored information media; access to contraceptive technologies
(Y3) sociality	(X3) freedom of expression; freedom of association	(X3) absence of political repression

For example, a large household survey in India found that nearly 50% of those who suffered calorie deficits were also not consuming an adequate amount of protein. By contrast, among those who sustained an adequate calorie intake, only 5% had protein deficient diets (Sukhatme, 1970).

The FAO has established minimum per capita calorie requirements on the order of 2,350 for Africa, 2,390 for Latin America, 2,210 for Asia, and 2,450 for the Middle East. However, these average energy requirements are not, in themselves, reliable guides for determining the nutritional status of a population, as FAO reports readily admit (see Srinivasan, 1981). Furthermore, the standard indicator of "daily calorie supply per capita as a percentage of FAO requirements" involves a great deal of guesswork (McGranahan et al., 1981) and, more importantly, fails to account for disparities in calorie consumption among different income classes (Reutlinger and Selowsky, 1976, pp. 10–11, 24).

Despite these measurement problems, there is no doubt that adequate nutrition is a (perhaps *the*) primary component of a BN bundle. For example, a "principal components analysis" of cross-country data from 110 LDCs found that calorie and protein consumption alone accounted for 76% of the total variation among eight BN indicators (Sheehan and Hopkins, 1979, pp. 54–55). Moreover, the synergism between malnutrition and infectious diseases has been well documented (Rosenberg et al., 1976; Scrimshaw et al., 1968). Undernutrition not only reduces the body's capacity to resist infection and infectious disease, but also decreases a person's capacity to absorb and utilize the limited amount of food one may consume. Furthermore, controlled field studies have demonstrated the remarkable impact of nutrition interventions in decreasing infant and child mortality (Berg, 1981; Lechtig et al., 1975; Mata et al., 1975).

2.6.b.   Safe Water/Sanitation

Safe water and sanitation are also BN, as both are necessary preconditions for reducing the incidence of waterborne and fecally transmitted diseases (e.g., cholera, dysentery, typhoid, diarrheal disease, tetanus, schistosomiasis) that often lead to mortality (especially among infants). Safe water and sanitation should be treated as a unit, as the health benefits of an improved water supply are likely to be severely diminished unless corresponding measures are taken in sanitation (Saunders and Warford, 1976, pp. 35–36). The World Bank estimates that in 1975 1.5 billion people did not have access to a safe water source and lacked adequate waste-disposal facilities (an especially acute health problem in urban areas).

Although a person can survive on one or two liters of water daily, it takes between 20 and 50 liters of safe water per day for food preparation and hygiene. The use of public standpipes, conveniently located, is clearly the most cost-effective delivery system for safe water. Neither boiling water nor individual household connections are economically viable solutions to the problem. Unfortunately the current availability of public standpipes is atrocious. For example, in Douala, Cameroon, there are only two standpipes for 50,000 persons! One study in Kenya found that nearly 20% of all rural households devoted more than six hours each day to collecting water (World Bank, 1980a).

As far as sanitation is concerned, there are many inexpensive options that effectively isolate human waste from habitats and water sources. The concept of appropriate "sanitation sequences" is a very promising solution to the current problem. By installing sanitation systems that are designed to minimize costs in the initial phase but can be eventually upgraded at a later date, facilities can be successively upgraded at a minimal cost in the long term. For example, a ventilated improved pit latrine built in year 1 could be upgraded to a pour-flush toilet with a soakaway in year 10 and finally upgraded to a pour-flush toilet with a small-bore sewer in year 20. If the costs for a sanitation sequence of this type were spread out over a 30-year period, the total economic costs (present value) per household would be U.S. $354 (at 1978 prices). By contrast, the introduction of a conventional waterborne sewerage system would cost $3,000 (present value) per household (Kalbermatten et al., 1982, pp. 52–57). Understandably, none of the low-cost sanitation sequences end up with conventional waterborne sewerage, common in MDCs. Not only is the cost of waterborne sewerage prohibitive, but it is not a technically viable option unless per capita water consumption exceeds 100 liters per day (Kalbermatten et al., 1980).

2.6.c. Primary Health Care

The concept of health cannot be easily operationalized for purposes of measurement. The constitution of the World Health Organization defines health as "a state of complete physical, mental, and social well-being and not merely the absence of disease or infirmity"; yet all of our available measures of health relate to the absence of health (e.g., the child mortality rate, life expectancy at birth, the number of physicians or hospital beds per capita). It has been estimated that an average person in an LDC suffers from serious ill health during 10% of his or her lifetime (Streeten et al., 1981, p. 131).

Because morbidity is difficult to quantify and systematic data from LDCs are not available, mortality is the only available indicator of illness. However, this limitation is less serious than it may seem, as high rates of mortality within certain age groups are strongly correlated with high rates of morbidity. Two indicators are especially important in this regard: the infant mortality rate (per 1,000 live births) and the life expectancy at birth. (The child death rate [ages 1–4] is less reliable due to underreporting, and the crude death rate is not an appropriate measure, because it reflects the age structure of a population more than local health conditions.) Yet even these conventional indicators mask the actual magnitude of health problems suffered by the poor, because statistics are not disaggregated according to income classes or urban/rural environments (see M. Lewis, 1981).

Certainly any concept of a BN bundle must include health care as a primary component. Given the magnitude and structure of the health problem in LDCs, it is commonly recognized that the high-cost, physician-dominated, curative health care systems found in MDCs are neither an effective nor an economically feasible model for LDCs. Consequently the concept of a low-cost, community-based, preventive approach to health care has emerged to supplement and expand current medical facilities in LDCs. This approach is known as primary health care.

The most distinctive feature of the primary health care concept is the utilization of "community health workers" who receive limited medical training in order to administer immunizations and routine medical treatments, to educate the community on health issues, and to serve as a liaison between the community and regional health centers. China has instituted the primary health care concept on a large scale and has experienced striking results. In spite of the fact that its population exceeds 1 billion people, China's primary health care program has produced dramatic advances in the health status of its citizenry, so that its health indicators now rival those of the United States in the 1930s (Morawetz, 1977, p. 49).

Pilot studies indicate that primary health care could be provided at the cost of only $2.50 to $4.00 per person a year (Streeten et al., 1981, p. 132). One proposal for a global implementation of primary health care recommends a four-tiered approach, involving (per every 1 million persons) the following: (1) 1,000 community health centers, each staffed by 5 community health workers; (2) 100 health centers, each staffed by 1 physician, 5 nurses, 5 medium-level personnel, and 10 community health workers; (3) 20 (100-bed) regional hospitals (located in poor districts), each staffed with 2 physicians, 5 nurses, and 25 medium-level personnel; and (4) 5 (300-bed) reference hospitals, each staffed by 15 physicians, 60 nurses, and 100 medium-level personnel (Norbye, 1974).

2.6.d.   Shelter/Clothing/Energy/Transportation

Shelter, clothing, energy, and transportation are also BN. I will refer to this class of human needs as "environmental needs." This is a particularly complex group of needs, because all four take on important symbolic significance (as indicators of social status) and are highly subject to variations in taste once some minimum threshold is passed. Hence the line between the basic and nonbasic provision of these four goods will be extremely vague, complicated by cultural standards and personal preferences that may generate artificial BN.

How would one go about defining minimum thresholds for these environmental needs? At least four kinds of thresholds may be relevant: (1) a heat-retention threshold; (2) a crowding threshold; (3) a social-interaction threshold; and (4) an access threshold.

A heat-retention threshold is clearly the most objective (and minimalistic) criterion for determining basic shelter, clothing, and energy needs. The human body has a remarkable ability to maintain an even body temperature in many different climates. A naked body exposed to calm, dry air ranging from 55° to 140°F can maintain a normal body temperature of between 98° and 100°F indefinitely (Guyton, 1982). Assuming that a comfortable skin temperature for most people lies somewhere between 70° and 75°F, there are numerous combinations of shelter, clothing, and energy use that could consistently maintain a comfortable *minimum* skin temperature. Clearly only the most cost-effective combinations could be recognized as a BN (e.g., it is not a BN to wear a mink coat or to heat a mansion).

The obvious problem with relying only on a heat-retention threshold in defining basic environmental needs is that most developing regions are located in tropical or semitropical regions. Hence the criterion is not very helpful in defining basic shelter, clothing, and energy needs.

A crowding threshold is significantly more helpful in defining basic shelter needs (however, it is not relevant to clothing, energy consumption, or transportation). Sociobiologists now realize that all major groups of vertebrates and some invertebrates exhibit territorial behavior by routinely advertising and defending their territory against would-be intruders of their own species (see E. O. Wilson, 1975, pp. 256–278, 564–565). Maintaining a norm of individual distance is one facet of territorial behavior.

Most animals maintain a more or less precise distance from members of their species (e.g., the swallow *Hirundo rustica* observes 15 centimeters; the gull *Larus ridibundus* 30 centimeters). With respect to Homo sapiens, the level of population density at which crowding is perceived varies greatly from one culture to the next (e.g., Mediterranean peoples, including the French, tolerate more density in restaurants and stand closer to one another in conversation than northern Europeans).

However, this cultural variance does not mean that a cross-cultural crowding threshold cannot be determined by some rough measures. It is certainly an area that warrants systematic study. We know that overcrowded, poorly ventilated habitats increase the risk of contracting airborne diseases (e.g., tuberculosis, pneumonia, diphtheria, measles, influenza). Moreover, it is likely that high population densities will have a negative impact on people's psychological well-being.

Two common indicators of occupational density in relation to shelter are the average number of persons per room or the number of square meters per person. Generally the former indicator is used, despite the obvious problem that room size varies markedly.

In Pakistan the average number of persons per room is 3.1, in Indonesia 3.0, and in Mexico 2.9. As high as these figures are, they understate the crowding problem of the low-income classes, because the figures represent national averages. For example, in India 34% of the rural families and 44% of the urban families live in a single room or share it with another family (Mabogunje et al., 1978).

Some Latin American countries express occupational density in terms of square meters per person (e.g., in Argentina the professed minimum housing standard is 8 square meters per person). This measure is obviously preferable because it eliminates the impact of variable room size upon occupational density. Evidence indicates that dwellings in burgeoning, uncontrolled, urban squatter settlements may typically have an average living space of only 3 square meters per person (McHale and McHale, 1978, p. 103). Even though it is not possible at this time to establish scientifically a minimum range of species-specific shelter density, clearly the minimum would lie above 3 square meters per person. (McHale and McHale [1978, p. 101] have recommended the figure of 10 square meters per person as a reasonable median target between U.N. proposals of 8.8 square meters in 1960 and 14.15 square meters in 1972.)

A third possible criterion in determining basic environmental needs is a social interaction threshold. It is obvious that shelter, clothing (including jewelry and ceremonial garb), energy consumption, and means of transportation are characteristic indicators of social status in any culture. The question is whether there is a functionally defined minimum status threshold that is *necessary* for social existence.

Clearly people ought to have enough environmental goods so that they can be assured of meeting fundamental norms of propriety that are embodied in their culture. These culture-specific canons of propriety are rarely transgressed and are considered integral to one's sense of personal dignity. For instance, in many societies, unless one has enough clothing to meet basic social expectations, it would be nearly impossible for a person to interact with others with dignity. I refer to this minimalistic level of social status as a "social interaction threshold."

The peculiar nature of this type of status threshold is that it cuts across income classes and is embedded in what might be termed the deep structure of the culture. Generally speaking, energy consumption, transportation, and shelter will be irrelevant to such a social interaction threshold; however, the threshold is certainly relevant to clothing needs in many societies and may even apply to important ritual acts that are considered mandatory by a culture (e.g., the ability to give a family member a decent burial).

Finally, a basic level of energy consumption and transportation could be determined by an access threshold that is necessary for meeting other BN. For example, a certain amount of energy will be necessary in food preparation, and some form of transportation (the most cost-effective) may be necessary to enable a person to reach a school or health care facility. While the actual dimensions of this access threshold will vary from one community to the next, this criterion could be roughly calculated if one had sufficient information about local diets, the proximity of clinics and educational institutions, and so on.

Fortunately the conceptual labyrinth of defining basic environmental needs is simplified somewhat insofar as public policy initiatives for shelter provision are concerned. With the exception of the poorest 10–20% of a LDC's population, most shelter improvements can be made within the budget constraints of the poor (Churchill, 1980). Moreover, recent evidence indicates that a significant amount of financial transfers takes place within the extended family to aid relatives who are building or upgrading their homes (Keare and Parris, 1982). However, these self-help improvements cannot take place on a significant scale unless appropriate land reform initiatives (both urban and rural) enable the poor to attain some sense of home ownership. The shelter needs of the lowest income groups can be met by low-cost rental accommodations and housing subsidy programs.

In summary, in spite of the many difficulties entailed in the identification of rough minima for basic environmental needs, at least four kinds of thresholds are capable of objective measurement (even though we lack the necessary data to define these minima). Of all three thresholds, only the heat-retention threshold is *essential* to physical survival. The access threshold would probably rank second in importance, because public goods such as health care and education are useless unless they are geographically accessible to the poor. (However this threshold is somewhat redundant in that both geographic and economic accessibility must be incorporated in any BN program.) Finally the crowding and social interaction thresholds embody important aspects of psychological well-being that may or may not be essential goods for physical survival, depending on how one views the relationship between psychological well-being and biological health.

2.6.e. Municipal Protection/National Defense

Finally, some mechanisms for municipal protection and national defense are necessary for physical survival, in order to protect citizens against violent attacks from other citizens and to insure the integrity of the state against intruders. Of all the BN essential to physical existence, this category is the most subject to abuse for several reasons.

First, there is a strong trend in LDC regimes to expand the concept of national security to encompass a whole range of internal security issues (not the least of which is the preservation of power by military and civilian elites). Hence the concept of municipal protection easily deteriorates into a synonym for state control.

Second, the fact that many LDC regimes are tacitly or explicitly controlled by military elites (as witnessed by the frequency of coups when the military's welfare is threatened), along with the political and economic signficance of arms transfers from MDCs to LDCs, has led to gross overestimations of external defense needs by LDC regimes (N. Ball, 1981). Moreover, there are indications that significant amounts of security expenditures are intentionally obscured in the national accounts of many developing countries (N. Ball, 1984). Consequently one cannot be satisfied with any concept of basic defense needs that relativizes these needs according to the felt needs of each regime.

The task of identifying basic internal and external defense needs according to objective (or semiobjective) criteria would certainly be difficult but not necessarily impossible.[4] Let us assume that basic defense needs are being determined in the context of a nonbelligerent state regime that has demonstrated a serious intent in meeting the basic needs of the population, in order to avoid the problems of the use of violence in revolutionary situations, preemptive defense by neighboring states, and foreign intervention for the purpose of blocking genocidal policies. Moreover, let us assume that basic internal defense needs are functionally related to the level of violent, noncooperative (i.e., criminal) behavior within a society,[5] and basic external defense needs are functionally related to the scope and severity of external threats to national security.

If the data were available, aggregate levels of violent, noncooperative behavior could be measured in terms of the probability that any random member of the society would suffer an act of violence.[6] Of course, it would be necessary to assign a set of arbitrary weights (w) to each probability estimate, as some acts of violence (e.g., assaults leading to death) are clearly graver than others (e.g., vandalism). Let us designate V for a violent act and distinguish among the following:

V_1 = assault leading to death;

V_2 = assault leading to physical impairment;

V_3 = assault with no physical but substantial psychological impairment;

V_4 = assault with no physical or psychological impairment;

V_5 = destruction or theft of property that decreases basic needs satisfaction; and

V_6 = destruction or theft of property that is irrelevant to basic needs satisfaction.

Given the above definitions, the actual weighted probability of violence (V_{awp}) in a certain time period (t) could be calculated as follows:

$$V_{awp}t = P(V_1)w_1t + P(V_2)w_2t + P(V_3)w_3t + P(V_4)w_4t + P(V_5)w_5t + P(V_6)w_6t. \quad (1)$$

Once the actual weighted probability of violence is determined, basic internal defense needs (ID_{bn}) can be defined in terms of the total expenditures needed to reduce the disparity between the actual weighted probability of violence in time period t ($V_{awp}t$) and a target weighted probability ($V_{twp}t_1$) in a subsequent time period (t_1). Letting C represent the costs required to reduce the actual weighted probability of violence by 0.001 in t_1,[7] the required investment for basic internal defense needs could be determined as follows:

$$ID_{bn} = Ct_1 [(V_{awp}t - V_{twp}t_1) 1,000]. \quad (2)$$

It is likely that the determination of basic external defense needs will be exceedingly more difficult than basic internal defense needs, owing to the strong perceptual component involved in any assessment of national security. Governments are usually able to generate unjustified anxiety about national defense whenever it suits their purposes. Nonetheless it would be theoretically possible to determine basic external defense needs by calculating a rough order of probability that a country will be invaded during any single time period, utilizing an expected utility model of conflict initiation (Bueno de Mesquita, 1981, 1985), which accounts for the historical propensities of neighboring countries to initiate belligerent conduct.[8] Given such a rough probability of foreign invasion for a particular time period, the required investment for basic external defense needs (ED_{bn}) could be defined in terms of the total expenditures needed to reduce the disparity between the actual probability of invasion in time period t $(I_{ap}t)$ and the target probability of invasion $(I_{tp}t_1)$ for a subsequent time period (t_1). Letting C represent the costs of reducing the probability of invasion by 0.001 in t_1,[9] basic external defense needs could be determined as follows:

$$ED_{bn} = Ct_1 [(I_{ap}t) - (I_{tp}t_1) 1,000]. \tag{3}$$

It may be objected that defense expenditures are based on more considerations than simply preventing foreign invasion. At least four other considerations may be relevant: (1) the promotion of national prestige, (2) the maintenance of hegemonic relationships with other states, (3) the positive impact of defense expenditures on economic development, and (4) the prevention of foreign dependency/domination. Obviously the first two hardly qualify as BN, as they are simply national preferences. To argue that the third consideration is relevant to basic external defense needs, one would have to show why military investment is preferable to other forms of investment on economic grounds. This would be impossible to argue for nearly all LDCs (with Israel as a possible exception), as defense expenditures are both import- and capital-intensive. Emile Benoit (1973) found a strong positive correlation between defense burdens and growth rates in his study of 44 LDCs. However Nicole Ball (1983) has emphasized that some methodological assumptions that informed the Benoit study are seriously flawed, and more recent statistical analyses have either failed to establish a positive correlation between economic growth and defense burden (excluding OPEC countries) or showed a strong negative correlation between the two (especially in the *least* developed countries). Finally the use of defense expenditures to prevent various forms of foreign domination or dependency is greatly complicated by the fact that there can be many forms (both formal and informal) of dependence/domination among states, ranging from simple import or export dependency to Finlandization. Let us assume that the only form of domination/dependency that is relevant to defense expenditures per se is cases in which foreign powers credibly threaten military intervention of some sort when a national regime acts autonomously in a way that neither undermines the security of its neighbors nor deprives its own citizens of life. For example, Argentina did not have a basic external defense need to protect itself from Britain when it seized the Falklands. Moreover, Uganda's Amin certainly did not have a basic external defense need to repel the invasion of Tanzania. If country-specific probabilities of foreign invasion are calculated on the basis that national regimes ought to act autonomously (given the aforementioned conditions), then the only relevant aspect of foreign domination in defining BN in external defense is incorporated in a general probability of invasion. Hence the probability of invasion is the only relevant criterion for determining basic external defense needs.

Given the large subjective dimension involved in the determination of basic internal and external defense needs (related to the necessity of assigning weights to various acts of violence, the need to assign target probabilities for both internal and external defense, and the strong perceptual component involved in calculating the probability of foreign invasion), the inclusion of this category may seem to create unnecessary complications for the basic needs concept. Obviously it is much easier to treat preparations for defense as simply a matter of national *preference* and thereby exclude defense considerations from the subject of basic needs. Yet, considering the overt and latent capacities for aggressive behavior among humans, it is difficult to avoid the conclusion that any cogent account of basic human needs must incorporate some need for collective defense.

If provisions for defense are considered a basic need instead of being a matter of country-specific preferences, this could have a profound effect on how defense expenditures are perceived relative to social expenditures in nutrition, safe water/sanitation, health care, and education. For example, let us say that a particular country faces the high probability of foreign invasion of .05 in a given time period. Even if analysts believed that an invasion would kill one-fifth of the population, the probability of war-related mortality would still be only .01 in peacetime. This compares to probabilities of infant mortality in many LDCs that range from .10 to .21.[10] Consequently, given reasonable probability estimates of internal and external violence, it is likely that the inclusion of defense needs in a basic needs bundle would underscore the importance of nondefense, social expenditures for the nation's well-being.

2.7. NEEDS RELATING TO INTELLECTUAL DEVELOPMENT

The X_2 variables necessary for the development of human intelligence consist of basic education/literacy, access to uncensored information media, and access to contraceptive technologies.

The concept of basic education has been introduced by Abdun Noor (1981).[11] In a sense, the concept of basic education is to the educational sector what primary health care is to the health sector. Noor describes the main components of a basic educational package as follows:

Communication skills and general knowledge, which at the basic level include literacy (if possible), numeracy, and general civic, scientific, and cultural knowledge, values, and attitudes;

Life skills and knowledge, which embrace hygienic practices, sanitation, nutrition, family planning, the environment, management of the family economy, and creating and maintaining the home; and

Production skills, which embrace all forms of activity directed toward making a living or the production of goods and services, at whatever level of sophistication (pp. 9–10).

Six criteria ought to regulate the design and distribution of a basic educational package:

First, it has a clear base in economic, social, health, shelter or nutritional human needs. Second, it is concerned with equity: there must be a high potential for equal distribution of whatever rewards are associated with educational outcomes (such as economic gain, improved health, and better nutrition). Third, it is linked directly to real employment opportunities, especially those involving a country's labor-intensive agriculture and industry. Fourth, it has a low cost per capita and per instructional unit. Fifth, it recognizes the aspirations of the learners, with responsive programs planned toward fulfillment of these aspirations. And sixth, it is of limited duration, with frequent completion points at which students may terminate (p. 10).

The concept of basic education presumes that organized educational instruction can take place within a formal, graded structure or in an innovative nonformal context (e.g., involving peer instruction, "learning by doing," use of folk media, distance teaching by radio). Both primary education (formal and nonformal) and adult literacy programs are key delivery systems of basic education.

At present only one-fifth of the developing world's 2.25 billion people are literate. Unfortunately the magnitude of illiteracy is not declining relative to population growth—there are 100 million more illiterate people than 25 years ago and 54 million more young people not attending school than in 1960! Current educational resources in most LDCs are strongly biased in favor of the rich, males, and higher education. The fact that government expenditures are skewed in favor of university education has tremendous distributive consequences, because of the much higher cost of higher education per pupil. For example, in Burundi a reduction of university enrollment of only 400 students would finance the provision of basic literacy for almost 100,000 primary age students (Noor, 1981, pp. 4–7, 26).

Two indicators are frequently used to measure the educational status of a country: the percentage of literate persons and the primary-school enrollment as a percentage of the primary school age group. While the first indicator is the most reliable to the two, literacy estimates suffer from the absence of a precise, international standard for cross-country comparisons. Moreover, censuses that produce data on literacy occur very infrequently (Brodsky and Rodrik, 1981; Sheehan and Hopkins, 1979, pp. 12–13).

The data on primary-school enrollments are extremely unreliable and usually overstate the extent of educational progress, owing to the low quality of education, teacher and student absenteeism, the high percentage of repeaters (averaging 15–20%), high dropout rates (only 50% of the entrants to primary school reach the fourth grade), and the fact that older children often enroll in primary school (and are counted as primary age children). Moreover, there are no established international standards as to the duration of primary school (in 1970 the most common official duration was six years, although 40% of LDCs had more or less than that) (McGranahan et al., 1981).

There seems to be an extremely important relationship between education and health. Literacy is consistently the most significant variable in explaining variations in life expectancy in cross-country analyses (Cochrane et al., 1980; Hicks, 1979). The primary mechanism that explains the correlation between education and health appears to be the way that the education of females impacts the health status of children. For example, controlled micro-level studies have shown that maternal education has a far greater impact on the health status of children than the educational level attained by the father.

The experience of Egypt seems to confirm the important impact of education on life expectancy. Egypt has made strong progress in nutrition and safe water supply; however, its life expectancy (53 years) is only slightly above the expected norm for its per capita GNP. The fact that only 40% of the population is literate may have depressed advances in life expectancy that otherwise may have taken place.

By contrast, the case of Tanzania seems to contradict the consistent correlation between literacy and life expectancy. Tanzania has made significant progress in water supply and literacy; however, its life expectancy still is only 45 years— the norm for its income class (Hicks, 1982). However, some caution must be exercised in using Tanzania as an exception to the rule. Presumably some lag time is necessary before recent educational advances will show up in decreasing life expectancies. The fact that most of the educational advances in Tanzania have taken place since the Arusha Declaration of 1967 suggests that data from Tanzania may eventually confirm the strong correlation between education and health.

Of course, basic education must never become a tool of the state for political indoctrination and repression, although clearly most formal education programs function as socializing institutions and typically convey subtle messages of class domination (Freire, 1983). Consequently opportunities for basic education must be complemented by access to uncensored information media.[12] Therefore it is appropriate to include this in the BN bundle.

Moreover, with the development of effective, economical contraceptive technologies within this century, it seems clear that couples should be given the opportunity to plan their families, as the denial of access to contraceptive technologies interjects a substantial zone of uncertainty in pursuing both individual and familial life plans. Therefore access to contraceptive technologies has been included in the BN bundle. Given the obvious moral dimensions of the decision to include access to contraceptive technologies within our time-relative BN bundle, this issue will receive further attention in the context of a discussion on the population crisis (see Chapter 6, section 6.4).

2.8.   NEEDS RELATING TO SOCIALITY

The X_3 variable necessary for the flourishing of human sociality is the absence of political repression. Logically it seems clear that *some* legitimate sphere of expression and association is absolutely necessary for the realization of human sociality. Yet it is important to note that freedom is a graded concept, itself comprised of varying degrees of freedom, ranging from the absence of physical restraint to the unrestrained publication of individual opinions. Moreover, it also needs to be emphasized that even the most free societies place certain informal and formal sanctions on the exercise of individual freedom (e.g., treason, shouting "fire" in a crowded theater).

By absence of political repression, I mean that individuals within a society are able to express themselves and associate freely, in a manner that does not contradict prominent social mores, without fear of political reprisal. A society would not need to be democratic to permit this degree of freedom of expression and association, although these freedoms will be obviously more secure in democratic societies than nondemocratic ones (see Chapter 8, section 8.2).

It may be objected that the notion of political repression values individual freedom over other (conflicting) kinds of goods and, therefore, is itself ethnocentric. For example, many ancient and contemporary societies have all too frequently placed severe restraints on individual freedom for the stated purpose of safeguarding "higher goods" (e.g., orthodoxy, eternal life, or political stability). In such cases, freedom was viewed as a threat to the social fabric (as defined by the dominant political and/or religious ideology).

Does this mean that the absence of political repression no longer qualifies as a universal basic need? No. Instead the issue rests on an interpretational question bearing on the perceived role of freedom in relation to the attainment of human sociality.

The distinctive innovation brought about by the Enlightenment faith in man (springing from ideological currents emanating from the Renaissance and the Protestant Reformation) was the belief that freedom is the true foundation of social stability, instead of posing a threat to social life. The remarkable spread of constitutional democracies and the rapid dissemination of the idea of individual human rights across the globe (along with the near disappearance of institutionalized slavery, racism, and colonialism) attests to the power (and truth) of this Enlightenment confidence in the freedom of thought and expression.

The fact that previous generations did not have an interpretational framework such as the one introduced by the Enlightenment, which encouraged them to treat freedom as the cornerstone of sociality, does not negate freedom of expression and association as basic human needs. Instead it confirms the fact that humans have displayed an uncompromising desire to preserve and reproduce stable social environments and have possessed a fundamental ambivalence concerning the role of freedom in the attainment of this goal. Obviously we have not yet resolved this tension between the individual expression of freedom and the preservation of a stable social order.

In defining the X_3 variable of our BN bundle negatively in terms of the absence of political repression, we are able to make more precise, cross-country comparisons of BN satisfaction than would be possible with a positive indicator (e.g., political participation). Even so, it will not be easy to construct measures of political repression that are capable of international comparison. For example, it is obvious that the criteria for political repression employed by Amnesty International and Freedom House are deficient in many respects (see Scoble and Wiseberg, 1981).

Perhaps the best instrument we have for the measurement of political repression at present is the three-dimensional measure devised by Bissell, Haignere, McCamant, and Picklo. They define political repression as "the use of coercion or the threat of coercion by authorities or their supporters against opponents or potential opponents in order to prevent or weaken their capabilities to oppose the authorities and their policies" (McCamant, 1981, p. 133). They suggest that the analysis of political repression thus defined must proceed on three tiers: (1) scope—the extent of restriction placed upon oppositional activity; (2) arbitrariness—the predictability with which coercive actions against the oppositional activities are executed; and (3) severity—the extent of harm done to those persons sanctioned by authorities for their oppositional activities or thoughts. Then for each of these dimensions they provisionally operationalize the extent of scope, arbitrariness, and severity on a 10-point scale. Although the work of Bissell, Haignere, McCamant, and Picklo is only a preliminary sketch of what valid, international measures for political repression might look like, it shows enough promise to suggest that objective, interstate measures of political repression may be available in the not-too-distant future.

2.9. SOME OMISSIONS: EMPLOYMENT, LEISURE, AND PARTICIPATION

Brief mention should be made of three items that are often considered BN yet were omitted in our discussion of a BN bundle: productive employment, leisure/recreation, and political participation. Perhaps the most notable omission in the above BN bundle is employment. The International Labor Office included employment "both as a means and as an end" in its list of BN. Most who write on BN follow this convention. It is clear that the implementation of BN programs (which are labor-intensive by definition) will generate many employment opportunities (e.g., community health workers, teachers). However, it is not readily apparent that formal employment is itself a BN.

First, although formal employment is a necessary means for many people to satisfy their BN, it is clearly not a universal means. For example, in industrialized welfare states, formal employment is no longer a precondition for the BN satisfaction of certain citizens (e.g., the severely handicapped, mothers with dependent children). Moreover, most nonliterate, traditional societies have mechanisms to distribute collective resources that certainly cannot be described in terms of the wage labor paradigm.

Second, formal employment not only fails as a universal means to BN satisfaction but also does not qualify as a universal end. People throughout history have occupied themselves with many creative, productive, and satisfying endeavors that could not be labeled as formal employment (e.g., child-rearing, hobbies, nonremunerative artistic activities). For instance, the way that many people anticipate and relish retirement suggests that one's productive energies need not be channeled in formal employment in order to lead a happy life. Moreover, the concept of job satisfaction presumes a fairly high degree of economic specialization. Even in the highly specialized economies of MDCs, job satisfaction is an elusive goal for many, due to boredom created by over-specialization, limitations on lateral and vertical mobility, poor employee-to-employee or employee-to-employer relationships, and the fact that some jobs (no matter how highly remunerated) will always be perceived as intrinsically less satisfying than others.

In light of the above considerations, it seems reasonable to conclude that employment itself is not a basic human need, even though employment-generation strategies for economic development will certainly be a crucial component of any attempt to implement the BNA.

Leisure or recreation is also sometimes listed as a BN. Obviously if the inclusion of leisure into a BN bundle simply means that humans are not machines and need moments for rest and play, then the inclusion is justified (as a necessary good for the development of sociality and, to some extent, intelligence). However, as Denis Goulet (1978, p. 239) notes, when writers refer to leisure, they usually have in mind a fairly ethnocentric concept. Western observers equate recreation or leisure with pleasurable consumption that is made possible by the discretionary household income generated by one's work. By contrast, recreational activities in traditional societies are often performed in the course of one's work (e.g., singing, games, dancing, play, conversation). Also many forms of recreation depend on only an imaginative appropriation of local resources and do not require special contrivances. Hence it seems reasonable to assume that moments of leisure/recreation will be structured in any human society, and that it is not necessary to treat this as a separate item in a BN bundle.

Finally, political participation is often regarded as a BN. While it is clear that local participation will be a crucial variable in the formulation and implementation of BN programs (see Lisk, 1985), it is not evident that political participation should be treated as an end in itself. On the one hand, there is little doubt that most people wish to exercise some influence over matters that affect those interests they perceive as critical to their well-being. On the other hand, voting behavior in many industrialized democracies and the behavior of workers in self-managed enterprises (e.g., Yugoslavia) suggest that the desire to participate in collective decision making is very uneven, particularly when one's perceived interests are not directly at stake. This would seem to indicate that political participation, by itself, is not a universal human need. Instead the *opportunity* to participate when one's own interests are affected in one way or another should be considered a BN. Presumably such opportunities for participation will develop naturally in sociopolitical contexts that are characterized by the absence of political repression (the X_3 good for sociality). Therefore it seems inadvisable to list political participation as a distinct item in a BN bundle.

2.10. THE PROBLEM OF INTRACLASS RANKINGS

While it does not seem necessary to establish intraclass rankings for BN of the X_2 or X_3 variety, an intraclass ranking is imperative for needs relating to physical existence (X_1), as most of the significant policy issues bearing on the allocation of scarce resources concern this class of needs.

In constructing intraclass ranks for needs relating to physical existence (i.e., minimal nutrition, safe water/sanitation, primary health care, shelter/clothing/energy/transportation, and municipal protection/national defense), it is necessary to identify a common denominator that will make intraclass comparisons possible. The most obvious common denominator here is the impact of BN shortfalls upon the longevity of human life. For the most part, the dramatic advances in life expectancy during the past two centuries in the West have come about through improvements in nutrition and public health programs (instead of sophisticated curative health care measures), and it is part of the accepted wisdom of our day that the human body easily has the capacity to survive into the early seventies with proper nutrition and care.

Maximizing the *quantity* of life has been an important hominid objective since our ancestors first roamed the African savanna. Clearly the survival instinct is the most powerful "innate drive" among humans, as well as most animal species. In this regard, it is interesting to note that the oft-mentioned trade-off between the quantity of life and the quality of life only becomes an influential factor in shaping an individual's decisions during old age or during periods of acute physical incapacitation or extreme emotional distress.[13] In a real sense it is appropriate to view the attainment of 70 years or so of life as the natural birthright of the human body, given advances in the fields of medicine, public health, and nutrition during this century.

In addition to the strong preference for life demonstrated by humans, it should be noted that a baseline number of years of lived existence are necessary prerequisites for developing the two species capabilities of intelligence and sociality. For instance, Piaget discovered that children did not reach the highest stage of mental functioning ("Formal Operational Intelligence") until they were 12–15 years old (Piaget, 1954; Inhelder and Piaget, 1958). Moreover, studies on cognition and moral development have suggested that the highest stages of moral reasoning cannot be reached prior to the late teens or early twenties (Duska and Whelan, 1975; Kohlberg, 1973; Kohlberg and Gilligan, 1971). In terms of human sociality, longitudinal studies on prosocial behavior have shown that human children make dramatic strides in developing empathetic and sharing abilities between ages 4 and 13 (Mussen and Eisenberg-Berg, 1977, pp. 20–23, 66). Additionally, psychologists and anthropologists have identified age-related life-cycle stages commonly manifest by humans from divergent cultures, stretching from early childhood through old age—stages that not only define the individual's changing role in the social order but also help make the universe meaningful (Erikson, 1968; Turnbull, 1983). Thus, in a significant respect, *basic* competencies in intelligence and socality cannot be achieved prior to ages 12–15, and a full, meaningful life has meant for most humans the opportunity to participate in the joys and tribulations of birthing a new generation and living long enough to insure the survival of their offspring, and, if fortunate, to enjoy their grandchildren.

It is important, though, to examine one serious objection to the idea that the length of life is the most appropriate indicator of whether an individual's BN for physical existence are being met. This objection concerns the relationship between mortality and morbidity: What is the worth of a long life if one is sick during much of one's productive years?

In response to this objection, it should be noted that there is a strong correlation between the general health status of a population and the average life expectancy achieved by the society (Morris, 1979, p. 41). In other words, high rates of morbidity are positively correlated with high rates of unwarranted or premature mortality, and vice versa. Moreover, health measures that fall under the heading of BN interventions (e.g., vaccinations) will obviously improve average life expectancies more than nonbasic medical procedures (e.g., cosmetic surgery).

If the longevity of life can be defended as the common denominator of all the needs related to physical existence, it would be possible to arrive at intraclass ranks on the basis of the ratio between the monetary investment in a particular BN category (BN) and the effect of that investment on increases in the life expectancy at birth in denominations of months (LE_{mos}). I shall to refer to this ratio as the BN Investment Ratio: BN/LE_{mos}. The purpose of the BN Investment Ratio is to identify the most cost-effective means of increasing the life expectancy of a community. For example, if a particular community is forced to choose between spending $50,000 during time period t for a child nutrition program or a sanitation project, the decision could be resolved by calculating the ratio between the dollar investment and the number of months such investment will add to the life expectancy at birth for a particular community. Hence if the child nutrition program will enhance the life expectancy at birth by 20 months and the sanitation project will increase the life expectancy at birth by 5 months, the child nutrition program would have priority, as the ratio yielded a lower dollar figure ($2,500) than the sanitation project ($10,000). If data were available, the same analysis could apply to all forms of BN investment within the X_1 category, ranging from defense expenditures to health programs.[14]

2.11.   LIFE EXPECTANCY AS A SIMPLIFYING CONCEPT

Hicks and Streeten (1979), in their survey of possible BN indicators, have suggested that life expectancy is a single measure that shows great potential for encompassing and integrating other BN indicators. In addition, the late Dudley Seers (1977) has recommended a broad application of the concept of life expectancy for social accounting systems, and the Overseas Development Council's "Physical Quality of Life Index" (PQLI) relies heavily on both the infant mortality rate and life expectancy at age one in constructing a scalar measure of development for cross-country analysis (Morris, 1979).

The major drawback with life expectancy at birth as a BN indicator is that it makes the questionable value judgment that only the aggregate number of years of life within a population are relevant to social welfare. For example, the life expectancy measure is indifferent to whether two individuals die at age 50 or whether one individual dies at age 10 and the other at age 90. However Jacques Silber (1983) has proposed a promising alternate indicator that accounts for inequalities in the distribution of life within a population: the ELL (Equivalent Length of Life).

The ELL measure applies indexes of income inequality developed by Atkinson and Kolm to the analysis of life tables. The major ethical component of the ELL concerns the selection of a value for parameter $\propto$. The higher the value for parameter $\propto$, the more sensitive the ELL is to inequalities in the distribution of life (hence lowering the aggregate equivalent length of life). For example, the life expectancy at birth (as normally computed) in Guatemala is 49.3 years as compared to 73.7 years in Sweden (i.e., the per capita aggregate years lived in Sweden are 1.5 times greater than in Guatemala). However, when Atkinson's inequality measure is used with a high value (0.50) for parameter $\propto$, the ELL for Guatemala is only 12.5 years in comparison to Sweden's ELL of 55.3 years (i.e., the equally distributed life spans in Sweden are nearly 4.5 times greater than in Guatemala). In spite of the complications involved in computing the ELL (e.g., the lack of reliable data, the problem of assigning a value to parameter $\propto$), the ELL is a far more sophisticated development measure than simple life expectancy at birth and holds much promise as a guide for BN investment.

2.12.   THE PROBLEM OF INTERCLASS WEIGHTS

I suggested in section 2.4 that interclass rankings in a BN hierarchy can be determined through logical deduction by assigning priority to those second-order goods that are essential prerequisites for the development of other second-order goods. With respect to the three core human attributes of biological existence, intelligence, and sociality, I argued that biological existence would rank first, intelligence second, and sociality third, given the fact that it is impossible to conceive of human sociality apart from human intelligence, but the distinctive features of human intelligence (including the capacity for symbolic communication) remain intact when isolated from social interaction.

Once these second-order goods have been rank-ordered, we must proceed to identify a weighting principle that will guide BN investment among the three levels of first-order goods (i.e., the BN categories themselves). At least three weighting principles may be relevant for this purpose: (1) the Lexicographic Principle, (2) the Serial-Incremental Reduction Principle, and (3) the BN Multiplier Principle.

The concept of a lexicographic (or lexical) ordering was first introduced by John Rawls (1971, pp. 42–43). The Lexical Principle holds that absolute weight should be given to the first item in an ordering until some target has been reached. Once that target has been achieved, absolute weight is transferred to the second item, and so forth. If the Lexical Principle were applied to a rank-ordered set of BN, it would mandate that all forms of BN investment should be directed toward the X_1 needs until some acceptable ELL target has been achieved before investment could take place in other BN sectors. The obvious problem with this approach is that the Lexical Principle is far too rigid and unrealistic to be useful in guiding BN investment priorities, because it ignores the existence of many important complementarities among BN interventions and disregards macroeconomic policies that must accompany BN programs if they are to be stable and successful.

The Serial-Incremental Reduction Principle would simply hold that BN investment should be distributed equally across all three classes of need, with the temporal distinction that the first category is the first to receive attention. Essentially a principle of this type simply holds that the rank-ordering of X_1, X_2, and X_3 needs simply dictates temporal priority, emphasizing that equal weight should be given to all three in a BN investment strategy. While this principle would help spread BN investment more evenly than the Lexical Principle, it is clearly unacceptable, due to the significant differences between the three classes in terms of the relative impact of BN shortfalls (e.g., starvation versus illiteracy).

The BN Multiplier Principle is the third possible weighting principle. Essentially it seeks to optimize important complementarities in BN interventions while still respecting the priorities set forth in a rank-ordered BN bundle. The principle holds that expenditures should be distributed in such a way as to optimize the linkages among different BN categories.

Obviously judicious BN investment will take advantage of such complementarities by investment in education (X_2) and expanding available mechanisms for political participation (X_3), as these forms of investment have a strong impact on the quantity of life in the X_1 category of needs. For example, as previously noted, literacy is the most highly correlated BN variable in relation to life expectancy at birth. To focus exclusively on the biological needs of the X_1 level to the exclusion of investment in basic education would clearly be ill-advised.

Therefore the Basic Needs Multiplier Principle is far more adequate than the other two weighting principles, because it optimizes the natural complementarities among the various items of a BN bundle.[15]

2.13.   THE PROBLEM OF EXTERNAL RANKINGS

Thus far the discussion on rank-ordering and weighting a BN bundle has focused on intraclass rankings (i.e., among X_1 needs) and interclass rankings (i.e., among X_1, X_2 and X_3 needs). Since both interclass and intraclass rankings are concerned with relative priorities within a BN bundle, they will be referred to as internal rankings. It is obvious that in addition to internal rankings, some external rank-order and weight must be assigned to a BN bundle (between basic and nonbasic goods) for the BNA to be operationally meaningful.

Let us assume that among a list of objectives for national policy, BN programs are ranked first in a government's budget priorities. At least three types of weighting principles may be relevant for a BN bundle's external rank: (1) the Lexical Principle, (2) the Principle of Expedience, and (3) the Principle of Recurrence. The first weighting principle would yield what Streeten and his associates (1981, pp. 54–55) have called a "pure BNA," and the second and third principles would produce a "mixed BNA."

The Lexical Principle, as discussed in the previous section, holds that the first item in a rank-ordered set of policy objectives should receive absolute weight until some designated goal is reached before moving on to investment in the second item, and so forth. Hence the Lexical Principle would assign infinite weight to expenditures earmarked for BN programs and zero weight to nonbasic policy objectives (until the BN objectives were fully achieved). For example, the Lexical Principle would appear to insist that the BN of the last 1% of a population should be met before expenditures were concentrated on raising the incomes of the other 99% above the BN threshold.

The Principle of Expedience simply leaves it up to policy makers or voters to assign a weight to BN investment that they deem appropriate. Hence the weighting problem is evaded by leaving the matter to be settled by the preferences of a particular decision maker, whether the decision maker is a benevolent dictator or some kind of social choice procedure.

The third weighting mechanism is the Principle of Recurrence. This principle holds that BN investment should proceed at levels that will optimize the stability of BN programs within a certain time frame. The Principle of Recurrence recognizes that many nonbasic macroeconomic objectives (e.g., balance of payments, inflation, growth in GNP) are critical pillars for the implementation of the BNA in the long term and will subvert BN policies if left unattended.

Obviously the choice of weighting principles will have a decisive impact on the determination of the BNA's time horizon. For example, the Lexical Principle would lead to a considerably shorter planning horizon for meeting BN than the Principle of Expedience. In this regard, it should be emphasized that there are positive intergenerational consequences produced by a telescoped time horizon for the BNA. It is unlikely that increased expenditures for well-designed BN programs will rob future generations of opportunities for growth. Instead it seems that satisfaction of BN at an early stage of development leads to a more equitable growth path at later stages—redistribution *before* growth instead of redistribution *with* growth (Morawetz, 1977, p. 71).

Nonetheless it is readily apparent that the Lexical Principle is far too inflexible to serve as a helpful guide in public policy situations. Ample evidence suggests that an application of the Lexical Principle to BN investment would be both politically and economically infeasible, given the importance of linking BN investment with nonbasic investment in the productive sectors of society within a judicious macroeconomic framework (see Morawetz, 1980; Stewart, 1985, pp. 14–35; Streeten et al., 1981, pp. 58–60). Hence the Principle of Recurrence is certainly the most promising candidate for the problem of external rankings.

2.14. SUMMARY OF THE THEORY OF BASIC NEEDS

The foregoing analysis has shown that it is possible to derive a universal set of basic human needs and a time-relative BN bundle (via the Principle of Technological Adaptation and the Principle of Optimal Coverage) from three species universals (biological existence, human intelligence, human sociality) that are grounded in the open genetic program of human life. Although the need categories of environmental needs (i.e., shelter/clothing/energy/transportation), municipal protection and national defense, and the absence of political repression pose substantial problems of definition and measurement, it seems reasonably clear that these problems could be resolved in due time, assuming the necessary data were available.

With respect to the problem of constructing internal and external ranks of a BN bundle (and applying a selected weighting principle to those rank-orderings), the following conclusions appear to be in order: (1) the determination of rough intraclass rank-orderings is possible, assuming that the necessary data are available, if life expectancy (particularly the ELL measure) is used to measure the impact of BN investment within bounded populations through the computation of BN Investment Ratios; (2) the assignment of weights for the determination of interclass rank-orderings is possible through the application of the BN Multiplier Principle; and (3) the determination of external ranks is possible through a weighting principle such as the Principle of Recurrence.

While certain aspects of the BN concept remain ill-defined and await further clarification, there is little doubt that this approach represents an advance over the kinds of theories of the good embraced by other approaches to distributive justice, both in terms of its apparent universality and its capacity for operational precision. We are now in a position to identify how this rudimentary theory of BN can be logically transformed into a universal development norm (the Basic

Needs Mandate) and a universal moral principle (the Basic Needs Imperative) that retain their validity from one culture to the next.

NOTES

1. David Miller (1976, pp. 127–128) has criticized Barry's instrumental interpretation of need-claims by devising a typology of three different categories of need statements: (1) instrumental needs (Barry's category), (2) functional needs, and (3) intrinsic needs. However, Galston (1980, pp. 162–163) has advanced some decisive criticisms against Miller's categories of functional and intrinsic needs that, in effect, collapse the latter two categories into Barry's instrumental category. While Galston proposes an alternate way of delimiting Barry's instrumentalist understanding of the concept of need, his arguments are not persuasive on normal linguistic grounds.

2. I concede, though, that tactile contact may be important for biological survival during infancy, given the increased incidence of crib deaths in orphanages where nurses do not regularly handle infants in the course of their care.

3. See Arellano (1985) on the importance of adequate coverage in BN programs. It should be noted that specific applications of the Principle of Optimal Coverage must conform to the Principle of Recurrence (see section 2.13) and are subject to the Replication Constraint and the Sociality Constraint (see Chapter 5, sections 5.3 and 5.4).

4. For example, an extensive discussion on recent attempts to formulate qualitative and quantitative measures for internal political instability appears in Andriole and Hopple (1984).

5. It is important to emphasize that a high degree of noncooperative behavior does not necessarily indicate that the state is unjust, as such conduct may reflect weaknesses in the cultural fabric of the society (e.g., a deteriorating family structure, the declining authority of traditional religious/moral beliefs).

6. It should be noted that Gurr and Bishop (1976) have proposed a typology of violence within and between nations that has used factor analysis to reduce 31 measures of violence to eight central dimensions (protest, internal war/revolution, external war, repression, social violence [denial of basic goods], foreign intervention, discrimination, and militarism).

7. I assume (unrealistically) that the total cost curve for internal defense needs is perfectly straight. It is likely that the smaller the probability of violence, the larger the marginal cost in reducing it incrementally.

8. There is evidence from 78 LDCs that arms transfers and overall rates of government expenditures for defense are primarily related to a country's previous involvement in interstate war (see Walker, 1979, pp. 157–206). Of course, a history of involvement in interstate wars may be irrelevant to a nation's current national security posture, as previous conflicts may have provided the occasion for instituting security enhancing measures.

9. I assume (unrealistically) that the total cost curve for external defense needs is perfectly straight. It is likely that the smaller the probability of invasion, the larger the marginal cost in reducing it incrementally.

10. Obviously the disparity between the infant mortality rate and the probability of foreign invasion would be somewhat lower than this comparison suggests, as the infant mortality rate affects a certain segment of the population, whereas a foreign invasion would affect the entire population.

11. However it should be noted that Coombs et al. (1973) previously formulated a concept of "minimum essential learning needs" that parallel's Noor's concept of basic education.

12. In using the term "information media" I mean to convey forms of literature that have the primary purpose of informing the reader about something, in contrast to media designed primarily for entertainment. In making this distinction, I wish to exclude certain types of media from the BN bundle that would clearly be inappropriate in certain cultural settings (e.g., pornographic literature in Muslim countries).

13. Of course, the trade-off between the quantity and quality of life also appears in the debates over the ethics of abortion and population control. Yet in these cases, the individual does not set a quality threshold (below which one would not want to live) for *themselves* but for others. It is likely that humans will nearly always set that quality threshold higher for others than they would for themselves, displaying a stronger individual preference for survival than they would impute to others.

14. I assume that it would be possible to incorporate the probabilities of mortality due to the internal violence (as measured by the actual weighted probability of violence) and the probability of mortality in peacetime with respect to the probability of foreign invasion into the computation of life expectancy at birth.

15. The previously defined Principle of Optimal Coverage presumes a weighting principle like the BN multiplier.

3
The Justification of the Basic Needs Mandate and the Basic Needs Imperative

3.1. THE OPEN GENETIC PROGRAM OF HUMAN LIFE

Since the publication of Edward Westermarck's imposing study of moral diversity across human cultures, *The Origin and Development of Moral Ideas* (1906), it has become part of the accepted wisdom of the academic community that moral relativity is an inescapable fact of life. Indeed the discovery of vast ranges of social, economic, political, and moral diversity among human communities is perhaps the most significant contribution of anthropology during this century— a contribution that has gone a long way toward debunking ethnocentric myths and has helped instill an appropriate sense of cultural humility.

While the reality of both cultural and ethical diversity cannot be disputed, does the presence of such diversity necessarily make moral relativism an inescapable fact of life? Recent investigations have forcefully argued against making a facile link between the perception of ethical diversity and theories of moral relativism either (1) by demonstrating the incoherence of relativist theories (Lyons, 1976; Nielsen, 1966), or (2) by making the case that moral relativity provides a foundation for a universal ethical principle such as the principle of equal worth (Wong, 1984). Hence there appears to be no *necessary* connection between the facts of ethical diversity and corresponding theories of moral relativism. Furthermore, if it could be shown that certain species capacities exponentially increase human adaptive capabilities and have been phylogenetically written into the structure of human existence, then we would have a strong foundation for constructing a global theory of distributive justice that both appreciates and transcends the magnitude of cultural diversity across human communities.

The discussion of sociobiology and neurobiology in Chapter 1, section 1.5.c. revealed that the distinctive features of human intelligence and human sociality were brought about by gene mutations and selection pressures associated with increased brain size and cortical sophistication, as well as various anatomical adaptations, including the underdeveloped birth and prolonged maturation of the human child, the near total suppression of estrus and the development of other features of human sexuality, and the capacity to vocalize a diverse repertoire of phonemes. These evolutionary developments, in conjunction with the sociological innovation known as the hunting and gathering way of life, have enabled humans to generate distinctive forms of culture—characterized by the extensive display of symbolic communication, altruism, empathy, reciprocity, long-term contractual relationships, and social cooperation.

These unique species capabilities, brought about by a constellation of adaptations conveniently subsumed under the headings of intelligence and sociality, have given humans a vast degree of environmental adaptability, enabling them to populate virtually every latitudinal zone of the earth's surface, as well as to live outside the earth's atmosphere and beneath its oceans. In essence, these adaptations have constituted a kind of "open program," phylogenetically written into the biological structure of human existence, which has enabled humans to gather information not contained in the genes and to store, recombine, and transmit that data through cultural evolution, thus attaining "a state of adaptedness," in spite of instabilities inherent within their respective habitats (Lorenz, 1981, p. 258).

3.1.a. The Problem of Maladaptiveness

Is it true that human intelligence and sociality are always adaptive in relation to the ultimate evolutionary goal of species survival? The history of species extinction and our knowledge of natural selection would tell us that no characteristic can be consistently adaptive, either losing its adaptive significance or becoming maladaptive. For example, the strong preference exhibited by human infants for food sugars suggests a genetically programmed behavior that was adaptive for humans in their early environment (Lumsden and Wilson, 1981, pp. 40–41). The strong taste preference for sweetness and aversion to bitterness encouraged humans to select ripe, nutritious fruit over spoiled or unripened fruit. Of course, the same taste preference now prompts many humans to consume more candy than ripe fruit (Williams, 1966). Moreover, the frequency of primitive phobias relating to the fear of strangers, snakes, spiders, closed spaces, heights, running waters, and thunderstorms among human infants and children suggests that the aversion to these traditional enemies in man's early environment was adaptive and genetically transmitted from one generation to the next. Unfortunately human infants and children do not display a similar aversion to the environmental threats of modern industrial societies (e.g., guns, knives, electric sockets).[1]

The fact that genetic evolution is unable to respond to rapid habitat changes or dramatic shifts in predator populations/behaviors and the tendency for plant and animal species to fall into the evolutionary trap of overspecialization (i.e., being too adapted to a particular habitat) suggest that no species characteristic can be consistently adaptive over time. Are there exceptions, though, to the general rule that biological characteristics are adaptive only with reference to certain constellations of environmental conditions?

I argue that the species capacities of human intelligence and human sociality are two such exceptions. Both capacities have produced widely divergent yet bounded forms of human culture and have been adaptive throughout the human evolutionary experience to date. Yet the following objections must be considered carefully.

It is self-evident that the cultivation of technical intelligence is not always in the evolutionary interests of humankind. The impressive technological accomplishments of the last hundred years have produced unparalleled threats to the earth's ecology in the form of the rapid depletion of nonrenewable natural resources, the population crisis, the specter of a nuclear holocaust, chemical warfare, and the potential abuses of genetic recombination. For example, it has been estimated that the United States alone has consumed more raw materials (including fuel) in the past 30 years than all of the natural resources consumed by hominids since our emergence from the African savanna (Uytenbogaardt, 1973). Moreover, the dark side of the reproductive success of humans (due largely to improvements in the transportation and public health infrastructures and increased nutrition) is the population crisis that confronts us today.

A similar mixed review could be offered with respect to human sociality insofar as aggression and altruism are concerned. The life-preserving adaptation of aggression, so essential to the survival of early man, is often dysfunctional in contemporary human societies, evidenced by intrafamilial physical and psychological abuse, crime, repressive governmental regimes, and interstate wars. Unfortunately, the maladaptive dimensions of human aggression have been magnified by recent technological innovations that intensify the sense of "personal distance" within the human community (Becker, 1975). Because of this increased range of "personal distance," empathetic emotions no longer play a major role in restraining aggressive conduct. Primitive hand-to-hand combat has been replaced with clinical ethos of sophisticated electronic displays at 30,000 feet. One pilot who flew in Vietnam put it like this:

For the pilot it's a set of coordinates. It's an altitude, it's a distance, it's flipping a switch, it's all these things that are so abstract. You depersonalize the enemy and you depersonalize the civilians. . . . You don't see the effect of what you do. Except the closer you get to the ground, the more that changes (Lavell, 1981).

Another problem related to sociality concerns the underdeveloped state of altruistic proficiencies among humans. Most instances of altruistic behavior in human interaction have taken the form of kin altruism (i.e., beneficent actions directed toward one's immediate family and relatives) and reciprocal altruism (i.e., beneficent actions motivated by the self-interested expectation that they will be reciprocated at some time in the future). In addition to these two common forms of altruism, there are clear indications that the challenges of the 21st century will require the rapid diffusion of a third form of altruism: species altruism (i.e., beneficent actions that are directed toward the survival and flourishing of one's own species and respect the habitats and genetic heritage of all life forms). Apart from the development of robust varieties of species altruism, it is doubtful that the human community will be able to negotiate the "K-transition," discussed in Chapter 11, section 11.1, during the first half of the 21st century. If the attainment of a generalized species altruism is not possible because of inherent genetic constraints, then human sociality is extremely maladaptive in our segment of the human evolutionary journey, and it is doubtful that our kind will be able to meet the momentous challenges posed by the 21st century.

Are the present and potential maladaptive dimensions of human intelligence and sociality the result of inherent flaws of our phylogenetic history or related to certain trends within human cultural evolution? On the one hand, if these maladaptive features of intelligence and sociality are rooted in human DNA, then intelligence and sociality are certainly not universally adaptive capacities. On the other hand, if these characteristics find their basis in human cultural evolution, then a case for their universal adaptiveness could be made.

One way of approaching this question is to consider the nature of three different facets of human cultural organization, which are currently maladaptive in some respect, in relation to our phylogenetic history: (1) technological development, (2) aggressive behavior, and (3) reciprocal altruism. More specifically, we must address three different questions: (1) Is there such a thing as a genetically determined technological imperative that holds, in the words of the physicist Dennis Gabor (1972, p. 43), that "if something *can* be made it *must* be made"? (2) Do humans have an innate tendency to commit socially destabilizing acts of aggression? and (3) Are altruistic behaviors by humans limited to self-interested forms of kin altruism and reciprocal altruism whose ultimate raison d'être is to promote the reproductive capability or genetic endowment of the altruist?

3.1.b. Technological Development and Maladaptiveness

Is there a genetic or logical reason why the capacity to create must necessarily exercise a determinant influence on the will to create? History provides overwhelming evidence that what humans conceive and what becomes technically and economically feasible, humans create. However, is this inclination to do everything that is technologically possible an instinctual or genetically determined trait? Obviously the answer is no.

It seems quite apparent that our desire to develop everything that has a shred of technological and economical feasibility has its foundation in cultural evolution, not genetic evolution. For example, the contemporary tendency to conceptualize progress in terms of technological advancement (as an end in itself) proceeds from a rather peculiar anthropocentric conception of human autonomy and nature that emerged from the Renaissance and intensified during the Enlightenment and the Industrial Revolution. This concept of man and nature understands human progress and destiny in terms of the advancing technological domination of nature. Accordingly this desire, if not lust, to dominate nature becomes legitimated as both an expression of and vehicle for human freedom and autonomy, and nearly every technological development is dubbed as a step forward for human progress. Yet as Goudzwaard (1979) suggests in his penetrating analysis of Western culture, the twin ideals of human freedom and the technological domination of nature are poised in an essential conflict, which he has termed "the dialectic of progress." Goudzwaard argues that in the process of seeking to dominate nature, humans have unwittingly relinquished much of their own freedom and autonomy in the process. Hence the technological domination of nature leads to self-domination, and progress legitimates a spurious love affair with technology that victimizes both humans and nature.

Even though it is quite clear that there is no "technological imperative" written into the human genetic code, there may be a genetic factor that influences one important aspect of our contemporary problems with technology. That possible genetic factor is the tendency for humans to confuse low-probability/low-consequence events with low-probability/high-consequence events (Lumsden and Wilson, 1981, p. 88). Because humans characteristically tend to underestimate the gravity of potential disasters, the cognitive recognition that certain forms of technological development could well conclude in ecological disaster may not result in any change of behavior—a particularly frightening thought in view of the nuclear arms race. Of course, the fact that humans lack the intuitive skills necessary for generating integrated probability judgments only underscores the importance of evolving cultural systems that will dethrone technological development from the commanding pedestal it now enjoys in most Western societies.

3.1.c. Aggression and Maladaptiveness

Certainly aggression is the most problematic and disturbing aspect of human behavior for modern sensibilities. Most of us would like to ignore it. For example, I suggest in Chapter 9, section 9.3 that economic theorists (of both neoclassical and Marxian vintage) have constructed theories of economic behavior that fail to account for human aggression and, accordingly, have overlooked some glaring discrepancies between theory and practice in both capitalist and socialist societies.

Do humans have an innate tendency to commit socially destabilizing acts of aggression? In responding to this question, it is important to emphasize at the outset that human beings are *not* the most violent members of the animal kingdom, as some have suggested (e.g., Lorenz, 1966). Hyenas, lions, langur monkeys, some species of ants and wasps are far more violent (in relation to members of their own species) than human beings (E. O. Wilson, 1975, pp. 245–247); and E. O. Wilson (1978, p. 104) has remarked that if hamadryas baboons had nuclear weapons, the world would be destroyed within a week! Our closest primate relatives are vegetarians (or nearly so), and it is a recognized fact that humans are facultative carnivores—meat-eating was a learned behavior, not instinctual (Crook, 1980, pp. 129–130). Furthermore, a growing body of evidence argues against the Freudian notion that aggression is an appetitive instinct that must find certain channels, such as violent sports or war, for the discharge of the internal tensions it creates (Sipes, 1975; Young, 1975).

The behaviors that are typically regarded as aggressive actions could be grouped into at least eight different categories: (1) territorial aggression, (2) dominance aggression, (3) sexual aggression, (4) parental disciplinary aggression, (5) weaning aggression, (6) moralistic aggression, (7) predatory aggression, and (8) antipredatory aggression (E. O. Wilson, 1975, pp. 242–243). When we think about socially destabilizing forms of aggression, it is generally the first three categories we have in mind. Hence we must ask whether there is an innate tendency for humans to practice socially destabilizing acts of territorial aggression, dominance aggression, and sexual aggression?

Territorial aggression involves signals and actions that are executed in the process of defending or conquering a particular territory. The most common and accepted manifestation of territorial aggression in nearly all human cultures has been the prerogative of self-defense. The near universal legitimation of aggression in defensive contexts and the uneven history of pacifism suggests that the so-called instinct of self-preservation has a strong genetic foundation that can only be superseded by heroic religious conditioning. Pacifist communities that are not protected by larger, nonpacifist societies have been among the most unstable of human history, and those who own pacifist convictions have great difficulty in cultivating them across the generations.

Irrespective of what one thinks about the genetic roots of defensive modes of territorial aggression, it seems clear that the defense of advertised territories is a socially stabilizing, albeit aggressive, maneuver. By contrast, one would expect that most socially destabilizing acts of territorial aggression involve individuals or groups who intentionally intrude upon the advertised territories of others. The issue is: Are humans genetically predisposed toward territorial aggression of an *offensive* nature?

The answer to this question seems to be a strongly qualified "yes." On the one hand, it is clear that humans, like most animal species, will employ aggression as an ecological strategy for gaining control of sufficient necessities of life, such as food and shelter, when faced with extreme conditions of crowding or scarcity (Bigelow, 1975; Corning, 1975; E. O. Wilson, 1978, p. 103). In this sense, it would probably be appropriate to conclude that there is an innate propensity for revolution among humans when they do not have access to the basic necessities of life and are aware of others who are hoarding such necessary goods.[2] On the other hand, it seems doubtful that humans are genetically predisposed to conquer indiscriminately for the sake of conquering, being driven by an insatiable, Hobbesian lust for power and control. The tragic manifestations of man's inhumanity to man throughout human history are better explained by the adaptive dimensions of war in the pre-nuclear era and other facets of cultural evolution, instead of linking them to the genes. Yet the following proviso must be made: There is a strong likelihood that humans are genetically predisposed, in some respect, to *learn* violence as a mechanism for conflict resolution, and that this predisposition is often linked to the tendency for humans to bifurcate members of their species into friend/in-group and stranger/out-group categorizations, often displaying an immense amount of hostility toward the latter (see E. O. Wilson, 1978, pp. 114–119). The extant anthropological evidence provides ample confirmation of the ability of humans to become proficient in violent behaviors in a brief period of time. For example, E. O.Wilson (1978, pp. 100–101) notes the following:

The most peaceable tribes of today were often the ravagers of yesteryear and will probably again produce soldiers and murderers in the future. Among contemporary !Kung San violence in adults is almost unknown; Elizabeth Marshall Thomas has correctly named them the "harmless people." But as recently as fifty years ago, when these "Bushman" populations were denser and less rigidly controlled by the central government, their homicide rate per capita equalled that of Detroit and Houston. The Semai of Malaya have shown an even greater plasticity. Most of the time they seem to be innocent of even the concept of violent aggression. Murder is unknown, no explicit word for kill exists ("hit" is the preferred euphemism), children are not struck, and chickens are beheaded only as a much regretted necessity. Parents carefully train their children in the habits of non-violence. When Semai men were recruited by the British colonial government to join in the campaign against Communist guerillas in the early 1950s, they were simply unaware that soldiers are supposed to fight and kill. "Many people who knew the Semai insisted that such an unwarlike people could never make good soldiers," writes the American anthropologist Robert K. Dentan. But they were proved wrong:

> Communist terrorists had killed the kinsmen of some of the Semai counterinsurgency troops. Taken out of their nonviolent society and ordered to kill, they seem to have been swept up in a sort of insanity which they call "blood drunkenness." A typical veteran's story runs like this, "We killed, killed, killed. The Malays would stop and go through people's pockets and take their watches and money. We did not think of watches or money. We thought only of killing. Wah, truly we were drunk with blood." One man even told how he had drunk the blood of a man he had killed.

Does the short learning curve that seems to characterize the ability of humans to respond violently in conflict situations constitute a socially destabilizing form of aggression? Intuitively, one would expect to answer the question in the affirmative. However, the ability of humans to acquire aggressive proficiencies quickly actually has the counterintuitive effect of facilitating the development of pacific cultural traditions. If humans faced a long learning curve in acquiring aggressive proficiencies, the risks of tranquility would be unacceptably high, as the cultural survival of more pacific communities would be constantly endangered by the prospect of aggressive intruders. By contrast, the short learning curve for aggression opens up new evolutionary pathways for the development of stable and peaceable strains of human culture.

Is aggression destabilizing when it is associated with the competition over necessary resources? Obviously displays of territorial aggression that emerge from the struggle over necessary and scarce resources typically involve the violation of another's territory/private property, leading to social destabilization in the short term. Yet it is just as apparent that such strategies often enhance the long-term stability of the society by yielding a more ecologically sound distribution of the goods necessary for survival, presuming that there was extensive hoarding of these resources by a minority of the population. Hence it seems likely that such offensive modes of territorial aggression actually contribute to long-term social stability, remaining dormant in most contemporary human communities, until it is triggered in conditions of extreme crowding or scarcity of necessary resources.

Unlike territorial aggression (which is primarily but not necessarily directed against an out-group), dominance aggression is typically employed against members of one's in-group for the purpose of creating or reinforcing a particular hierarchy or pecking order. Obviously such hierarchies frequently help stabilize a social situation by identifying centers of power and routinizing authority. Therefore one might be led to believe that most forms of dominance aggression are inherently socially stabilizing.

The problem is, of course, distinguishing between forms of dominance aggression that have a long-term stabilizing influence versus those that may appear to be stable in the long term but carry within them the seeds of destruction. For example, slavery has never been a stable social institution among human communities in the long term (yet it is extremely stable within ant colonies [E. O. Wilson, 1978, pp. 80–82]), whereas the widespread use of compulsory rituals or coercive institutions to sanction social rules is a regular feature of nearly all forms of human organization.

The role specialization made possible by the development of symbolic modes of communication and extensive social cooperation has embedded complex hierarchical structures within human cultures, allowing individuals to be dominant in some social contexts and submissive in others. Consequently human social systems are characterized by "two-way" power relations that yield degrees of autonomy and dependence, so that "even the most autonomous agent is in some degree dependent, and the most dependent actor or party in a relationship retains some autonomy" (Giddens, 1979, p. 93; cf. Dumont, 1983). Therefore power relations that lose their semblance of reciprocity and are widely perceived as oppressive are highly unstable.

In contrast to territorial aggression, there does not seem to be a genetic predisposition among humans either to learn or to perform acts of dominance aggression. While human history is certainly littered with plenty of instances where individuals sought to dominate others for their own gain, humans hardly display anything like an inherited Hobbesian lust for power. On the contrary, if we can speak of any genetic determinants relating to dominance aggression, it would be the recurring tendency for humans to learn obedience and to respond deferentially to authority.

The famous Stanford experiments conducted by Milgram (1974) and his associates, involving contrived memory experiments using electric shocks, provide distressing testimony of the ease at which normal people abandon their own moral sensibilities in order to satisfy the dictates of an authority figure. As Milgram suggests, it is tempting to understand a predisposition for obedience as a by-product of the human evolutionary experience, given the hunter-gatherers' need for simple and efficient modes of social organization in unpredictable and hostile environments. Of course, not a few individuals have shrewdly exploited the aptitude of humans to learn obedience and revere authority for their own benefit. Niccolò Machiavelli was the first to work out the implications of this social datum for political theory. Unfortunately the tendency for humans to obey and revere authority has had draconian consequences in the form of totalitarianism—a gruesome innovation of the 20th century. Presumably the increased degree of social isolation and anomie that has accompanied modernization has made it easier for people to surrender their individual identities to a collectivity as a means of overcoming feelings of insignificance and isolation (Arendt, 1958).

Probably the most striking aspect of social hierarchies in human communities is their remarkable plasticity. The exceptional variance in the definition and function of hierarchies across human societies suggests that cultural variables are the primary determinants of dominance aggression, instead of genetic factors. Whereas maleness, stature, and physical strength and adroitness were critical factors in the social hierarchies of traditional hunting and gathering societies, hierarchies in modern industrial societies depend mostly on the ability to project confidence and competence ("presence"), communication skills, bureaucratic savvy, and, to an increasingly diminished extent, maleness. The prerequisites for dominance in one culture do not apply in another. Consequently we should look to cultural evolution as the determinant of dominance aggression, not the genes.

Finally, it is readily apparent that sexual aggression has taken many diverse forms among the human species. Its blatant manifestations include female rape and the physical abuse of females, with its more subtle forms being evident in the role-exploitation and strategic dependency that often characterizes male/female relationships. While culture is certainly the primary factor in explaining behavioral differences between males and females, there seems to be some genetic-hormonal basis for these differences. Numerous studies indicate that boys, from two years old onward, are typically more physically venturesome, aggressive, and concerned about dominance status than their female counterparts; whereas girls are typically more attentive to social stimuli (from as early as six months of age), less venturesome and more affiliative than boys (Freedman, 1974; Josephson and Colwill, 1978; Maccoby and Jacklin, 1974; Parsons, 1980). These early behavioral differences between males and females have even been found among the ?Kung San of the Kalahari Desert, a hunter-gatherer society that evidences no differences in the rearing of boys and girls (Blurton-Jones and Konner, 1973).

Assuming that there is some genetic basis underlying the tendency for males to be more sexually aggressive than females, does it follow that males are genetically hard-wired to display sexual aggression? No. Clearly aggression was a part of an adaptive reproductive strategy for our early ancestors, where numerous males competed for access to a limited number of desirable females. However such aggressive behaviors are characterized by considerable plasticity across individuals and cultures, and obviously they have lost their adaptive significance in contemporary social contexts. The display of physical aggression is generally anathema in both the romantic and arranged concepts of courtship. The fact that humans have been able to evolve courtship rituals that do not depend on violent behaviors suggests that there is no genetic imperative that enshrines male sexual aggression as a permanent fixture of the human species.

In summary, of the three forms of aggression that are potentially socially destabilizing, only territorial aggression is a behavior that seems to have a strong genetic basis and can be overcome only by stringent religious convictions. It has been suggested that the short learning curve that characterizes the ability of humans to learn violence has the counterintuitive effect of opening up new evolutionary pathways for the development of stable and peaceable strains of human culture. Moreover, displays of territorial aggression provide a system of checks and balances that discourage both rapid social change (through the defense of existing territorial claims) and extensive hoarding behaviors by a small minority of the population (leading to a more ecologically sound distribution of resources). Hence there is no reason to conclude that aggression represents a bestial flaw that severely diminishes the adaptive properties of human sociality.

3.1.d. Reciprocal Altruism and Maladaptiveness

Are altruistic behaviors among humans limited to self-interested forms of kin altruism and reciprocal altruism whose ultimate raison d'être is to promote the reproductive capability or genetic endowment of the altruist? On the one hand, if genetic evolution has produced bounded varieties of human sociality that restrict the range of altruistic behaviors to the fundamentally self-interested forms of kin selection and reciprocal altruism, then human sociality is currently maladaptive in relation to several contemporary distributive justice problems faced by the global human community (which typically are not amenable to resolutions based on simple reciprocity). On the other hand, if humans have the capability to achieve more disinterested forms of altruism, such as species altruism (i.e., beneficent actions that are directed toward the survival and flourishing of one's own species and respect the habitats and genetic heritage of all life forms), then human sociality retains its adaptive properties.

The writings of E. O. Wilson seem to suggest that genetic hard-wiring makes it highly improbable, if not impossible, for humans to rise above self-interested varieties of altruism. Wilson (1978, pp. 155–156) distinguishes between "hard-core" and "soft-core" altruism, defining the former in terms of self-annihilating, sacrificial action and understanding the latter as simply enlightened self-interest. Hard-core altruism is typically directed toward close relatives and is a strategy designed to enhance the survival of the altruist's genes, in spite of the fact that the individual has sacrificed his own reproductive capability by his altruistic act. By contrast, soft-core altruism simply amounts to assisting someone in distress with the expectation that the person will also come to the aid of the altruist, if that becomes necessary in the future. Sociobiologists usually refer to hard-core altruism as "kin selection" (Hamilton, 1964; E. O. Wilson, 1975, pp. 117–120) and soft-core altruism as "reciprocal altruism" (Maynard Smith, 1983; Trivers, 1980). Figure 3.1 illustrates the relationship between relatedness and altruistic behavior as construed by most sociobiologists.

There is no question that both kin selection (or kin altruism) and reciprocal altruism are necessary components of human sociality (although there are grounds for doubting that altruism is the appropriate term to describe these behaviors). The problem with these categories does not lie with their empirical validity but with the claim that they exhaust the possible range of altruistic behaviors. For example, sociobiologists have typically adopted a Humean perspective in their understanding of the relation between human reason and altruistic behavior (i.e., reason is a slave to the passions). Yet there is much evidence that indicates that human ratiocination—itself a product of natural selection—has given humans "the power to defy the selfish genes of our birth" (Dawkins, 1976, p. 215), including the capacity to transcend the evolutionary categories of altruism (P. Singer, 1981). Indeed, as Ernst Mayr (1988, p. 77) has noted, "the shift from an instinctive altruism based on inclusive fitness to an ethics based on decision making was perhaps the most important step in humanization." Moreover, much empirical data points to the fact that environmental factors play a considerable role in shaping altruistic behaviors (Mussen and Eisenberg-Berg, 1977). Game-theoretical models of nonselfish behavior and some empirical data related to blood donations as well as postdisaster behavior suggest that altruistic behavior sometimes exhibits the characteristics of an epidemic, what Collard (1978) has termed the "contagion thesis" of altruism. Of course, this says nothing of the literature in moral philosophy that has tried to grapple with the behavioral and moral dimensions of disinterested, self-sacrificial, "supererogatory acts" (Urmson, 1958; Feinberg, 1970, pp. 3–24; Raz, 1975). In sum, it seems both simplistic and gratuitous to assume that wide ranges of altruistic behavior among humans can be collapsed into an undifferentiated biological model of either crude or enlightened self-interest.

In light of the foregoing considerations, it seems appropriate to conclude that the distinctive capacities of human intelligence and sociality, constitutive of the

Figure 3.1
The Correlation Between Social Relationships and Altruistic Behaviors

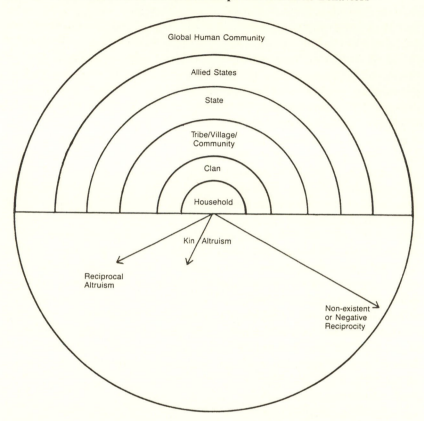

Source: Adapted from David Barash, *Sociobiology and Behavior* (New York: Elsevier, 1977), p. 316.

open genetic program of human life, have placed the human species on a vast adaptive plateau. Consequently the development of the species capacities of intelligence and sociality is logically good in relation to our evolutionary experience, according to the following syllogistic argument:

Premise 1:   Environmental adaptation is good for the human species.

Premise 2:   The development of human intelligence and sociality significantly enhance the capacity of humans to adapt to their environment.

Conclusion: The development of human intelligence and sociality are good for the human species.

Of course, the degree to which the human species can remain on this adaptive plateau depends on whether or not Homo sapiens are able to generate and perpetuate cultural forms that enhance the species capacities of intelligence and sociality. Indeed the pressing questions facing the global human community are nearly exclusively preoccupied with cultural evolution and only tangentially related to genetic evolution. Consequently our attention must be drawn to human cultural evolution, and, more specifically, to the ways in which human cultures can affirm their essential diversity while enhancing the universal species capabilities of intelligence and sociality. This brings us directly to the question of formulating a universal development norm that is, at one and the same time, broad enough to span diverse cultures yet substantive enough to undergird the open genetic program of human life.

3.2. THE PROSPECT OF A UNIVERSAL MORAL PRINCIPLE

The task of constructing and justifying a universal moral principle founded on the open genetic program of human life cannot proceed without extensive reference to Alan Gewirth's (1978) Principle of Generic Consistency. As previously discussed in Chapter 1, section 1.5.b., Gewirth's moral theory represents a powerful synthesis between the naturalistic and Kantian ethical traditions.

For Gewirth the starting point of moral reflection is action or, more precisely, human agency. Action is to moral philosophy what empirical data are to the natural sciences. Gewirth defines action in a morally neutral way and argues that all morally relevant action must have two invariant or "generic" features: (1) voluntariness (referring to an agent's ability to control their behavior); and (2) purposiveness or intentionality (referring to any goal or end of an agent). These generic features of action mean that freedom and well-being are necessary goods for any agent.

The notions of freedom (or voluntariness) and well-being (or generic purposiveness) exhaust the generic goods of action. Well-being, according to Gewirth, consists of three goods: basic goods, nonsubtractive goods, and additive goods. Basic goods are those aspects of well-being that "are the proximate necessary preconditions of his performance of any and all of his actions" (p. 53). Nonsubtractive and additive goods refer to the quantitative dimension of generic goods. The particular contents of nonsubtractive and additive goods will depend upon each individual's conception of the good and their immediate socioeconomic context. However, when viewed generically-dispositionally, nonsubtractive goods comprise those abilities and conditions that are necessary for not losing what an agent regards as good (e.g., food security programs), and additive goods refer to those abilities and conditions that increase or advance an agent's purpose-fulfillment (e.g., education). The categories of nonsubtractive and additive goods are quantitative notions that refer to the loss or gain of goods and, as such, aim at describing in a value-neutral manner an agent's "level of purpose-fulfillment."

Using a well-defined concept of rationality (i.e., agents are able to trace logical entailments and avoid self-contradiction), Gewirth organizes this process of rational reflection on the nature of human agency according to what he calls a "dialectically necessary method" (p. 44). The strength of this (Socratic) dialectical process—which attempts to translate an agent's informal, practical judgments into equivalent formal, linguistic expressions—is that one is able to enter the agent's own perspective. Gewirth claims that his dialectically necessary method reveals that an agent with the capacity to trace logical entailments and who values logical consistency will affirm the validity of a substantive, categorical moral principle, on pain of contradiction, which he calls the "Principle of Generic Consistency": "Act in accord with the generic rights of your recipients as well as of yourself" (p. 135). The function of this categorical, supreme moral principle is to provide "the justification of all correct moral judgments and rules" (p. 7).

Gewirth's defense of the PGC is detailed and, by any standard, impressively constructed. The core argument consists in defending the logical entailments of a series of statements, where the subject of these claims is the agent.

He or she begins by establishing that all purposive action is both valuational (agents act for purposes they construe as being good, where "good" is a value-neutral concept and simply refers to a pro-attitude of an agent toward his or her actions) and has freedom and well-being (in its three dimensions) as its generic or invariant features.

Hence, when an agent (actually or prospectively) claims (1) "I do X for purpose E" (as all choosing, purposive agents must), it follows that (2a) "E is good" and (2b) "My freedom and well-being are necessary goods." Because the agent necessarily views his or her own purposes as good (2a) and recognizes that certain goods are necessary preconditions for the realization of these purposes (2b), it logically follows, according to Gewirth, that (3) "I have rights to freedom and well-being." Gewirth interprets the movement from statement 2b to statement 3 as simply reflecting the agent's prudentially motivated realization that *any* purposive action requires freedom and well-being, thereby necessitating, ipso facto, the agent's conclusion that he or she has "rights" to these generic goods. Hence statement 3 emerges from the structure of human action instead of proceeding from an exogenous theory of rights.

Once the veracity of statement 3 is established, Gewirth demonstrates that statement 3 logically entails (4) "all other persons ought at least to refrain from interfering with my freedom and well-being." Gewirth justifies this move on the basis of the formal structure of rights claims ("A has a right to X against B by virtue of Y" [pp. 65ff.]), which locates individual rights-claims in a correlative relationship with one's moral obligations to others.

Once the entailments from statement 1 to statement 4 are established, Gewirth introduces what he calls the Logical Principle of Universalizability (i.e., "if some predicate P belongs to some subject S because S has the property Q [where the "because" is that of sufficient reason or condition], then P must also belong to all other subjects S_1, S_2, ...S_n that have Q" [pp. 105ff.]). This Logical Principle of Universalizability, in turn, yields the Criterion of Relevant Similarities ("if one person S has a certain right because he has quality Q . . . , then all persons who have Q must have such a right"). Once the truth of the Criterion of Relevant Similarities is accepted, Gewirth proceeds to demonstrate that statement 4 entails (5) "all prospective agents have rights to freedom and well-being," because being a prospective purposive agent is the sufficient condition (Q) for the possession of generic rights (P). From statement 5 it logically follows that (6) "I ought at least to refrain from interfering with the freedom and well-being of any prospective purposive agent."

Finally, in light of the transactional structure of action (which involves agents as well as the recipients of their actions) and the fact that often negative moral obligations logically imply the existence of positive moral obligations (where an agent ought to assist his recipients in having "freedom and well-being whenever they cannot otherwise have these necessary goods and he can help them at no comparable cost to himself" [p. 135]), it follows from statement 6 that (7) "I ought to respect the freedom and well-being of any (and every) prospective purposive agent." The imperative form of statement 7 is the PGC: "Act in accord with the generic rights of your recipients as well as yourself."

All things considered, the PGC is an egalitarian universalist moral principle that is derived from nonmoral (logical and prudential) considerations. The PGC prescribes an "Equality of Generic Rights," where strict equality obtains at the level of basic and nonsubtractive goods and the equality of opportunity determines the allocation of additive goods (pp. 206, 246–247). As such, the PGC does not impose an obligation of positive beneficence at the level of additive goods. However the PGC does consider such assistance morally obligatory at the level of basic and nonsubtractive goods, that is, if no "comparable cost" is incurred by the agent rendering such aid (where comparable cost is defined as risking one's basic/nonsubtractive goods to prevent the loss of another's basic/nonsubtractive goods).

Since Gewirth's theory synthesizes different features of the Kantian and naturalistic ethical traditions, it is important to explore whether any typical weaknesses of these respective traditions survive in his "modified naturalism."

First, let us examine the Kantian element in Gewirth's theory, which I take to be his affirmation of logical consistency as a necessary feature of practical reason. For Gewirth the criterion of noncontradiction has overriding and categorical force, forging the critical, justificatory link between his "normative structure of action" and the PGC. Hence Gewirth's understanding of rationality plays an undeniably critical role in establishing the PGC as the supreme moral principle.

Gewirth's strong Kantian commitment to the worth of consistency has been criticized as being an exogenous value commitment that he has imported to his theory of rationality, instead of proceeding from the intrinsic qualities of human rationality itself. For example, Galston (1980, p. 50) argues that Gewirth's concept of rationality avoids forms of radical skepticism (e.g., Nietzsche) that devalue the significance of ratiocination in human behavior and aspirations.

The crux of this criticism turns on whether one is referring to rationality as a structural concept or a behavioral concept. From a *structural* standpoint, it seems clear that both the principles of noncontradiction and transitivity form the groundwork of *any* exercise in rational reflection. From a *behavioral* standpoint, rational considerations may have little to no influence in determining the motivation and structure of a particular action, in relation to other factors (e.g., emotions, power, social status) that may influence an action. Yet the fact that people do not always uphold the principles of noncontradiction and transitivity in their actual behavior does not disqualify these characteristics as necessary features of human rationality. Instead it simply affirms the truth of Aristotle's insight that "moral weakness" is an unrelenting fact of life where human behavior is concerned.

Turning to the naturalistic element in Gewirth's theory, the most common criticism is that Gewirth has imported a moral notion of rights into his logical defense of the PGC (Galston, 1980, pp. 50–51; MacIntyre, 1981, pp. 64–65). The problem concerns the transition from statement 2b ("My freedom and well-being are necessary goods") to statement 3 ("I have rights to freedom and well-being"). Essentially the criticism goes like this. The concept of rights is built on the idea that individuals can advance (potentially) sanctionable claims on the behavior of others (which obviously must be recognized as legitimate claims by the claimant's audience). It is clear, though, that many of the purposes for which an agent may act will not be sufficient to compel others to guarantee that he has the requisite generic goods to achieve those purposes.

Hence, as the criticism goes, how does an agent's pro-attitude toward his or her own ends (and his or her corresponding perception that freedom and well-being are necessary means to accomplish those ends) become a morally compelling rights-claim for others? The obvious answer seems to be that individual claims upon others become morally compelling only when they are universalized (thereby limiting the class of legitimate rights-claims), which does not take place until step 5 of the argument ("all prospective agents have rights to freedom and well-being"). Consequently, because the transition from step 2b to step 3 appears to presuppose step 5 (universalization) as a necessary condition, in what sense can we say that statement 2b entails statement 3?

Gewirth (1978, pp. 68ff.) anticipated this objection and took pains to refute it by clarifying that the term "rights" need not necessarily refer to moral or legal concepts and has simply a prudentially based meaning in statement 3 ("I have rights to freedom and well-being"). However there is a distinction, he notes, between mere demands and rights-claims, as the latter require some sort of justificatory reason for them to be intelligible. The justificatory rationale behind statement 3 is that the agent realizes that *any* purposive action he or she may wish to initiate (irrespective of the ends toward which the act is aimed) requires freedom and well-being as necessary conditions. Hence the justificatory reason that makes statement 3 more than an arbitrary demand is grounded in the facts of human agency, not in some sort of universalization procedure. Consequently this objection to Gewirth's theory does not appear to be decisive.[3]

3.3.   PROBLEMS WITH GENERIC GOODS

The primary difficulties facing Gewirth's moral theory concern neither his methodology nor the structure of his logical argument. Instead the principal problems center upon Gewirth's understanding of generic goods, as well as his initial decision to select human agency as the *only* morally relevant, universal feature of human life (which tends to bias the determination of certain critical questions by giving "agency" priority over "being").[4]

As discussed previously, Gewirth argues that human agency requires the generic goods of freedom and well-being (in its three dimensions of basic goods, nonsubtractive goods, and additive goods). Basic goods consist of those aspects of well-being that form the necessary preconditions of action. Nonsubtractive goods comprise those abilities and conditions that are necessary in order to safeguard one's level of purpose-fulfillment at the level of basic goods, and additive goods refer to those abilities and conditions that increase an agent's level of purpose-fulfillment.

At all three levels of well-being, Gewirth regards freedom as an essential prerequisite for human agency. Although he notes that freedom and well-being are coextensive in many respects, he emphasizes that the conceptual autonomy of freedom is crucial. Gewirth does not argue for any priority of freedom over well-being (at any level of purpose-fulfillment) or vice versa, as there is no logical way that one can limit the other, since freedom and well-being exhaust the generic features of action. Consequently it seems proper to conclude that Gewirth treats freedom as a necessary, undifferentiated, and discontinuous (i.e., it cannot substitute for something else) member of the set of generic goods at any level of well-being. Gewirth concedes, though, that in cases of extreme scarcity, it may be permissible to invoke nondemocratic procedures in the short term to prevent starvation or to prevent other basic harms; however, such measures are permitted only in extraordinary situations for a limited duration (p. 321).

The discontinuous relationship between freedom and well-being at any level of purpose-fulfillment seems like an unusually strong claim for the worth of freedom. One wonders whether Gewirth's strong affirmation of the worth of freedom is due, in part, to his prior decision to make human agency the only morally relevant common denominator of human life. The contention that agents cannot rationally justify a limited sphere of freedom for the sake of increased well-being is strained, at best. For example, at the level of basic goods, it would seem to be a rational choice for an individual to limit their sphere of unforced choice voluntarily (beyond simply the suspension of democratic social choice procedures) for the sake of sheer biological survival, suggesting that freedom is in a continuous relationship to well-being. Moreover it seems likely that persons undergoing severe deprivation will characteristically value additional increments of material well-being more than political freedom or the freedom to migrate.

One way of focusing this question about the worth of freedom at low levels of material well-being is to ask the question: If I were a peasant in the poorest income decile in China or India in 1949 (and had knowledge of the future developments within both countries), in which country would I prefer to live, ceteris paribus? The same question could be asked with respect to Cuba and the Dominican Republic in 1959. The fact that the answers to such questions do not seem immediately self-evident suggests that Gewirth's discontinuous valuation of freedom is highly suspect.

In addition to the problem of selecting an appropriate starting point for moral reflection on naturalistic grounds, Gewirth's concept of nonsubtractive goods introduces numerous problems of definition and implementation. Essentially the notion of nonsubtractive goods is a security concept, in that it holds that all agents need to retain their present stock of basic goods as a foundation for increasing their stock of additive goods. The fact that Gewirth's concept of nonsubtractive goods has strong affinities with the notion of security introduces substantial definitional problems into his theory of generic goods. As discussed in Chapter 2, section 2.2, security is a highly relative and an extremely difficult concept to operationalize, as it represents a function of perceived past instabilities in need-satisfaction, perceived prospective instabilities, one's individual propensity to take risks, and one's ideological resources. Moreover, the difficulties involved in defining security would be seriously compounded by any attempt to define an international security threshold. This would raise the dual problems of (1) defining a universally valid propensity for Homo sapiens to accept risk, and (2) determining universally valid, age-specific, threshold probabilities that indicate acceptable degrees of failure in the continuation of individual longevity.

A final problem facing Gewirth's theory of generic goods concerns his appropriation of John Rawls' "lexical principle" in constructing the internal and external rank-orderings and weights among his set of generic goods. Gewirth's use of the lexical ordering principle introduces two major difficulties into his theory of generic goods concerning: (1) the problem of defining the hierarchical relationship between nonsubtractive and additive goods in relation to the variance of individual propensities to accept risk, and (2) the problem of implementing feasible intranational and transnational resource transfers in accordance with the PGC.

Gewirth claims that an internal (intraclass and interclass) hierarchy among generic goods can be determined "by the degree of their indispensability for purposive action" (pp. 62–63). He calls this the "Criterion of Degrees of Necessity for Action" (p. 343). Not only does this hierarchy exist between these three components of well-being (i.e., first basic, then nonsubtractive, and so forth), but there exists an intraclass hierarchy for the class of basic goods (p. 63). Gewirth weights his interclass rank-ordering among the three dimensions of well-being according to Rawls' (1971) notion of a lexicographic or lexical ordering. The lexical principle holds that absolute weight should be given to the first item in a class ordering until some target has been reached. Once that target has been achieved, absolute weight is transferred to the second item, and so forth.

While the lexical ordering between basic goods and nonsubtractive goods is clear and does not require further comment, there is a major problem with a lexical hierarchy between nonsubtractive and additive goods that concerns the variable factor of individual propensities to accept risk. Given the fact that the notion of nonsubtractive goods is primarily a security concept and the PGC requires a lexical ordering between nonsubtractive and additive goods, then one is forced to conclude that rationality is inherently risk-averse (assuming that the PGC is a logical extension of human rationality). Clearly such a claim is not warranted on the basis of human experience.

The problematic aspects of the lexical principle not only appear with respect to internal orderings among generic goods, but also encroach upon the external ordering between generic and nongeneric goods. For example, in relation to the BNA, the PGC would mandate what Streeten and his associates (1981, p. 55) have termed a "pure BNA." In other words, all forms of investment irrelevant to BN programs would be given zero weight until the BN of the entire population were met. Consequently it would be immoral, according to the PGC, to pursue economic and social policies that raised the incomes of 95% of the population if the BN of 5% of the population were unmet. Furthermore, Gewirth's lexical hierarchy among basic, nonsubtractive and additive goods would require an implementation sequence for the BNA that would be roughly consistent with the lexical hierarchy (i.e., all members of a population should have basic goods before delivery systems for nonsubtractive or additive goods are established).

The obvious problem with a pure BNA is that it is too rigid to be a realistic policy objective. No credible implementation sequence for the BNA could be executed in strict compliance with the PGC's lexical ordering. Moreover, it would be economic and political suicide for any policy maker to assign such absolute weight to BN programs that other forms of investment in nonbasic sectors of the economy received little or no attention. Unless BN problems are complemented with judicious macroeconomic policies, their impact and longevity will be severely limited. What a pure BNA gains in clarity is far outweighed by what it loses in feasibility; only some kind of "mixed BNA" (where BN programs must compete with nonbasic fiscal priorities) offers a reasonable hope for implementation.

The problem of the PGC's endorsement of a pure BNA is exacerbated by the fact that the PGC prescribes an undifferentiated moral obligation to provide assistance, unless such assistance would threaten the basic or nonsubtractive goods of the person giving the aid. In Chapter 5, I argue that the "comparable cost" criterion, while relevant in many contexts, is not an appropriate decision rule in situations that require assistance to be given over a lengthy period of time (i.e., diachronic moral obligations). Consequently the PGC seriously overstates the bounds of moral obligation because it does not account for time as a morally relevant dimension of positive beneficence. For example, the PGC, in relation to the lexical ordering principle, would require both individuals and countries to sacrifice *all* of their nonbasic expenditures/objectives until all individuals within their sphere of influence had satisfied their BN—an expectation that is clearly unreasonable.

In sum, Gewirth argues that the PGC, in conjunction with the Criterion of Degrees of Necessity for Action, mandates interclass lexical orderings among generic goods and an external lexical ordering between generic and nongeneric goods. It has been argued that Gewirth's use of the lexical ordering principle creates major difficulties concerning (1) the definition of the hierarchical relationship between nonsubtractive and additive goods and (2) the implementation of viable intranational and transnational resource transfers in accordance with the PGC. Moreover, because Gewirth's category of nonsubtractive goods is primarily a security concept, it faces significant conceptual problems related to the variance of individual propensities to accept risk and the definition of appropriate, age-specific, international threshold probabilities that indicate permissible degrees of failure in the continuation of individual longevity. Additionally the strong valuation that Gewirth assigns to freedom, as an undifferentiated, discontinuous, and necessary member of the set of generic goods at all levels of well-being, is highly suspect and appears to be the logical outcome of his initial decision to select human agency as the only morally relevant common denominator of human life.

3.4. THE BASIC NEEDS MANDATE AND THE BASIC NEEDS IMPERATIVE

The foregoing analysis of Gewirth's moral theory has revealed several substantial problems that all relate directly to his theory of the good (i.e., generic goods). It would seem that a more adequate theory of the good would resolve the problems facing his moral system.

The PGC finds its ultimate justification in a descriptive account of the structure of human action that involves the generic goods of freedom and well-being. However, if one were to substitute the three species universals of existence, intelligence, and sociality for Gewirth's concept of generic goods, would it not be possible to recover the essential line of Gewirth's argument without subverting its logical power and conceptual integrity?

Given Gewirth's initial decision to make human agency the only feature of the human species that is relevant to a theory of morality, the PGC emerges from a series of logically entailed claims that the individual makes about his or her own requirements for agency and that, in turn (through the Logical Principle of Universalizability and the Criterion of Relevant Similarities), compel the agent, on pain of contradiction, to respect and promote the preconditions for another's agency. If, however, the starting point for moral reflection is the open genetic program of human life, the analytical and persuasive power of Gewirth's argument would be significantly amplified and the structure of the argument would be somewhat simplified. Additionally this approach avoids the problem that PGC is relevant to human action only inasmuch as a person elects to function as a prospective, purposive agent (see Gamwell, 1984, pp. 60–66). Obviously one can neither elect to be a human being nor deny oneself membership in the human race while still remaining a living creature.

A reformulation of Gewirth's essential line of argument based upon the open genetic program of human life could proceed as follows. Any human being, by virtue of being a member of Homo sapiens, is logically constrained to affirm the following (actually or prospectively):

> As a human being, I require the goods necessary to maintain and develop
> my species-capacities for existence, intelligence, and sociality.   (1)

Since the phrase "to maintain and develop my species-capacities for existence, intelligence, and sociality" is synonymous with the phrase "to meet my basic needs," statement 1 can be simplified to statement 1a:

> As a human being, I require the goods necessary to meet my basic
> needs.   (1a)

From statement 1a it follows that

> As a human being, I have a right to the goods necessary for meeting
> my basic needs.   (2)

Here, as with Gewirth's argument from step 2b to step 3, the use of the term "right" simply reflects the individual's prudentially motivated realization that there are certain essential prerequisites for the maintenance and development of his or her capabilities as a human being, instead of proceeding from an exogenous theory of rights.

Once the validity of statement 2 is recognized, it follows that

> All other persons ought at least to refrain from interfering with the
> satisfaction of my own basic needs.   (3)

As with Gewirth's original argument, this move is justified on the basis of the formal structure of rights claims ("A has a right to X against B by virtue of Y"), which locates individual rights-claims in a correlative relationship with one's moral obligations to others.

In view of the Logical Principle of Universalizability (i.e., "if some predicate P belongs to some subject S because S has the property Q [where the "because" is that of sufficient reason or condition], then P must also belong to all other subjects $S_1, S_2, \ldots S_n$ that have Q"), statement 3 logically entails the following:

> **All human beings have the right to meet their basic needs.**   (4)

Statement 4 is a universal development norm that I call the Basic Needs Mandate.

In addition to the development norm of the BNM, it is possible to derive a moral principle similar to the Principle of Generic Consistency by proceeding within Gewirth's logical framework. From statement 4 it logically follows that

*I ought at least to refrain from interfering with the basic needs of any
other human being.* (5)

In view of the interactive relationship among human individuals and societies
across the globe and given the fact that often negative moral obligations logically
entail the existence of positive moral obligations (where an individual or an
association of individuals can assist other human beings to meet their basic needs
without depriving themselves of their own basic needs, consistent with the three
diachronic constraints outlined in Chapter 5), it follows from statement 5 that

I ought to respect the basic needs of any (and every) human being. (6)

The imperative form of statement 6 is a universal moral principle that I call the
Basic Needs Imperative:

**Act in accord with the basic needs of other human beings as well as
yourself.** (7)

3.5. THE BNM AND BNI AS SPECIES-ETHICS

While the BNM and BNI employ a minimalistic notion of human rationality
and are derived in a manner similar to the PGC, these principles have access to
a larger field of relevant data than the PGC, because the BNM and BNI are
grounded in the open genetic program of human life instead of simply human
agency. Furthermore, both principles find their ultimate ground in the transspecific goal of evolutionary survival.

The identification of the BNM and the BNI as species-ethics introduces a kind
of duality that opens up the possibility of developing balanced varieties of humanism on nonanthropocentric grounds. On the one hand, Homo sapiens are
probably the only life forms within our solar system who actually have the
capability to execute courses of action conforming to the BNM and the BNI.
Yet, on the other hand, there is a transspecific dimension inherent in both
principles that permits us to reconcile claims about human uniqueness with an
affirming and noninstrumentalist view of earth's ecosystems. This constructive
duality is explained, in part, by the fact that the BNM and BNI find their
evolutionary ground in the transspecific goal of environmental adaptation; yet
the principles can only be formulated, justified, and deployed by species who
have attained fairly sophisticated powers of ratiocination.

As species-ethics, the BNM and BNI prohibit policies or actions that lead to
the extinction of other plant or animal species, as it would be logically inconsistent for any species ethic to sanction courses of action that would lead to the
extinction of other species.[5] Whereas any species may legitimately compete with
other species over a particular ecological niche, the complete destruction of
another species is morally impermissible. The argument here is closely related
to the first premise of the syllogistic argument that appears at the end of section
3.1. The first premise holds that "environmental adaptation is good for the

human species." Given the fact that environmental adaptation is a desirable goal for any species and since Homo sapiens are a subset of all earth's plant and animal species, the first premise can be restated as follows: "Environmental adaptation is good for any species." Once the equivalence between these two statements is accepted, it becomes incongruous to develop a species-ethic that is predicated on the elimination of other species, as this would deny the essential interdependence of our biosphere and would necessitate the justification of supraspecific criteria that endorse the existence of certain species and legitimate the extinction of others.[6] Therefore the BNM and the BNI require a generalized respect for the habitats and genetic heritage of all plant and animal species. Given the fact that humans have been notorious angels of extinction during their sojourn on earth, presumably beginning with the extinctions of over 50 genera of megafauna (large mammals weighing more than 100 pounds) during the late Pleistocene, it is of the utmost importance for us to cultivate a generalized respect for all life forms.

As species-ethics that are relevant to only one known species at this time, the BNM and the BNI require the development of fairly sophisticated powers of ratiocination. For humans, the development of rational capabilities was itself a by-product of natural selection, triggered by any one (or combination) of several distinctive innovations, including the use of tools and weapons, the advent of hunting and gathering, or the adoption of a socioreproductive system that involved food sharing and central place foraging (Issac, 1983). With the extraordinary expansion of the human neocortex, which more than doubled in the brief transition from Homo habilis to Homo sapiens, a quantum leap in neurological circuitry took place. As a result, hominids developed markedly enhanced capabilities to conceive and execute courses of intelligent behavior. This enhanced capacity to behave intelligently reflected the maturation of four primary factors that contribute to the occurrence of intelligent behavior (see Chapter 1, section 1.5.c). "Sapientization" or the maturation of this four-factored cognitive organization has facilitated the development of the capabilities of self-representation and symbolic communication and, thereby, has opened up a multitude of evolutionary pathways through cultural evolution.

The extraordinary powers of discretion and adaptation made possible by cortical sophistication created a wide berth for human responsibility. The moral norms and directives that have evolved in human communities are exceedingly more comprehensive than those required to facilitate genetic evolution (e.g., the promotion of genetic fitness by incest taboos and gene survival by kin altruism), and clearly have their primary impact in shaping cultural evolution.

The enhanced sphere of choice and adaptation made possible by the development of human intelligence imposes a special obligation on our species: humans should adopt a K-reproductive strategy whenever possible (except in extreme situations when this would lead to the extinction of the species, e.g., in the aftermath of a nuclear holocaust). The distinction between r- and K-selection was first developed by MacArthur and Wilson (1967) as a model of

Table 3.1
Comparisons Between r-Selection and K-Selection

Characteristic	r-Selection	K-selection
Climate	Variable	Constant
Availability of Resources	Unpredictable	Predictable
Habitat	Transient	Stable
Mortality	High	Low
Competition (both within a species and between species)	Weak (unimportant)	Strong (important)
Energy Utilization	Emphasizes Quantity	Emphasizes Quality
Population Size	Varies Dramatically	Steady (close to carrying capacity)
Age at Reproduction	Younger	Older
Number of Offspring	Many	Few
Parental Care	Poorly Developed	Well Developed
Social Grouping	Poorly Integrated	Well Integrated
Altruism	Rare	Common

Source: Modified from David Barash, *Sociobiology and Behavior* (New York: Elsevier, 1977), p. 183.

density-dependent natural selection in connection with their work on the colonization of islands.[7] Where natural selection favors high population growth and productivity, as in the case of an initial period of colonization, r-selection or r-strategies become the most influential (''r'' is the symbol used to signify the rate of population increase). By contrast, K-selection becomes prominent when the habitat of a species is at or near its ecological carrying capacity (''K'' represents the carrying capacity of a habitat). In K-conditions, natural selection favors K-strategists who utilize resources more efficiently and allocate parental investment increasingly for rearing offspring instead of reproduction. In short, an r-strategy for reproduction emphasizes the quantitative dimensions of life by producing as many offspring as possible, whereas a K-reproductive strategy focuses on increasing the quality of life by limiting the birth rate. Table 3.1 presents a comparison of the major differences between r-selection and K-selection.

In light of the tremendous environmental pressures that Homo sapiens have placed upon earth's ecosystems, there is an urgent need for humans to embrace a K-reproductive strategy without reservation. For example, at present trends of fuelwood consumption in LDCs, tropical and subtropical forest cover will decline by 40% from 1975 to the year 2000. The long-term effects of this disturbing trend will be the serious erosion of fragile laterite topsoil, the extinction of many rare plant and insect species, the decline of arable land, and eventually it could play havoc with the composition of the earth's atmosphere. It has been estimated that between 500,000 and 2,000,000 plant and animal species (15% to 20% of all species on the planet) could become extinct by the year 2000 due to pollution and the deterioration or loss of forest habitats (U.S. Council on Environmental Quality and the Department of State, 1980).

In sum, the BNM and BNI, as species-ethics, do not permit us to construe our unique status on the planet as license to trample the habitats of more fragile species and to ignore the interconnectedness of life. To do so is not only a prescription for disaster but also a denial of the essential interdependence of the biosphere.

We are now ready to examine the implications of the problem of paternalism for the BNM, as well as the relationship between the BNI and divergent ethical traditions.

3.6. THE BNM AND THE PROBLEM OF PATERNALISM

A significant moral problem facing the BNM, as a universal development norm, is the problem of paternalism. Even if the BNM is based on a reading of the human good that is universally valid and capable of rigorous justification, this would not mean that such a theory of BN could be imposed upon human communities according to the arbitrary will of some external authority. Laying claim to a universal theory of the good is one thing; imposing such a valuational system upon others is quite another.

Most of the recent literature on paternalism has focused on establishing criteria that delimit justified forms of paternalism from unjustified forms, instead of issuing a blanket condemnation of all paternalistic behaviors or policies (see Dworkin, 1971; Fotion, 1979; Gert and Culver, 1979; Husak, 1981; Kelman, 1981; Kleinig, 1984; Lee, 1981; Sartorius, 1983). Gewirth (1978, pp. 304ff.) himself discusses the issue of paternalism with respect to his distinction between the "optional-procedural" justification of social rules (e.g., voting) and the "necessary-procedural" justification of social rules (based on rational consent independent from individual preference orderings). Necessary-procedural justifications provide a kind of "constitution" for the distribution of generic goods (which conforms to the PGC). However, Gewirth emphasizes that such a constitutional framework does not justify dispensing with social choice procedures for determining specific kinds of legislation.

In considering the issue of paternalism in relation to the BNM, it is essential to make two sets of distinctions: (1) between strong and weak paternalism; and (2) between positive and negative paternalism (Kleinig, 1984, p. 14).

Strong paternalism (which often has coercive overtones) involves X's imposition of a good upon Y while disregarding Y's capacity to select that good himself. By contrast, weak paternalism involves X's imposition of a good upon Y that is predicated on the reasoned perception that Y is unable to select that good for himself (due to inadequate information, a reduced capacity for agency, etc.).

Positive paternalism refers to contexts in which X acts in a paternalistic fashion toward Y for the purpose of securing a positive benefit for Y. Conversely, negative paternalism describes situations in which X's rationale for some paternalistic act is rooted in a concern to protect Y from some harm.

In attempting to get at the heart of the distinction between legitimate and illegitimate forms of paternalism, Kleinig (1984) has constructed a comprehensive typology of the possible justifications for paternalistic policies or behaviors. He categorizes these justificatory arguments under the following headings: (1) Arguments from Interconnectedness, (2) the Argument from Future Selves, (3) Consequentialist Arguments for Paternalism, (4) Consent-based Arguments for Paternalism, and (5) the Argument from Personal Integrity.

In light of his examination of paternalistic justifications, Kleinig concludes that all of the major categories have significant weaknesses, except for the final category. The Argument from Personal Integrity is essentially a construct of the best features of the four other methods of justification. Kleinig's argument proceeds as follows:

Where our conduct or choices place our more permanent, stable, and central projects in jeopardy, and where what comes to expression in this conduct or these choices manifests aspects of our personality that do not rank highly in our constellation of desires, dispositions, etc., benevolent interference will constitute no violation of integrity. Indeed, if anything, it helps to preserve it. . . . We can differentiate passing and settled desires, major and minor projects, central and peripheral concerns, valued and disvalued habits and dispositions. The argument in question maintains that where a course of conduct would in response to some peripheral or lowly ranked tendency, threaten disproportionate disruption to highly ranked concerns, paternalistic grounds for intervention have a legitimate place. Strong, no less than weak, paternalism may thus find a toe hold (p. 68).

Kleinig emphasizes that the Argument from Personal Integrity, or any other paternalistic justification, does not sanction a rampant disregard of human preferences. He insists that paternalism must not function as "a substitute for persuasion and education, but a strategy of last resort" (p. 70). Toward this end, he has identified five maxims that are general rules of thumb for the determination of whether or not a paternalistic imposition is justified:

(1) In general, negative paternalism is to be preferred; (2) In general, the "weaker" the paternalism, the more likely it is that it can be justified; (3) In general, the more serious the threatened detriment to welfare, the more likely it is that paternalism will be justified; (4) In general, the higher the risk involved the more compelling the case for paternalism; and (5) In general, the more difficult it is to repair the harm or detriment, the more likely it is that paternalism will be justified (pp. 75–76).

It is interesting that the most extensive survey on paternalism to date has arrived at a conclusion that has strong affinities with the BNM and the theory of basic needs that supports it. Clearly the provision of basic human needs is central to any well-differentiated notion of personal integrity. If the promotion of personal integrity is paternalistic, then this certainly gives new meaning to the term.

Fortunately the BNA has some built-in safeguards against paternalism. Because successful BN programs require community participation and a real sense of local ownership in the development process, the BNA cannot afford, on strategic grounds, to resort to paternalistic impositions, even though such impositions may actually be morally permissible. Unless BN initiatives are accepted and owned by the community (even though they may be initiated and encouraged by outside bureaucrats), the programs are doomed to failure (see Lisk, 1985; Salmen, 1987). Presumably this operational requirement of the BNA will prevent the sorts of paternalistic excesses that are hypothetically possible.

In essence the BNM provides a kind of "virtual constitution" for development policy.[8] As such, the BNM does not replace democratic social choice processes, market valuations, or the decisions of planners and policy makers, but instead establishes general objectives and parameters for public policy formation. Therefore the BNM neither amounts to an unjustified paternalistic imposition of development priorities upon local communities nor sanctions the disregard of decentralized participatory institutions, but instead aims only at promoting essential human rights. In short, the BNM speaks for those who do not have a voice—those excluded from political processes and the economically disinherited—for the purpose of securing the same basic human rights the rich and powerful enjoy. If that is paternalistic, then so is the Bill of Rights of the U.S. Constitution and many other legal instruments that democratic societies hold dear.

3.7. THE BNI AND DIVERGENT ETHICAL TRADITIONS

The function of the BNI as a universal principle of morality is to provide an Archimedean point from which to evaluate all ethical principles, moral ideals/virtues, social policies, and cultural systems. It is a supreme moral principle by virtue of its universality, not supreme in the sense that it evokes the highest level of moral conduct in humanity (e.g., as a religious ethic of sacrificial love). Consequently the BNI neither replaces nor summarizes the repositories of moral wisdom embodied in the religious and secular traditions of Homo sapiens, but instead provides a touchstone by which these ethical traditions can be evaluated. The intent of the BNI is to clarify and enliven humanity's rich and diverse assortment of moral traditions, not to reduce them to their least common denominator.

As a universal ethical principle, the BNI must find support from within a variety of ethical traditions, not only for it to be recognized as a global ethical principle but also for the sake of its implementation. Bare ethical principles are rarely able to inspire the energy and devotion necessary for carrying them out.

It is a truism that "principles without virtues are impotent," in the same way that "virtues without principles are blind" (Frankena, 1973, p. 32). Just actions do not occur in a vacuum of moral character, but instead thrive upon the religious and moral ideals that belong to the human heritage. One cannot ignore the important interdependent relation between agent-oriented ethics of virtue and the BNI's act-oriented ethic of duty.[9]

Consequently the BNI should not be construed as an alternative ethical system that competes with the current religious and secular traditions of earth's human population. Instead the intent of the BNI is simply this: for one to be a good Muslim, Christian, Buddhist, Jew, Taoist, Hindu, Marxist, atheist, or capitalist, one must act in accordance with the BNI or some indigenous moral principle congruent with the BNI (e.g., the Golden Rule), in addition to respecting the canons of belief and conduct prescribed by each respective tradition. Since the BNI is a species-ethic, it has the potential to weave the fundamental ethical commitments of many different traditions together in such a way that preserves the distinctiveness of each tradition while extending the scope of moral obligations, which are normally reserved for those within the in-group, to those who are deemed outsiders.

We are now ready to mine some of the implications of the BNM and the BNI for a unified theory of global development.

NOTES

1. Lumsden and Wilson (1981, pp. 82–85) relate an interesting experiment carried out by Chalmers Mitchell. When Mitchell carried snakes through the London zoo, the monkeys were greatly agitated and ran away in haste, whereas the lemurs (which come from Madagascar, which does not have any species of poisonous snakes) ran to the front of the cages to observe the snakes.

2. The level of aggressive behavior seems to be positively correlated with the degree of concentration/defensibility of the scarce resource in question. For example, food shortages will only stimulate aggressive behavior when stockpiles can be defended, whereas general hunger will tend to generate apathy and asociality. See E. O. Wilson (1975, pp. 249–250).

3. Gamwell (1984, pp. 58–60) has also formulated a helpful defense of this aspect of Gewirth's theory.

4. This bias of agency over being is clearly evident in Gewirth's discussion of abortion, where the "physically separate existence" and increased range of movement experienced by infants is construed as being a decisive moral consideration that justifies abortion on demand yet prohibits infanticide (Gewirth, 1978, p. 142).

5. It should be emphasized that species extinction is a familiar occurrence in evolutionary history, due to changes in climate, habitat, and predator populations. Obviously species extinctions that are caused by factors beyond human control fall outside the scope of both the BNM and the BNI.

6. The only possible criterion that could qualify would be that of complexity (i.e., more complex [higher] life forms have a stronger claim to survival than less complex [lower] life forms). For example, if the very existence of a small insect threatened the

survival of certain primate populations (perhaps humans), it would be morally permissible to destroy the insect species. Of course, the likelihood of interspecific problems of this magnitude is extremely remote. Moreover, the criterion of complexity is an especially precarious one, not only because of the difficulties involved in defining and measuring complexity, but also because the criterion could theoretically justify the extinction of the human species by more advanced extraterrestrial life forms.

7. The terms ''r'' and ''K'' are derived from the logistic equation $dN/dt = rN (K - N)/K$, where N is the population size, r is the intrinsic rate of increase, and K is the carrying capacity of the habitat.

8. For the concept of the ''virtual constitution,'' see Mishan (1975, p. 385). Benjamin Higgins (1981) has adapted Mishan's concept of the virtual constitution to the BNA in an interesting manner.

9. An ethic of virtue focuses on certain agent-states in the appraisal of moral problems; whereas an ethic of duty focuses on the performance of a moral responsibility, irrespective of the intentions or motives involved. See Dyck (1973), Foot (1979, pp. 1–18), and Schenck (1976).

4
Assessing the Feasibility of the Basic Needs Approach

4.1 THE MATTHEW ARNOLD SYNDROME

The emergence of the BNA as a new paradigm of economic development occurred at a time when many development economists and planners were entertaining growing doubts about the adequacy of aggregate growth-oriented approaches to development. For about 15 years (1955–70) growth in aggregate GNP had been the received indicator of economic development (Morawetz, 1977, pp. 7–9). This "trickle-down" approach held that the cost of short-term socioeconomic inequalities would be outweighed by the benefits of larger shares for everyone in the long term. Even as late as 1969 the Pearson Commission, reporting to the president of the World Bank, endorsed the dominant paradigm of economic development by essentially recommending that the development policies of the postwar period were sufficient to meet the needs of LDCs within a reasonable period of time, that is, if MDCs increased their aid commitments (Commission on International Development, 1969).

By the decade of the 1970s a shift in perspective became apparent. There was a growing recognition that the distribution-blind, aggregate growth approach simply was not working. Upon closer analysis the Brazilian miracle turned out to be a distributional nightmare (Fox, 1983), and evidence from other rapidly growing countries (e.g., Pakistan, Nigeria) indicated that the benefits of growth were trickling up faster than they trickled down. Adelman and Morris (1973) even went so far as to conclude that growth actually impoverished, in *absolute* terms, the poorest 40% of the population during an LDC's initial spurt of growth. They suggested that for a sharply dualistic economy it would take two generations for the poorest 40% to recover their absolute losses, returning to their pre-growth level of welfare. This assertion by Adelman and Morris sparked a heated debate among many development economists (Morawetz, 1977, pp. 42–43; Lal, 1976).[1]

With mounting, legitimate disillusionment over the traditional growth-oriented approach to development, a number of alternate development concepts and strategies came to the fore, including the New International Economic Order (Rothstein, 1979; Streeten, 1982), the Unified Approach (U.N. Research Institute for Social Development, 1974), dependency theory (Muñoz, 1981), appropriate technology (McRobie, 1981; Schumacher, 1973), no growth or steady-state economics (Daly, 1977; Kohr, 1973), and redistribution with growth (Chenery, 1974). It is in this environment that the BNA formally took shape.

The significance of the BNA is that it maps development issues within a broad interpretive framework and makes the struggle against absolute poverty the central objective of economic development. As a consequence, the poverty-oriented focus of the BNA is considerably more prominent than in alternate approaches to development. Moreover, the BNA represents an attempt to establish a kind of global moral community as an alternative to the fragmented global order that currently exists (Little, 1982, pp. 271–272).

The problem facing us is that there is no such thing as an "international community" in the fullest sense of the term. In a sense, we are caught in what Denis Goulet has aptly termed the "Matthew Arnold Syndrome": the feeling that we are, in the words of the poet, "wandering between two worlds, one dead, the other powerless to be born."

The present global institutions are relics of an earlier age and no longer work; they are already dead, although not yet interred. And alternative new institutions, albeit often portrayed in the form of desirable scenarios, do not yet exist: worse still, they seem powerless to be born (Goulet, 1983, p. 614).

Is the BNA a noble idea whose time has not yet come? Is it destined to become a passing fad in the annals of development thought? Is it a truly feasible development program, given the current institutional landscape that characterizes the global order (or disorder)?

4.2 PROBLEMS OF IMPLEMENTATION

Proponents and critics of the BNA both admit that the political/institutional impediments hindering its global implementation are formidable. A brief list of some operational problems surrounding the BNA is sufficient to underline the real world obstacles it must confront.

1. The BNA would require substantially higher rates of official development assistance (ODA) from MDCs, earmarked for countries with low absorptive capacities (i.e., low-income LDCs), at a time when aggregate aid flows from members of the Organization for Economic Cooperation and Development (OECD) have experienced a secular decline (relative to gross national product [GNP]) since 1965. Presumably a kind of Global Marshall Plan for low-income LDCs would be required by any large-scale implementation of the BNA. A provisional estimate of the total costs (capital and recurrent) necessary for meeting core BN (food, safe water and sanitation, housing, health, and basic education)

within *low-income* LDCs would involve an annual investment rate of between $30 and $40 billion (1976 prices) over a 20-year period (Burki and Voorhoeve, 1977; Streeten and Burki, 1978). This figure amounts to 80–105% of the average gross domestic investment of low-income LDCs and 85–110% of their average governmental resources. Clearly massive infusions of aid would be necessary to supplement the contributions from LDCs. However, as large as the figure of $30–40 billion per year seems, if the United States increased its present ODA flows from the present level of 0.24% of its GNP to 1.3%, it could foot the entire annual bill of $40 billion while maintaining its present aid commitments. (The average level of ODA for Arab OPEC countries is 1.6% of their GNPs.)

2. The BNA would require new aid flows to be significantly restructured toward recurrent, labor-intensive expenditures, constituting a radical departure from the present norm of one-time, capital-intensive expenditures that are often used as a means of financing MDC exports and rarely utilize labor-intensive, appropriate technologies (see Cassen et al., 1986, pp. 49–66, 285–291; Tendler, 1975, pp. 43–49, 54–79). BN programs are especially reliant upon the long-term provision of funds from MDCs and/or LDCs to cover recurrent costs, so that projects do not deteriorate shortly after they are established. MDCs are reluctant to provide these funds, as such expenditures are perceived as consumption-oriented instead of being capital investment and are less spectacular than capital-intensive projects, having considerably less public relations value. Generally speaking, funding for recurrent costs by LDCs has been unstable and sporadic in the health and education sectors (in contrast to agriculture and transportation), partly attributable to the limited tax bases of low-income LDCs (Gray and Marens, 1983; Lim, 1983).

3. A global implementation of the BNA would entail an increased degree of intervention (or intrusion) in the domestic affairs of LDCs by MDCs (or multilateral institutions). This intervention could take the form of tying poverty-oriented conditions to aid disbursements and monitoring their effectiveness. Such intervention would, no doubt, offend Southern elites, who could be expected to insist uncompromisingly on absolute state sovereignty. Streeten and his associates (1981, p. 177) believe that MDC-sponsored BN programs could be harmonized with state sovereignty by channeling ODA through multilateral institutions and by allowing LDCs themselves to monitor each other's progress (similar to the mechanism used with the Marshall Plan). Moreover, Hansen (1977) suggests that if MDCs unilaterally offered large amounts of ODA through a multilateral agency (available to any LDCs that met certain standardized performance criteria, negotiated between the agency and its recipients), Southern elites would be constrained to set aside their insistence on noninterference.

4. The BNA is malfitted for the present structure of international finance. Both private and public nonconcessional loans mainly benefit the middle-income LDCs. The effectiveness of concessional loans is diminished by the fact that the resources of the International Development Association (the World Bank's soft loan affiliate) are already spread too thin and regional development banks are

often either overpoliticized (e.g., the African Development Bank) or dominated by MDCs (e.g., the Asian Development Bank) (see Fordwor, 1981; Krasner, 1983).

5. From its inception the BNA sparked concern among many LDC policy makers that the focus on BN may divert attention away from trade reforms and other proposals clustered under the banner of a New International Economic Order (NIEO). Advocates of NIEO have proposed far-reaching structural reforms relating to debt relief, technology transfer, the expanded use of Special Drawing Rights (SDRs) within the International Monetary Fund (IMF) as a mechanism for resource-transfers to LDCs, the establishment of nonreciprocal preferential tariffs benefiting LDCs (General System of Preferences), the stabilization of commodity prices through a buffer stock mechanism (Integrated Program for Commodities), the establishment of international codes that regulate the activities of multinational corporations, and the creation of a Third World Secretariat. Because there is reason to believe that, in the minds of MDC policy makers, concessions in trade may substitute for ODA, the implementation of the BNA could detract from LDC efforts to negotiate trade reforms (Little, 1982, p. 365). In spite of this problem, though, it seems appropriate to regard the BNA and NIEO as complementary approaches to economic development (Leipziger, 1981a; Streeten, 1979). Long-term BN programs presuppose some type of NIEO reforms; and, conversely, meaningful reforms in international trade must be guided by BN objectives so that the ensuing benefits are distributed equitably. (Whereas the rich producers within a particular country and the middle-income LDCs as a whole stand to benefit the most from trade reforms and debt relief, the impact upon low-income LDCs and the poor would be relatively negligible [Rothstein, 1979, pp. 116–117; Weintraub, 1979].) Hence the BNA complements the NIEO reforms by focusing on the critical problem of intrastate distribution and, conceivably, could even pave the way for MDC concessions in trade (due to the unprecedented level of cooperation the BNA would require from both MDCs and LDCs).

6. Owing to the substantial involvement of the public sector in implementing BN programs, the implementation of the BNA on a global scale could intensify problems of macroeconomic adjustment and stability (e.g., inflation, balance of payments, debt servicing, exchange rate adjustment), unless BN programs are underwritten by substantial inflows of ODA and complemented by well-designed structural adjustment programs. Given the current monetarist bias of the IMF in the construal of its stabilization programs, it is clear that the IMF policy prescription for stabilization would frequently be at odds with the development objectives of the BNA (David, 1985; Dell, 1982). Moreover, because the BNA would tend to restructure a domestic economy away from the production of nonbasic goods to basic goods, some detrimental macroeconomic repercussions (associated with demand-pull inflation and balance-of-payments problems) would be likely, because the income elasticities of demand for basic goods are typically higher than their short-run supply elasticities. Presumably, though, these negative

effects could be minimized through effective supply-management policies (Streeten et al., 1981, pp. 42–45, 58–60).

7. Because BN programs require sensitive administrative mechanisms that are fine tuned to local needs and perceptions, the BNA must cope with persistent problems relating to decentralization (Bryant and White, 1982, pp. 155–203), corruption (Myrdal, 1970, pp. 208–252), the planning process (Dey, 1982; Kornai, 1975, 1979), and project management (Rondinelli, 1976). These problems are intensified by the fact that civil service professionals often fail to solicit the opinions and suggestions of the local community and to involve the community members in the design of development projects or programs. Moreover the BNA's mandate of reaching the poorest, most vulnerable groups in a population is complicated by the fact that the most severely affected are usually difficult for the occasional visitor or civil service professional to identify (Chambers, 1981) or are denied normal legal protections, such as refugees (Karadawi, 1983).

8. A global implementation of the BNA would eventually have to enter the labyrinth of land reform in both rural and urban contexts—an effective yet difficult redistributive instrument that can be easily subverted by powerful elites (Eckstein et al., 1978; King, 1977; and World Bank, 1975b; however see Prosterman and Riedlinger [1978] for some constructive proposals).

9. Inadequately designed BN policies can have strong disincentive effects on agricultural productivity, particularly if urban-biased agricultural price policies are employed to accomplish BN objectives (Schuh, 1979). Typically agricultural price policies in LDCs are designed to keep the prices of agricultural produce artificially low in order to keep urban, middle-class consumers happy (usually the most politically powerful group in LDCs, next to the military establishment). Unfortunately such agricultural price policies impose an implicit tax on the rural population (the precise opposite of agricultural price support programs in many MDCs) and reduce overall agricultural productivity. For example, Tanzania's program of *ujamaa* (Ki-swahili for "familyhood") socialism has been severely hampered by ill-conceived agricultural price policies (see Ellis, 1982; Stewart, 1985, pp. 192ff.)

10. BN programs may often be constrained by resistance from local vested interests, as in the case of physicians restricting the use of community health workers in Latin America (de Kadt, 1982).

11. An inevitable reality facing all BN programs is that there will always be some leakage from such programs, either in the form of waste or trickle-up effects that benefit nontargeted groups (Austin, 1980, p. 88; Burki and ul Haq, 1981).

12. Because BN objectives may sometimes be at variance with individual preferences, they are likely to be subject to substitution effects that subvert the intended aims of BN programs, as in the case of supplemental feeding programs for children (i.e., parents who reduce the amount of food allocated to children

Figure 4.1
The Sleeping Giant Effect

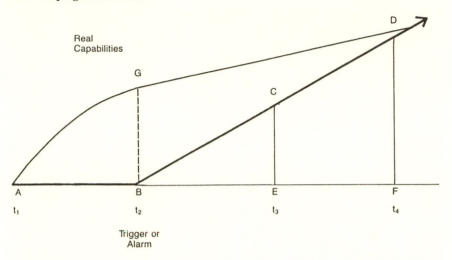

Real
Capabilities

Trigger or
Alarm

in proportion to what they receive at school) (Knudsen, 1981; Selowsky, 1979a, b).

These are formidable problems. They touch every strata of policy formation: international, regional, national, and local. Worse yet, well-intentioned initiatives that emerge from any one of these levels can be effectively derailed by resistance or the lack of coordination at other levels of policy formation.

Do these operational problems doom the BNA? Admittedly, the collective weight of these difficulties tempts one to respond in the affirmative. Yet to do so would effectively shut down future possibilities for meaningful institutional reform. While the force of these problems can hardly be overstated, they are not necessarily insurmountable.

For example, one could imagine that several of the international reforms (e.g., increased and restructured aid flows) could be achieved within a relatively telescoped time frame due to something like a sleeping giant effect. Such an effect would be predicated on a sharp discrepancy between actual sociopolitical conditions and the real capabilities brought about by rapid technological change. Figure 4.1 depicts a sleeping giant pathway (*ABCD*) across four time periods (t_{1-4}). Line *AGD* represents the real capabilities brought about by technological change. During t_2 a substantial discrepancy appears between sociopolitical realities and actual capabilities, signified by the broken line *BG*. This discrepancy, which I shall refer to as the ''G factor,'' constitutes a necessary precondition for the sleeping giant effect. At point *B* in the pathway, a well-placed or timely trigger combines with a high G factor to create a strong sleeping giant effect, evidenced by the progress attained during t_3 and t_4 (represented by *CE* and *DF*). Presumably if the G factor is low or if the trigger is ill-timed, the overall effect would be significantly diminished. The virtue of the sleeping giant pathway is the sheer rapidity and momentum of the effect. The pent-up dissatisfaction, energy, and creativity that typify cultures with high G factors can be unleashed and powerfully focused with the proper trigger.

Admittedly there would probably be considerable debate among historians as to whether sleeping giants actually exist, as it is often the *observers* of sleeping giants who are asleep, not the giants themselves. Nonetheless there does seem to be some limited confirmation of a sleeping giant effect in history. For example, one is tempted to understand Mohammed's proclamation as a kind of ideological trigger that sparked the explosion of Arab culture across the sleepy, disconnected Arabian Peninsula. Moreover, the impact of Calvinism upon the swift expansion of capitalism across Northern Europe appears to be a clear instance of a sleeping giant effect, although the association between Protestantism and capitalism is by no means clear once we leave Northern Europe. Additionally the rapid diffusion of socialist ideals since Marx and Engels penned the "Communist Manifesto" suggests a kind of sleeping giant effect. Presumably the doctrine of communism functioned as a kind of ideological trigger that exploited the wide discrepancy between the abusive conditions typical of early capitalism and the new capabilities for political organization that were made possible by (1) the industrial mode of production, (2) the rising prominence of the nation-state, and (3) the technological feasibility of large-scale bureaucracies through improved systems of communication, transportation, and surveillance.

It seems quite apparent that since 1960, or thereabouts, the G factor for earth's human population has been increasing steadily, being subjectively experienced as a contradiction between what is and what could be. Presumably the G factor will increase for the remainder of this century and, perhaps, will exceed a critical threshold during the first half of the 21st century. This suggests that we may be close to a major sleeping giant effect within the next two or three decades. Whether there will be appropriate triggers to spark the effect remains to be seen.

In this regard, it is possible that the BNA itself could function as a kind of ideological trigger for the sleeping giant effect, given the strong humanitarian appeal of the BNA (Streeten et al., 1981, pp. 40–41). For instance, the Scandinavian countries have emphasized humanitarian justifications for foreign aid as opposed to arguments appealing to national interests (Arnold, 1982). It seems more than coincidental that these same countries have the largest aid budgets (relative to per capita GNP) of all OECD countries (e.g., in 1985 Norway gave almost four times more ODA than the United States).

Presumably it is often not possible to predict the eventual outcomes of a sleeping giant effect. (For example, who could have predicted the eventual sociopolitical significance of Mohammed's proclamation or the "Communist Manifesto"?) Consequently, what appears to be an intractable problem from our present standpoint may be significantly less formidable once a sleeping giant effect has begun.

Whether the international community is able to formulate an effective response to absolute poverty remains to be seen. Realism warrants extreme caution in constructing hopeful scenarios of the future. Yet responsible realism must never be pressed into service for the purpose of denigrating real, albeit improbable, options for meaningful global change. If realism is the beginning of insight and constructive action, then vision is the catalyst for discovering horizons of the thought and action that are neither immediately apparent nor entirely plausible in relation to our present standpoint. Vision without realism is presumptuous and naive, but realism without vision lacks imagination and courage. Responsible realism must hold vision and realism in a creative tension without giving way to either gratuitous optimism or cheap pessimism.

4.3 SOME COUNTRY EXPERIENCE

Despite the formidable obstacles facing a *global* implementation of the BNA, there is country-specific evidence that suggests the BNA is a viable program of national development for even the poorest countries to adopt. Sri Lanka, China, and the Indian state of Kerala stand out as notable examples of LDCs that have pursued BN-type programs, to varying degrees, in the course of their national development. All three states have per capita GNPs ranging from less than $260 to $360 per year. The fact that they have made impressive strides in the satisfaction of material BN with limited economic resources suggests that national wealth is not a decisive prerequisite for the implementation of the BNA.

4.3.a Sri Lanka

Sri Lanka, as a democratic, mixed economy, has made impressive advances in social welfare without resorting to coercive measures for redistribution. With an annual per capita GNP of only $360 (1984), Sri Lanka has social indicators that rival those of countries with per capita GNPs of well over $1,000. The life expectancy at birth is 70 years (1984); the adult literacy rate is estimated at 85% (1977); and the rate of infant mortality per 1,000 live births is 37 (1984) (World Bank, 1982, 1984). These impressive social achievements were purchased at the per capita cost of only $15 per year (Isenman, 1980).

It would be a mistake to interpret Sri Lanka's history of social investment as the outcome of self-consciously pursued BN policies. Instead its social programs resulted from more-or-less ad hoc political pressures since its independence in 1948. Consequently these social programs were not targeted exclusively for the poor. The key to Sri Lanka's success seems to be that these nontargeted social programs had effective coverage in the poor and rural districts of the country.

The centerpiece of Sri Lanka's social programs is its long-standing food ration and subsidy program (on the average of 2–4 lbs. of subsidized rice per month, of which 1–2 lbs. were free). The food ration and subsidy program has placed an increasing fiscal burden on the government because of the rapid growth in population since the country's independence (in the 1970s the program absorbed

18–25% of total government expenditures [Morawetz, 1980, p. 351]). As a consequence, in 1973 the ration program was reduced by 15%. With the combined effect of these cutbacks and high international food prices owing to the world food crisis of 1973–74, the crude death rate in Sri Lanka increased from 7.7 to 8.9 persons per 1,000 in 1974. By the end of 1977 the United National Party (UNP) gained control of the government and limited the coverage of the ration and subsidy program to the poorer half of the population—a politically risky measure. In September 1979 the government announced that the food ration and subsidy program would be replaced by a targeted food stamp program.

Despite Sri Lanka's notable accomplishments in nutrition and health, the record in other sectors is not so impressive. For example, even though the adult literacy rate was 85% in 1977, the country entered its period of independence with an exceptionally literate public (58% in 1946) (Morawetz, 1980, p. 345). Because the educational system is geared toward university education and is inspired by the British model (emphasizing the humanities as opposed to technical education), Sri Lanka has a serious problem with educated unemployment (Cole, 1976, pp. 41–55; Richards, 1981).

In terms of macroeconomic performance, Sri Lanka has experienced moderate to poor rates of growth. During the 1960s the annual Gross Domestic Product (GDP) grew by 4.4% (only 3.5% when corrected for the declining terms of trade due to static tea prices). Between 1970 and 1977 the rate of growth in GDP decreased to 3%, much of which reflected a surge of growth in the service sector. In the face of poor monsoon rains from 1971 to 1973 and the high food and petroleum prices on the international market, Sri Lanka's balance-of-payments situation continued to deteriorate, increasing its external public debt to 32% of its GNP by 1975. These adverse economic circumstances were further aggravated by imprudent fiscal and monetary policies on the part of the government (Khatkhate, 1982).

The recent poor growth experience of Sri Lanka could be attributed to a number of factors; however, the country's expenditures for the food ration and subsidy program are often singled out as the culprit. For example, one study found that given certain simplifying assumptions, if the food ration and subsidy program was discontinued from 1963 to 1969 and *directly* invested in poverty-focused capital formation (a big assumption), it would adversely affect the incomes of the poorest 40% of the population during the first six years; however, after the six-year period, the increased income would outweigh the foregone food subsidy (Jayawardena, 1974). However, Martha de Melo (1981) has conducted similar simulations on Sri Lanka and found that a discontinuation of the rice subsidy would slightly benefit estate workers and the rural landless after ten years; but the incomes of small farmers would decline and total rice consumption would be 8% less than the base year. In general, cross-country data suggest that BN programs do not generally trade off with economic growth; instead they serve as a prelude to high growth rates in the future (Hicks, 1979).

4.3.b   China

With over one-fifth of the world's population and a per capita GNP of $310 (1984), China has made dramatic strides in nutrition, health care, and education. The life expectancy at birth in China is 69 years (1984), and its infant mortality rate has declined from 250 per 1,000 live births in 1949 to only 36 in 1984. Whereas in 1949 there was only one hospital bed for every 24,201 people in rural areas, by 1982 the ratio was reduced to one for every 658 people (Perkins and Yusuf, 1984, p. 146). Whereas only 25% of school-aged children were enrolled in primary education programs in 1949, the enrollment ratio is now 93%. The adult literacy rate has jumped from less than 20% in 1949 to 66% (1979) (World Bank, 1983, pp. 134–135).

China's phenomenal success has often been attributed to its autarkic development path and its extensive agricultural collectivization. However it seems likely that an early conventional land reform program and China's three-tiered health system and immunization program were far more important factors behind the Chinese success story.

During the communists' struggle for power in the late 1940s, a large-scale coercive land reform program was initiated, primarily as a means of securing the political allegience of the peasantry. In what became the largest land reform program in human history, nearly one-half of the arable land (46.7 million hectares) was redistributed to about 65% of the rural population. The landlord class—which comprised only 4% of the population but owned 50% of the land— was, in effect, liquidated by these measures. Approximately 800,000 landlords were executed (Perkins and Yusuf, 1984, p. 92). However the land redistribution was not a panacea for correcting long-standing rural inequalities. Because draft animals and farming implements were not generally included in the land reform package, the poor farmers still remained in a disadvantaged position, despite their absolute gains. This predicament, though, was temporary, as Mao viewed the land reform as only a prelude to collectivization.

Beginning in 1952 a nascent form of socialism was introduced throughout the countryside in the form of mutual aid teams, where some animals, tools, and reclaimed land were owned jointly. These teams quickly gained universal acceptance due to the obvious benefits of cooperation and the fact that private landholdings were not threatened. By 1954 over 68.4 million households belonged to these mutual aid teams. Soon the mutual aid teams (composed of 6– 10 households) were integrated into larger, semisocialist producers' cooperatives (20–40 households). About 91% of the rural population (110 million families) were enrolled in these producers' cooperatives by May 1956. Earlier that year the semisocialist producers' cooperatives began to be converted into advanced or socialist producers' cooperatives (100–300 households). Essentially these advanced cooperatives were the equivalent of collective farms, where private ownership of land (with the exception of small private plots), implements, and animals were forfeited. Income was determined on the basis of one's labor. Collectives were subdivided into production brigades and production teams. By December 1956, 110 million households belonged to these collective farms.

During the Great Leap Forward (1958), China's 740,000 collectives were merged into 26,000 rural communes (averaging nearly 5,000 households each). Private plots were abolished and communal services (e.g., dining halls, nurseries, laundries, schools, clinics) were established. The agricultural mismanagement of the Great Leap Forward and adverse weather conditions brought famine to much of the country during the "three bitter years" (1959–61). More than 16 million people died of starvation. Morale among the agricultural workers was low, and the size of many communes was reduced (by 1971 the communes averaged 1,900 households). Also private plots were reestablished (10–30% of a peasant's income) and some free markets were permitted across the countryside. The practice of communal feeding was abandoned in favor of the traditional family pattern, and a complex work points system was established to determine a laborer's income. By 1971 about 90% of the arable land was cultivated communally, 5% consisted of private plots, and another 5% was owned by state farms (mainly for land reclamation purposes) (King, 1977, pp. 252–278).

In retrospect, it seems that Mao's conventional land reform program of the early 1950s had a much greater impact on the redistribution of income than the later cooperatives and communes. Using data from the 1930s as a baseline, Dwight Perkins (1978) discovered that the real income of the poorest 20% of the rural population rose almost 90% as a result of these land reform measures. Yet while collectivization had little impact on income distribution, it did provide a convenient rural infrastructure for primary health care (e.g., barefoot doctors) and education.

In addition to its massive land reform program, China's remarkable growth in its industrial sector has been a notable feature of Chinese development since 1949. During its First Five-Year Plan (1952–57), China devoted most of its national investment to the industrial sector, especially in heavy industry. The policy was extremely effective; industry grew at a rate of 20% per year. Soon, however, Mao became dissatisfied with this one-sided economic policy and gave more attention to agricultural development: "walking on two legs." Still the priority was to be given to heavy industry. It has been estimated that between 1949 and 1973 China's GNP experienced an average annual increase of 6% real growth, while agriculture has grown at only 2% (Perkins, 1978).

Unfortunately the strong emphasis on industrialization and stringent restrictions on migration to urban areas combined to retard the development of China's countryside. Despite the fact that 80% of the Chinese population reside in rural areas, state investment in agriculture has been very low, consuming only 6.8% of the government budget in 1981 in comparison to the 40.3% allocated to heavy industry (Perkins and Yusuf, 1984, p. 14). Moreover, strict controls on rural-to-urban migration meant that the benefits of industrialization did not trickle down to the rural areas through the partial absorption of rural labor in the industrial sector. These factors, combined with the varying resource endowments of each province, have created significant interregional inequalities in income, even though the ratio between the lowest incomes in relation to the highest incomes *within* a particular region are typically only 1:4 or 1:5. (However Chossudovsky [1986, p. 63] reports that within many rich agricultural provinces there is an income differential of 1:7 and an interregional income differential of 1:100 [i.e., the incomes of the poorest farmers in less affluent regions in relation to the richest farmers in the most affluent regions].) Additionally, there is a persistent and widening gap between the welfare of the peasantry and urbanites.

Certainly the most striking accomplishments in China's development experience have been in the fields of health care and population control. China pioneered the concept of low-cost and wide-coverage primary health care. With a per capita investment in health care of only $4 per year (World Bank, 1983, p. 8), the Chinese government has been able to improve the health status of its 1 billion inhabitants to the point that its health indicators now rival those of the United States in the 1930s—a stunning achievement (Morawetz, 1977, p. 49). Through a three-tiered health care system (consisting of brigade-level cooperative health stations staffed by paramedical personnel known as barefoot doctors, commune health centers, and county general hospitals), China has been able to strike an effective mix of preventive and curative health care that integrates Western medical practices with aspects of traditional Chinese medicine.

The promotion of mass immunization campaigns since the 1960s has been especially influential in improving the health status of the population. All children have access to five vaccines: Bacillus Calmette-Guerin against tuberculosis, oral poliomyelitis vaccine, diptheria and tetanus toxoids combined with pertussis, and the measles vaccine (Young and Prost, 1985). The success of China's three-tiered approach to primary health care, coupled with modest improvements in safe water and sanitation, is evidenced by the fact that health problems have shifted from infectious and parasitic diseases to typical MDC health problems such as cancer, heart disease, and respiratory diseases from smoking and air pollution. This shift has been called the "epidemiological transition" or China's second health revolution. Cholera, plague, and venereal disease—endemic to the Chinese countryside prior to 1949—are now eradicated, and considerable progress has been made in reducing the incidence of malaria, tuberculosis, schistosomiasis, ancyclostomiasis (hookworm), and trachoma (World Bank, 1983, pp. 29–30). As the focus shifts to curative approaches to medicine, the role of barefoot doctors is gradually declining (Perkins and Yusuf, 1984, p. 142).

China's remarkable success in health care is matched by impressive inroads in reducing fertility. Since the early 1970s, China's population control programs have reduced the rate of population growth from above 3% in the mid–1960s to a current level of 1.2% (the average for low-income LDCs is 2.4%) (World Bank, 1983, p. 59). This stunning achievement was accomplished by a mix of economic incentives and disincentives, the universal availability of contraceptive devices, peer pressure, legal minimum ages for marriages (22 years old for men and 20 years old for women), and the government's promotion of the one-child family as a social ideal. Other important contributing factors in the reduction of population growth have been China's elaborate health care infrastructure, the attendant decrease in infant mortality, and increased educational opportunities for women.

With the pragmatic economic and political reforms inaugurated by Deng Xiaoping in 1978, China embarked upon a new and ambitious program of market socialism that has enhanced productivity and promoted economic decentralization. As a result of these reforms, the growth in national income jumped to 6.8% per year from 1979 to 1984 (World Bank, 1985, p. 1). Of special importance was the introduction of the "production responsibility system," which had the effect of making rural households the basic unit of agricultural management and production. Under this system, the farm household has considerable latitude in allocating economic resources and selling agricultural produce at local markets once a modest government quota has been met. Many of the administrative controls exercised by the commune and brigade have been dismantled. The commune and the brigade are being transformed into the township and village, respectively. Furthermore, the prices for the government's grain quota have increased substantially. Since 1978, the annual growth of the gross value of agricultural output has exceeded 7%—more than twice the rate of agricultural growth in the past 20 years. Interestingly, these reforms have led to *greater* income equality in rural areas, apparently because the production responsibility system was first introduced within the poorest regions and they were the first to benefit. Unfortunately, though, the increased productivity generated by these reforms has been accompanied by a sharp decline in subscriptions for rural cooperative medical insurance and a decrease in primary school attendance, as parents often keep their children home to work on the farm (World Bank, 1985, p. 30).

In sum, the Chinese experience demonstrates that wide-coverage BN programs can be implemented on a large scale with minimal per capita expenditures. China's progress in the fields of health, population control, and education is nothing less than remarkable. Moreover, with the introduction of the "responsibility system" in rural areas, it is hoped that agricultural production will increase to the extent that chronic malnutrition will be eliminated. One wonders what China would have been like today if the early land reform program had not been followed by rapid agricultural collectivization, if more capital investment had been devoted to the countryside, if the 1978 reforms had come 20 years earlier instead of the Great Leap Forward, and if there had never been a Cultural Revolution.

4.3.c Kerala

The Indian state of Kerala, with a per capita income significantly under the per capita GNP of India ($260), has made remarkable progress in meeting BN in health and education. Despite the fact that Kerala has the highest population density in India (with a total population of 25.4 million) and ranks ninth in per capita income among the 22 states of India, Kerala not only outdistances the other Indian states in BN performance, but also surpasses the performance of many countries with per capita GNPs in excess of $1,000 (Panikar and Soman, 1984, pp. 2–3). For example, an analysis of the major Indian states in relation to the Physical Quality of Life Index—which is a single-scale measure of the infant mortality rate, the adult literacy rate and life expectancy at age one—has shown that if Kerala is assigned a PQLI index of 100, the next highest Indian state achieves a PQLI rank of only 61.6 (Punjab). In comparison to Kerala, the vast majority of Indian states have PQLI ranks of less than 40 (Rajeev, 1983, p. 11).

The life expectancy at birth in Kerala has increased from 42.3 years in 1950 to 65.3 years in 1979 (the life expectancy at birth for all of India is 54 years), and the rural infant mortality rate has declined from 120 infant deaths per 1,000 live births in 1950 to 39.6 infant deaths in 1980 (Sankaranarayanan and Karunakaran, 1985, pp. 16–17). Moreover, the adult literacy rate has risen from 47.4% in 1951 to 70.4% in 1981 (the adult literacy rate for all of India is only 36.2%). Of special significance is Kerala's extremely high female literacy rate of 66%, compared with 25% for all of India. These significant improvements in health and education have been accompanied by a dramatic decrease in the birth rate among the rural population (from 37 births per 1,000 in 1966 to 26 per 1,000 in 1978). As a consequence, Kerala's population increase between 1961 and 1971 fell from 26% to 19% between 1971 and 1981 (Zachariah, 1984).

What policies or programs were influential in Kerala's impressive BN performance? Although a definitive answer to this question awaits further research, several contributing factors may be noted.

To begin with, Kerala's progressive land reform program has played an important role in upgrading the status of landless agricultural workers and creating a middle class of smallholder owner-cultivators. Since the 11th century, the region comprising present-day Kerala was dominated by a feudal agrarian structure that was reinforced by the caste system. When three coastal states in the southwest corner of the Indian subcontinent were merged into a single administrative unit in 1956, which became known as Kerala, land reform became an important political goal for the newly established government. During that early period, a flurry of land reform legislation was enacted, including the Kerala Stay of Eviction Proceedings Act of 1957, the Kerala Land Tax Act, the Kerala Agrarian Relations Bill of 1957, the Jenmikkaram Payment Abolition Bill, the Kerala Conservancy Act, and the Kerala Relinquishment Act. However, it was not until the passage of the Kerala Land Reforms Act of 1963 that tenants throughout the state were given the legal right to land tenure (which the landlord could revoke only if he utilized the land for personal cultivation). Unfortunately, though, little was done to implement the provisions of this act until the Land Reforms (Amendment) Act of 1969. The act included strict provisions against the landlord's resumption of land for "personal cultivation" and landlordism was effectively abolished. The Land Reforms Act of 1969 lowered the ceiling on landholdings to ten acres and provided tenants with the full rights of land-ownership. From then on, the creation of tenancies was illegal.

It appears that the social group that benefited the most from the Land Reforms Act of 1969 was the landless agricultural workers (hutment dwellers) who traditionally lived on land belonging to others. This group, comprising 30% of the labor force, gained permanent rights to their house sites and land immediately adjacent to their homes (for personal cultivation) and benefited from an increase in agricultural wages (due to the Minimum Wage Act and other agrarian legislation). Furthermore, the tenants who became owner-cultivators overnight have obviously netted substantial gains from the legislation. However, it is unlikely that their economic situation improved appreciably, as the benefit of not having to pay rent to landlords was offset by the increased wages of farm workers (which accordingly increased the costs of cultivation) (Zachariah, 1984, pp. 16–17).

Perhaps the most important consideration relating to Kerala's success in meeting BN concerns its substantial investment in primary education. A comparison between school enrollments in Kerala and other Indian states reveals very high rates of enrollment and retention at the primary level and comparatively low enrollments in middle school. This profile is consistent with the state's strong interest in primary education, as exemplified by the high per student investment at the primary level in Kerala—the highest of all Indian states (Nair, 1979). Government expenditures for primary school education have increased tenfold between 1961–62 and 1980–81, and approximately 40% of the state's budget is devoted to all levels of education (Rajeev, 1983, pp. 68, 86). Obviously Kerala's emphasis on primary education has played a major role in increasing the adult literacy rate.

Kerala's investment in primary education has been complemented by an expanding health care infrastructure and health education programs. Since 1957–58 a large portion of the state government's budget has been devoted to health care (12.5–16%). The total number of hospital beds increased from 13,000 in 1960–61 to 29,000 in 1980–81 (120 beds per 100,000 persons). Between 1957–58 and 1975–76 the number of primary health centers grew from 68 to 163. The large number of public and private hospitals and clinics in Kerala make health care accessible to all of the rural population. Between 1957 and 1977, the annual average growth rates in the number of inpatients and outpatients were 6.02% and 5.06%, respectively, compared to an overall population increase of 2.34% per year. Currently the state government allocates approximately 15% of its budget for health care. Moreover, private expenditures on health care have even exceeded the government's health budget (Panikar and Soman, 1984). These improvements in the health infrastructure have been complemented by the state's ongoing program of health education, sponsored through the State Health Education Bureau.

Insofar as nutrition is concerned, Kerala's public distribution of foodgrains through fair price shops, which are normally confined only to urban areas in other Indian states, is accessible to virtually all of the population. The price of rice on the open market is significantly higher than the rice sold through the fair price shops. In addition, the state sponsors a number of nutrition intervention schemes for designated target groups. These programs include the Special Nutrition Programme for Pre-School Children, the Applied Nutrition Programme, the Special Feeding Programme, and the School Mid-day Meals Programme. Despite these efforts, anthropometric surveys have revealed that a substantial number of children suffer from severe malnutrition (4.8%). Yet, even so, Kerala has the lowest rate of severe malnutrition among all Indian states (Panikar and Soman, 1984).

Family planning programs have met with exceptional success in Kerala. The official family planning program has yielded fertility declines across all major socioeconomic groups—both rich and poor, literate and illiterate. A total of 88% of women in Kerala are familiar with birth control methods. Certainly the high degree of female literacy in Kerala has been a decisive factor in the success of the family planning program, as knowledge of contraceptives is positively correlated with years of schooling (Zachariah, 1984, pp. 39, 106–107, 145).

Finally the highly politicized nature of public life in Kerala seems to be a contributing factor in the country's BN performance. This intensity of political expression has led to a heightened degree of responsiveness on the part of the state government in delivering social services. As K. C. Zachariah (1984, p. 15) suggests,

the political awareness and the politicization of all issues, even those affecting only a small minority of the population, may be responsible for better delivery of government services than would otherwise be the case. Newspapers and political leaders explain the services and benefits available, along with the eligibility requirements. And what people are eligible for, they obtain—by application, appeal, or agitation.

In summary, the Indian state of Kerala has made impressive progress in meeting BN, particularly in the fields of health and education. While much remains to be done, especially in the fields of nutrition, safe water, and sanitation, the accomplishments that have been wrought thus far by this democratic state have been quite remarkable. Moreover the recent sharp decrease in Kerala's fertility rate provides support for the essential complementarity between BN programs and measures to control population growth (Chapter 6, section 6.4).

In this brief survey of three low-income LDCs that have pursued BN-type policies, the following conclusions seem in order: (1) it is possible to make substantial progress in the satisfaction of BN with very limited economic resources; (2) neither collectivization nor a dramatic redistribution of income appear to be necessary prerequisites for successful BN programs (see also Stewart, 1985, p. 209); (3) effective BN programs must enlist the participation of the groups those programs are intended to serve; and (4) unless BN programs are complemented by rational macroeconomic policies, their effectiveness will be seriously hampered in the long term.

While none of the countries surveyed is an ideal model for the BNA, all of them point to the fact that BN programs are feasible for even low-income LDCs, and BN policies can improve the quality of human life appreciably. In one case, the satisfaction of material BN was accompanied by a significant loss of political freedom (China). In each case, with the possible exception of Kerala, imprudent macroeconomic policies have diminished the effectiveness and stability of BN programs. In Sri Lanka the inflexibility of its educational curricula has led to a severe underutilization of its human resources. In China, Mao's preoccupation with collectivization and the creation of the New Socialist Man/Woman, as well as the myopic focus on industrialization, clearly diminished the overall health of the economy.

In sum, BN policies should not be lumped together with other economic policies and evaluated as one seamless garb. BN programs are intrinsically more difficult to implement and manage than well-defined, capital-intensive development projects (e.g., roads, electrification, telecommunications, dams) because of their labor-intensive structure, their dependence on recurrent financing, and their profound political implications. Hence the potential for economic mismanagement will always be greater with BN programs. However, one should evaluate such programs on their own merit, not on the basis of the poor macroeconomic management that often accompanies BN programs.

4.4   A MACROECONOMIC FRAMEWORK FOR THE BASIC NEEDS APPROACH

One of the problems surrounding assessments of the BNA's feasibility concerns the inability of mainstream macrotheory to capture the benefits of poverty-focused development initiatives, and, conversely, to reflect the productivity costs associated with acute poverty. Therefore it is necessary to locate the BNA within a macroeconomic framework that is sensitive to the spillover benefits associated with BN programs.

4.4.a   An Enhanced Production Function

Let us begin our consideration of the implications of the BNA for macrotheory by developing an enhanced version of the traditional production function. Beginning with a traditional production function that understands the aggregate output (Y) as the combination of the factors of capital (K), labor (L), and natural resources/land (R), so that

$$Y = f(K, L, R), \tag{1}$$

let us introduce two other independent variables in the production function: (1) the impact of the choice of technology in determining the composition and magnitude of the output (Sen, 1960); and (2) the autonomous role of the Schumpeterian entrepreneur in stimulating innovation and economic growth (Schumpeter, 1939, 1965). With the addition of technology (T) and entrepreneurial capacity (E) as independent factors of production, we may revise the traditional production function as follows:

$$Y = f(K, L, R, T, E) \tag{1a}$$

Using this expanded production function, let us assume that we are working with an LDC that is a semiclosed market economy (which permits capital outflows) and proceed to define individual functions for capital, labor, technology, and entrepreneurship.

Drawing upon the work of Montek Ahluwalia and Hollis Chenery (1974), let us disaggregate the capital stocks within an economy in order to reflect their distribution across income groups and their relative yield in terms of generating employment.[2] At the outset, let us distinguish between two basic types of capital stocks: (1) capital stocks that utilize hired labor (i.e., linked capital); and (2) capital stocks that do not utilize hired labor (i.e., nonlinked capital). Using the subscript e to denote linked capital stocks that are deployed in such a manner that employment/job creation is a secondary outcome and the subscript n to signify nonlinked capital stocks that do not utilize hired labor, the capital stock function within an economy can be depicted in the following manner:

$$K = f(K_e, K_n) \tag{2}$$

In addition to the distinction between linked and nonlinked capital stocks, it is necessary to reflect how these capital stocks are distributed across income groups. Obviously any attempt to depict the real-world distribution of capital stocks would be extremely involved. However, for purposes of this discussion, let us distinguish among four income groups: (1) the first group representing the richest income decile of the population; (2) the second group representing a nascent middle class, consisting of the next three lower income deciles of the population; (3) the third income group representing the marginally poor, comprised of the middle-income quintile of the population; and (4) the fourth income group including the lowest two income quintiles of the population (i.e., the poorest 40%). Obviously this is an extremely rough categorization. However, it is not altogether unrealistic to adopt a four-tiered characterization such as this one in portraying the distribution of income within developing countries. For example, 1976 data on income distribution from Kenya show that the group 1 decile enjoys 45.8% of the household income, group 2 has an average of 11.2% per decile, group 3 averaged 5.7% per decile, and group 4 holds an average of only 2.2% per decile (World Bank, 1986, p. 226). Similar portraits hold for nearly every LDC that collects data on income distribution (e.g., Zambia, Indonesia, Philippines, Thailand, Peru, Mauritius, Turkey, Brazil, Mexico, Costa Rica).

By combining the above four-tiered categorization for income distribution (using the subscripts 1, 2, 3, and 4 to represent each income group) with the elementary capital stock function, we may rewrite equation 2 as follows:

$$K = f(K_{e1}, K_{n1}, K_{e2}, K_{e3}, K_{e4}, K_{n4}),$$ (2a)

where K_{n1} primarily represents capital stocks that are devoted to foreign investment and have no discernible impact on domestic employment, K_{n4} consists of capital stocks used for self-employment (e.g., ownership of land, draft animals, or agricultural implements by smallholder farmers), and all of the capital stocks of income groups 2 and 3 accumulate within the domestic financial system (consisting of home mortgages, interest-bearing time deposits and domestic securities) and hence may be construed as a form of linked capital.

With respect to the labor stock function, there is a growing body of evidence, emerging from human capital studies, that highlights the important relationship between consumption and productivity within low-income groups (Belli, 1971; Colclough, 1982; Liu and Wong, 1981; Lockheed et al., 1980; Pinera and Selowsky, 1981; Rati and Schultz, 1979; Selowsky, 1981). These studies suggest that the productive capabilities of labor are significantly enhanced by improvements in consumption relating to nutrition, health, and education (presumably up to some consumption threshold or productivity plateau). Therefore the labor stock function could be conceived as follows:

$$L = f(Pop_L, N, Hea, Ed_n, Ed_f),$$ (3)

where Pop_L represents the number of people in the labor force, N stands for the nutritional status of the population, Hea signifies the health status of the population, and Ed_n and Ed_f denote opportunities for nonformal and formal education, respectively (e.g., basic literacy and numeracy).

Insofar as the technology function is concerned, there are strong indications, proceeding from the literature on "appropriate technology," that the choice of technologies can have salutary or perverse effects in the development process (see Carr, 1985). While certain industries have more problems with technical rigidity than others, there are indications that such rigidities may have more to do with the *scale* of production than the nature of the industry itself (Forsyth et al., 1980). This evidence suggests that the efficient range of factor choice in a production mix diminishes with an increasing scale of production, because production technologies usually must be capital-intensive in order to be efficient on a large scale. Hence, what could be called the "Principle of Diminishing Factor Choice to Scale" holds that the smaller the scale of production, the larger the efficient range of factor choice in a production mix; the larger the scale of production, the smaller the efficient range of factor choice in a production mix. This scale-dependent aspect of production may explain, in part, the empirical evidence that indicates an inverse relationship between the size of the firm and its willingness to employ appropriate technologies (World Bank, 1978). In addition, there is a substantial amount of anecdotal evidence that suggests that firm managers often prefer capital-intensive technologies over labor-intensive technologies owing to their desire to improve the asset base of the firm, to gain a perceived sense of modernization, or to reduce potential labor relations problems. Moreover, often scarce capital inputs are subsidized through government protection of certain industries, exchange rate policies, tied foreign assistance, and factor-price distortions.

In light of the above considerations, it seems warranted to make technology an independent factor of production, instead of being reduced to a dependent variable that is determined by factor-price relationships. Therefore, we could define a technology function as consisting of both capital-intensive technologies (T_K) and labor-intensive technologies (T_L) so that

$$T = f(T_K, T_L). \tag{4}$$

Figure 4.2 depicts two alternate growth paths in relation to the choice of technology. The production possibilities curve AB identifies the technologically feasible combinations of capital and labor for a particular society; the vertical axis represents capital inputs and the horizontal axis signifies labor inputs. The capital-intensive growth path (T_K) crosses the production possibilities frontier at point C, requiring capital resources equivalent to E and labor resources equivalent to G. By contrast, the labor-intensive growth path (T_L) crosses the frontier at point D, yielding a mix of capital and labor resources equivalent to F and H, respectively. All other things being equal, the increased labor utilization brought about by the labor-intensive growth path (T_L) would be the preferred growth path in country-contexts of relative labor abundance and capital scarcity (i.e., typical LDCs).[3] Yet some of the biases inherent in neoclassical growth theory would recommend the capital-intensive growth path (T_K) as the preferred option, as FE represents the additional increment of capital accumulation/savings for the country. On this view, additional increments on the vertical axis have greater relevance for economic growth than gains on the horizontal axis; the additional level of employment (GH) represents consumption, not investment in human capital. Certainly any understanding of economic growth that focuses on capital accumulation to the exclusion of human capital formation is highly suspect.

Finally the entrepreneurship function posits a relationship between the entrepreneurial capacity of an economy and the variables of nutrition (N), health (Hea), nonformal education (Ed_n), formal education (Ed_f), material incentives (In_m), and nonmaterial incentives (In_n), so that

$$E = f(N, Hea, Ed_n, Ed_f, In_m, In_n). \tag{5}$$

The variables of nutrition, health, and formal/nonformal education are clearly important preconditions for entrepreneurial insight and activities. Moreover, the importance of these variables for an economy's entrepreneurial capacity increases with broadened definitions of the entrepreneur, which, as T. W. Schultz (1980) has argued, should include nontraditional groups such as farmers and housewives.

Figure 4.2
Technology Choice and Alternate Growth Paths

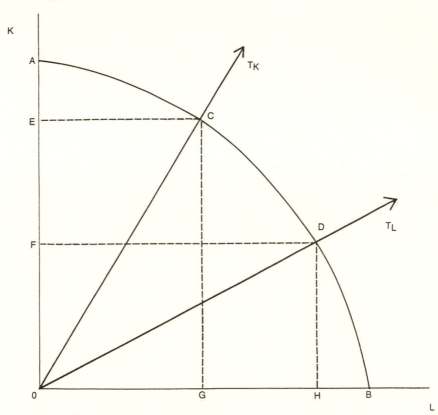

In addition, the presence of incentives, both material and nonmaterial, are clearly important factors in stimulating entrepreneurship. Insofar as material incentives are concerned, it is clear that all market economies will provide a sufficient degree of market disequilibrium for the entrepreneurial spirit to thrive, assuming that there are few legal or economic barriers for new entrants. With respect to nonmaterial incentives, it appears that a central, if not decisive, factor in entrepreneurial motivation is the desire for autonomy or freedom from control by others and the felt need to be an innovator (Ronen, 1983).

To summarize the foregoing discussion, I have suggested that a macroeconomic framework for the BNA would utilize the following:

1. an enhanced production function,
   $Y = f(K, L, R, T, E)$;
2. a capital stock function,
   $K = f(K_{e1}, K_{n1}, K_{e2}, K_{e3}, K_{e4}, K_{n4})$;

3. a labor stock function,
   $L = f(Pop_L, N, Hea, Ed_n, Ed_f)$;
4. a technology function,
   $T = f(T_K, T_L)$; and
5. an entrepreneurship function,
   $E = f(N, Hea, Ed_n, Ed_f, In_m, In_n)$.

where,

Y	=	output
K	=	capital
L	=	labor
R	=	natural resources, including land
E	=	entrepreneurial capacity
T	=	technology
K_{e1}	=	linked capital owned by the richest income decile that generates domestic employment
K_{n1}	=	nonlinked capital owned by the richest income decile that does not generate domestic employment (i.e., primarily capital stocks invested in foreign countries)
K_{e2}	=	linked capital owned by the nascent middle class that generates domestic employment
K_{e3}	=	linked capital owned by the marginally poor group (middle quintile) that generates domestic employment
K_{e4}	=	linked capital owned by the poorest 40% of the population that generates domestic employment
K_{n4}	=	nonlinked capital owned by the poorest 40% that is utilized for self-employment
Pop_L	=	labor force
N	=	nutrition
Hea	=	health
Ed_n	=	nonformal education
Ed_f	=	formal education
In_m	=	material incentives
In_n	=	nonmaterial incentives
T_K	=	capital-intensive technologies
T_L	=	labor-intensive technologies.

4.4.b. Disaggregating the Harrod-Domar Model

The advantage of an enhanced production function such as this one is that it broadens the conceptual range of our thinking about economic growth. Instead of focusing on one factor of growth, such as land (physiocrats), trade (mercantilists), labor (classical economists, Marx), or capital (Harrod-Domar), a multifactoral analysis has a significantly better chance of comprehending the complexity of development realities and offering meaningful solutions (Streeten, 1967).

Nonetheless, despite the inherent weaknesses of one-factored analysis, it is difficult to escape the conclusion that capital accumulation will play a major role in defining both the magnitude and contours of economic growth. Unfortunately, though, the highly influential formulation by Harrod and Domar,

$$g = s v \tag{6}$$

(where g signifies growth, s stands for an incremental change in aggregate savings, v is a fixed output-capital ratio), is far too aggregative and abstract to be useful in analyzing growth patterns within LDCs. The lack of disaggregation within the Harrod-Domar model has encouraged the development of two unfortunate biases within modern growth theory: (1) the tendency to ignore the distributional pattern of capital stocks across an economy; and (2) a prejudicial presumption in favor of allocations of capital to firms/industries/sectors with the highest output-capital ratios (v).

Returning to our capital stock function, let us distinguish among six output-capital ratios corresponding to each of the capital stocks. Let a refer to the output-capital ratios for linked capital stocks that create domestic employment, and b stand for output-capital ratios for nonlinked capital stocks. Using our four-tiered income analysis, the output-capital ratios pertaining to each income group would be the following:

Group 1 (10th income decile): a_1, b_1

Group 2 (7th through 9th income deciles): a_2

Group 3 (5th and 6th income deciles): a_3

Group 4 (1st through 4th income deciles): a_4, b_4.

On the basis of these output-capital ratios, the aggregate output (Y) from the seven capital stocks could be written as follows:

$$Y = f(Y_{Ke1}, Y_{Kn1}, Y_{Ke2}, Y_{Ke3}, Y_{Ke4}, Y_{Kn4}), \tag{7}$$

$$
\begin{aligned}
Y_{Ke1} &= a_1 K_{e1} \\
Y_{Kn1} &= b_1 K_{n1} \\
Y_{Ke2} &= a_2 K_{e2} \\
Y_{Ke3} &= a_3 K_{e3}
\end{aligned}
$$

$$Y_{Ke4} = a_4 K_{e4}$$
$$Y_{Kn4} = b_4 K_{n4}.$$

Using the following notation,

$Y_1, Y_2, Y_3, Y_4 =$	incomes of the rich (group 1), middle class (group 2), marginally poor (group 3), and poorest 40% (group 4)
$W_1, W_2, W_3, W_4 =$	total wage income accruing to the rich, middle class, marginally poor, and poorest 40% income groups
$wi_1, wi_2, wi_3, wi_4 =$	share of wage income accruing to the four income groups from linked capital stocks
$P_1, P_2, P_3, P_4 =$	total nonwage income (i.e., profits, interest, rents) accruing to the four income groups
$pi_1, pi_2, pi_3, pi_4 =$	share of nonwage income accruing to the four income groups from linked capital stocks

the total income from each group could be written as follows

$$Y = Y_1 + Y_2 + Y_3 + Y_4, \tag{8}$$

where

$$Y_1 = W_1 + P_1$$
$$Y_2 = W_2 + P_2$$
$$Y_3 = W_3 + P_3$$
$$Y_4 = W_4 + P_4.$$

Furthermore, the wage income from linked capital stocks for each of the income groups would be the following (assuming that people from higher income groups are not engaged in wage labor by entrepreneurs from lower income groups):

$$W_1 = wi_1 Y_{Ke1}$$
$$W_2 = wi_2 Y_{Ke1} + wi_2 Y_{Ke2}$$
$$W_3 = wi_3 Y_{Ke1} + wi_3 Y_{Ke2} + wi_3 Y_{Ke3}$$
$$W_4 = wi_4 Y_{Ke1} + wi_4 Y_{Ke2} + wi_4 Y_{Ke3} + wi_4 Y_{Ke4}. \tag{9}$$

The nonwage income on both linked and nonlinked capital stocks could be written as follows:

$$P_1 = pi_1 Y_{Ke1} + Y_{Kn1}$$
$$P_2 = pi_2 Y_{Ke2}$$

$$P_3 = pi_3 \, Y_{Ke3}$$

$$P_4 = pi_4 \, Y_{Ke4} + Y_{Kn4}, \tag{10}$$

where,

$$pi_1 = 1 - (wi_1 \, Y_{Ke1} + wi_2 \, Y_{Ke1} + wi_3 \, Y_{Ke1} + wi_4 \, Y_{Ke1});$$

$$pi_2 = 1 - (wi_2 \, Y_{Ke2} + wi_3 \, Y_{Ke2} + wi_4 \, Y_{Ke2});$$

$$pi_3 = 1 - (wi_3 \, Y_{Ke3} + wi_4 \, Y_{Ke3}); \text{ and}$$

$$pi_4 = 1 - wi_4 \, Y_{Ke4}.$$

In formulating an aggregate savings equation for these four income groups, it is necessary to consider the impact of consumption on productivity within low-income groups. As previously mentioned in the discussion on the labor stock function, a growing body of evidence suggests that improved consumption of basic goods within low-income groups is associated with increased productivity. Unfortunately the critical relationship between consumption and productivity in low-income groups has not found explicit expression in contemporary formulations of economic theory, except in a few instances (e.g., Mirrless, 1975). Yet when consumption at certain income levels is viewed as a form of savings or investment, there are profound implications for the way that macroeconomic aggregates, such as consumption and savings, are conceptualized. This would suggest the existence of a human capital consumption coefficient, denoted h (where $0 \leq h < 1$), which represents the average marginal productivity value of additional increments of consumption by low-income groups within a population (i.e., groups 3 and 4 in this model).

If such a human capital consumption coefficient exists (and it seems readily apparent that it does), then the traditional consumption aggregate of

$$C = cY \tag{11}$$

where C is aggregate consumption, c is the marginal propensity to consume, and Y is aggregate income, should be rewritten as follows:

$$C = cY - ([h_3 \cdot \Delta Y_3] + [h_4 \cdot \Delta Y_4]), \tag{11a}$$

where $h_3 < h_4$, $0 \leq \Delta Y_3$, $0 \leq \Delta Y_4$, $\Delta Y_3 = Y_3 t_1 - Y_3 t$, and $\Delta Y_4 = Y_4 t_1 - Y_4 t$. Similarly the traditional savings aggregate

$$S = sY, \tag{12}$$

where S is aggregate savings, s is the marginal propensity to save, and Y is aggregate income, should be reformulated as follows:

$$S = sY + ([h_3 \cdot \Delta Y_3] + [h_4 \cdot \Delta Y_4]), \tag{12a}$$

where $h_3 < h_4$, $0 \le \Delta Y_3$, $0 \le \Delta Y_4$, $\Delta Y_3 = Y_3 t_1 - Y_3 t$, and $\Delta Y_4 = Y_4 t_1 - Y_4 t$. Assuming an identity between savings (S) and investment (I), such that

$$S = I, \tag{13}$$

equations 11a and 12a suggest that there exists a shadow rate of investment which is mistakenly incorporated into the consumption aggregate of macro-economic formulations. If this is true, the impact of the human capital consumption coefficient (h) must be reflected in our savings equation for the four income groups.

Given the above equations, we can formulate the aggregate savings equation as follows:

$$S = sY_1 + sY_2 + sY_3 + sY_4 + (h_3 \cdot \Delta Y_3) + (h_4 \cdot \Delta Y_4), \tag{14}$$

where s is the marginal propensity of each group to save, and $h_3 < h_4$, $0 \le \Delta Y_3$, $0 \le \Delta Y_4$, $\Delta Y_3 = Y_3 t_1 - Y_3 t$, and $\Delta Y_4 = Y_4 t_1 - Y_4 t$. It should be emphasized that although the marginal propensities of upper income groups to save will be higher than low-income groups, it is possible to raise the marginal propensities of the lower income groups through institutional reforms that grant them access to banks/credit unions and provide sufficient incentives to save (Vogel and Burkett, 1986). Moreover, much of the savings of the richest income group will likely accumulate in capital stock K_{n1}, consisting primarily of foreign investments that do not generate domestic employment.

In light of the prominent role of the public sector in sponsoring BN programs, it is necessary to enhance equation 14 by accounting for the productivity gains associated with government BN initiatives. Let G_{bni} refer to government investment in BN programs targeted to the poorest 60% of a population (groups 3 and 4). Moreover, let us assume that we have sufficient data to predict the income effect of G_{bni} upon household budgets, so that it is possible to calculate a rough coefficient for household consumption (H_c), where $0 \le H_c < 1$, for each of the low-income groups (H_{c3}, H_{c4}). By computing the contribution of government BN expenditures to the budgets of low-income households ($G_{bni} \cdot H_c$), it would be possible to calculate the investment value of government BN programs based upon the human capital consumption coefficient for groups 3 and 4 (h_3, h_4). Therefore we could account for the impact of public sector BN expenditures on aggregate savings as follows:

$$S = sY_1 + sY_2 + sY_3 + sY_4 + (h_3 \cdot \Delta Y_3) + (h_4 \cdot \Delta Y_4) + G_{bni} ([H_{c3} \cdot h_3] + [H_{c4} \cdot h_4]). \tag{14a}$$

This enhanced savings equation suggests the existence of a non-Keynesian BN multiplier effect that is associated with public-sector BN programs, as well as growth/redistribution policies designed to increase the household income of low-income groups. Depending on the magnitudes of the human capital consumption coefficient (h) and the household consumption coefficient (H_c), as well as the increase in real income among low-income households (ΔY_3, ΔY_4), government BN programs and growth/redistribution policies targeted for low-income groups could have a tremendous productivity impact on a nation's development. What looks like consumption would actually be a significant investment in the future.

The probable existence of a non-Keynesian BN multiplier effect also underscores the significant opportunity costs associated with highiy unequal distributions of income and wealth. These opportunity costs are most pronounced in connection with the nonlinked capital stocks held by the richest income group (K_{n1}), as this stock has little or no impact on domestic productivity and employment. Consequently it would seem appropriate to reflect these costs in our aggregate savings equation by assigning a shadow price to the opportunity costs (C_o) associated with the K_{n1} capital stocks. Hence equation 14a could be expanded as follows:

$$S = sY_1 + sY_2 + sY_3 + sY_4 + (h_3 \cdot \Delta Y_3) + (h_4 \cdot \Delta Y_4) + G_{bni} ([H_{c3} \cdot h_3] + [H_{c4} \cdot h_4]) - (C_o \cdot K_{n1}), \tag{14b}$$

where $0 \leq C_o \leq 1$.

The concept of a BN multiplier effect takes on added significance when one factors in the impact of population growth upon economic growth. Assuming the following notion,

$$N_1, N_2, N_3, N_4 \quad = \quad \text{number of people in groups 1, 2, 3 and 4}$$
$$r_1, r_2, r_3, r_4 \quad = \quad \text{rate of population growth for groups 1, 2, 3 and 4}$$
$$t, t_1, \ldots, t_n \quad = \quad \text{time periods,}$$

the impact of population growth upon economic growth could be written as follows:

$$Y_1 t_1 \quad = \quad Y_1 t_1 \ / \ N_1 t \ r_1 t$$
$$Y_2 t_1 \quad = \quad Y_2 t_1 \ / \ N_2 t \ r_2 t$$
$$Y_3 t_1 \quad = \quad Y_3 t_1 \ / \ N_3 t \ r_3 t$$
$$Y_4 t_1 \quad = \quad Y_4 t_1 \ / \ N_4 t \ r_4 t. \tag{15}$$

In light of the high rates of population growth characteristic of group 4, the income effect of BN programs ($G_{bni} \cdot H_c$) becomes all the more critical in improving, if not simply maintaining, the income posture of the poorest 40%. Additionally, it is clear that we will not be able to make significant progress in fertility declines without substantial investment in education and increased opportunities for employment, particularly for females (see Chapter 6, section 6.4).

Returning to the previous discussion concerning Harrod-Domar output-capital ratios, it seems reasonable to assume that the following relationship holds among the six output-capital ratios of their respective capital stocks:

$$b_1 > a_1 > a_2 > a_3 > b_4 > a_4. \tag{16}$$

Consequently, the optimization of strictly capital resources would require an allocation favoring the upper income groups. However, in light of a presumed BN multiplier effect and its potential impact on fertility declines, the productivity value of scarce capital resources would be much greater if capital was allocated in favor of low-income groups (e.g., agricultural extension programs, improvements in transportation/marketing infrastructures, food preservation/processing programs, development of small-scale village industries, enterprise enhancement programs for the urban informal sector). This would be especially true in view of the capital outflows and opportunity costs associated with the K_{n1} capital stock. Additionally, an increased allocation of productive resources to lower income groups would lessen the need for recurrent government expenditures for BN programs (assuming that such programs were structured to foster self-reliance instead of dependency). Furthermore, the complementarities between the labor and entrepreneurship functions suggest that BN programs will have spillover benefits in terms of enhanced labor quality and entrepreneurial capacity, as both functions share the variables of nutrition, health, and formal/nonformal education. Moreover, there is evidence that the informal sector of LDCs has a significant and underutilized capacity for job creation (Levitsky, 1986) and entrepreneurial development (Page and Steel, 1984, pp. 22–23).

4.4.c   The Basic Needs Matrix

In crafting a wide range of creative delivery systems for basic goods and services, it is necessary to enlist the resources of both the public and private sectors. Many of the public services presently available in MDCs and LDCs are provided through the cooperation of the government and the private sector as either a producer or buyer of such services. For example, Figure 4.3 illustrates how the public and private sectors function as either producers or buyers of educational services.

The concept of a BN matrix is a helpful way of illustrating various modalities for BN delivery systems and the opportunities for public- and private-sector participation. Using m to represent a mean level of income and g to signify a Gini coefficient for the distribution of income or consumption, a BN matrix could be defined as follows:

Figure 4.3
Government and Private Sectors as Buyers and Producers of Educational Services

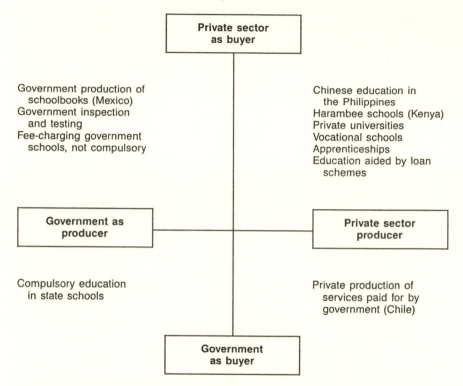

Source: Gabrial Roth, *The Private Provision of Public Services in Developing Countries* (New York: Oxford University Press, 1987), p. 65.

$$\text{BN Matrix} = f(HIm, HIg, H_{bnc}\,g, H_{bnp}, G_{bni}, M_{bn}), \tag{17}$$

where, HIm represents the mean level of household income, HIg stands for the extent of inequality (as measured by a Gini coefficient) in the distribution of household income, $H_{bnc}\,g$ denotes the extent of inequality (as measured by a Gini coefficient) in the distribution of basic goods and services *within* the household, H_{bnp} represents the marginal propensity of households to allocate income for BN consumption, G_{bni} indicates the magnitude of government investment in BN programs, and M_{bn} denotes the capacity of markets to supply basic goods and services.

Figure 4.4 depicts the supply and demand dimensions of the BN matrix by locating equation 17 within a 2 × 4 matrix. On the supply side, basic goods and services may be provided either directly through government programs (G_{bni}) or indirectly through public-sector initiatives that utilize the private sector in supplying basic goods and services (M_{bn}). On the demand side, the level of

Figure 4.4
Supply and Demand Aspects of a BN Matrix and Respective Delivery Systems

		Demand-Side			
		H_{lm}	H_{lg}	H_{bncg}	H_{bnp}
Supply-Side	G_{bni}	I	II	III	IV
	M_{bn}	V	VI	VII	VIII

Zone	Examples of Delivery Systems
I	direct general subsidies (income or in-kind)
II	direct targeted subsidies (income or in-kind); land reform programs (urban and rural); provision of public services in low-income areas (e.g., health, water and sanitation, education)
III	on-site supplementary child nutrition programs
IV	nutrition/health education; primary education; adult literacy programs
V	macroeconomic policies which promote overall economic growth
VI	agricultural price policies which benefit rural populations; extension and credit programs designed to increase the output of smallholder farmers and support small entrepreneurs in the informal sector ; partial subsidization of foodstuffs which are typically consumed by low-income households
VII	tax incentives for firms which convey in their business advertising that increased consumption of basic goods among all family members is a source of pride and elevated social status
VIII	competitive pricing of basic goods and services; infrastructure improvements which increase market access

consumption of basic goods and services will be influenced by the mean level of household income (HIm), the pattern of income distribution *among* households (HIg), the pattern of consumption *within* households ($H_{bnc}\ g$), and the marginal propensity of households to consume basic goods and services (H_{bnp}). Each of the eight zones of the matrix represents a class of delivery systems for the provision of basic goods and services.

The significance of the BN matrix is that BN programs may be devised around a multiplicity of delivery systems in both the public and private sectors. While most BN programs will probably come in the form of direct public-sector involvement, there are many opportunities to utilize the private sector in the design of BN delivery systems.

Of course, it should be emphasized that country-wide implementations of the BNA may precipitate some degree of macroeconomic instability insofar as demand-pull inflation and balance-of-payments problems are concerned. For instance, the fact that income elasticities of demand for certain basic goods (e.g., food) are higher than their short-run supply elasticities suggests that demand-pull inflation will be a fact of life for development strategies that emphasize BN objectives, unless appropriate supply-management policies are devised. Moreover, low-income LDCs that implement BN programs may face substantial balance-of-payments problems, unless such programs are accompanied by substantial infusions of external development assistance. This problem becomes particularly acute in light of the pronounced tendency of the IMF's stabilization programs to diminish the long-term effectiveness of development programs through the blanket imposition of fiscal austerity (e.g., insisting that governments cut subsidies on foodstuffs and basic goods).

What are the implications of the foregoing macroeconomic framework for the BNA? It would appear that the primary implication for the BNA is that well-designed BN policies will enhance the productivity of a nation's economy, instead of diminishing overall economic growth. The probable existence of a human capital consumption coefficient and a non-Keynesian BN multiplier effect suggests that the traditional macroeconomic aggregates of consumption and savings must be reformulated in order to reflect a shadow rate of savings/investment (implicit in BN programs), which has been mistakenly incorporated into the consumption aggregate. Moreover, the common variables of the labor and entrepreneurship functions (N, Hea, Ed_n, Ed_f) suggest that BN programs will have beneficial spillover effects in terms of improving the quality of labor resources and increasing the entrepreneurial capacity of the economy.

Secondary implications of the model for the BNA include the following:

1. an important trade-off exists between labor intensity and the productivity of capital, and this tension should not necessarily be resolved by allocating scarce capital resources to firms/industries/sectors having the highest output-capital ratios;

2. there are significant opportunity costs associated with one of two capital stocks held by the richest income group within LDCs (K_{n1});
3. with increases in capital stocks held by lower income groups, the productivity costs associated with lower output-capital ratios would be offset by a variety of benefits, relating to (a) more appropriate factor mixes in production processes, (b) enhanced labor productivity and diffusion of entrepreneurial skills, (c) an eventual decrease in recurrent government expenditures for BN programs, and (d) a decrease in the rate of population growth; and
4. there is a wide range of BN delivery systems within both the public and private sectors for the provision of basic goods and services, as indicated by the BN matrix.

In short, the long-term interests of economic growth and development are best served by addressing the long-term interests of the poor. While the provisions of BNA would probably create some degree of macroeconomic instability insofar as demand-pull inflation and balance-of-payments problems are concerned, the costs of these macroeconomic adjustments are a small price to pay for long-term economic stability and growth. Consequently, the BNA is not only a program in behalf of the poor, but also provides a secure foundation for a prosperous and durable international economic order.

NOTES

1. The major problem with the conclusions of Adelman and Morris was that they relied exclusively on cross-sectional comparisons, instead of utilizing longitudinal data on income distribution (although admittedly the data are very sparse and unreliable). What little longitudinal data do exist do not appear to support Adelman and Morris's claim for absolute impoverishment (Ahluwalia et al., 1979). However Griffin and Khan (1978) claim that data from seven Asian countries indicate that the *rural* poor, especially the landless, have suffered absolute declines in their standard of living during the course of aggregate economic growth. Clearly the debate over absolute impoverishment is far from over.

2. I have adapted much of Ahluwalia and Chenery's macroeconomic model for this presentation.

3. Of course, countries that have the capability to adopt aggressive export-promotion development strategies may find it more advantageous to pursue a more capital-intensive growth path.

5
Human Responsibility and Duties to Provide Assistance

5.1. THE PARAMETERS OF GLOBAL OBLIGATIONS

A powerful aspect of the BNM and BNI as species-ethics is that they map moral obligations on the basis of membership in the human race, instead of determining those obligations with reference to certain human subgroupings (e.g., family, community, state). As a consequence, the BNM and BNI do not consider natural ethnic and geographic groupings, as well as arbitrary national boundaries, to be morally significant insofar as compliance to these universal principles is concerned.

Since the BNM and BNI mandate action in accordance with the basic needs of other human beings as well as one's own basic needs, they support an extensive moral regime of global human rights and corresponding duties aimed at safeguarding those human rights. In view of the logical correlativity between rights and duties (i.e., my right to X imposes a duty upon you to respect that right), the BNM and BNI raise the critical issue as to how far one is morally obligated to respect the BN of other human beings. One would expect that the sort of global moral regime that the BNM and BNI envision will not respect artificial distinctions between security rights (i.e., negative freedom) and subsistence rights (i.e., positive freedom), but instead will regard the human person as both an autonomous moral agent and a social being who requires certain basic goods for survival and development. Consequently the BNM and BNI not only prohibit policies/actions that *deprive* others of their basic goods, but also prescribe policies/actions that *promote* basic goods.

To what extent does the BNI, as a universal moral principle, obligate individuals to become actively engaged in efforts to assist others in meeting their BN? Often moral philosophers have answered questions of this type by stating that persons have a moral obligation to assist others in need unless they will suffer some comparable harm in the course of providing such assistance (Aiken,

1977; Gewirth, 1979; Shue, 1980; P. Singer, 1977a). I will refer to this as the Principle of Comparable Harm. The classic case in the ethics literature refers to a person drowning in a lake, and a bystander must decide whether or not she will jump in and save the drowning individual. According to the Principle of Comparable Harm, it is clear that the bystander should jump in and rescue the person if she knows how to swim and is in good physical condition. However, if there is a high probability that the bystander will drown in the course of rescuing the individual (due to poor health or an inability to swim), the Principle of Comparable Harm would exempt that bystander from the moral duty to rescue the drowning individual.

The problem with the Principle of Comparable Harm is that it fails to account for the important variable of time in the construal of moral duties to provide assistance. The Principle of Comparable Harm is well suited for *synchronic* moral obligations that demand responses spanning a brief period of time. It is not an appropriate principle, though, for *diachronic* moral obligations that require us to reinstate a moral response continually over a period of years, if not decades.

The distinction between synchronic and diachronic moral obligations is justified on both logical and consequentialist grounds. First, there is a logical difference between moral obligations that must be performed in a discrete time period (t_1) and those that must be replicated over an indefinite period of time $(t_1 \ldots t_n)$. For example, there is a substantial difference between the commitment involved in adopting a child versus babysitting a child, even though both commitments entail similar duties of care and protection. Second, on consequentialist grounds, it is clear that a high degree of discipline, strength of character, and social reinforcement are typically required to reinstate a commitment to provide assistance over a lengthy period of time. For instance, the commitment shown by an individual toward his or her invalid spouse or severely disabled child is a powerful testimony to the strength of human love. Yet it is a commitment that can be sustained only by the intense devotion between husband and wife or parent and child and, not infrequently, is sorely tested as the years pass by.

In light of the foregoing considerations, it seems appropriate to conclude that the Principle of Comparable Harm should be the decisive criterion in mapping synchronic duties to provide assistance. However, no such direct application can be made with respect to diachronic moral duties. Instead the Principle of Comparable Harm must be qualified by three kinds of constraints that pose justifiable limitations on the extent to which we are obligated to provide assistance to other human beings over extended time periods: (1) the Sphere of Influence Constraint, (2) the Replication Constraint, and (3) the Sociality Constraint.

5.2.   THE SPHERE OF INFLUENCE CONSTRAINT

The Sphere of Influence Constraint simply holds that one is morally obligated to assist those individuals within our sphere of influence. Because ''ought implies can," we cannot be held morally responsible to aid those who are beyond the reach of our influence. It should be emphasized, though, that in an age of split-second communications and international governmental/nongovernmental agencies, there are only a few regions of the world that actually lie outside of our sphere of influence. Therefore the Sphere of Influence Constraint is a relatively insignificant factor in establishing limitations on moral duties to provide assistance to others. Even in exceptional cases where the extent of one's influence is extremely weak (e.g., 80% of the famine assistance from a donor country is being taken by the military in the recipient country), the Sphere of Influence Constraint would not abrogate the moral obligation to give aid (unless rough calculations of BN Investment Ratios demonstrated that the opportunity costs of such aid disbursements were high enough to justify an alternative use of these resources).[1]

5.3.   THE REPLICATION CONSTRAINT

The Replication Constraint attempts to optimize the impact of altruistic behaviors, enlightened governmental policies, and aid flows by permitting measures that will enhance the stability or repetition of those courses of action or policies over time.[2] In essence, the Replication Constraint recognizes that diachronic moral duties to provide assistance must be formulated with reference to an individual's life plan or salient national goals. To deny the existence of individual preferences or national priorities is hardly a credible course for any theory of morality to chart and would introduce significant degrees of instability in actions or policies designed to provide assistance. It is the task of moral theory to establish parameters for individual preferences and national priorities, not to ignore them.

The Replication Constraint holds that compliance to the BNM and BNI should be structured in a way that maximizes the total amount of possible assistance over a significant period of time. In other words, the Replication Constraint sanctions exemptions from the Principle of Comparable Harm inasmuch as those exemptions promote stability in the capacity of individuals or nations to perform their diachronic moral obligations to provide assistance. For example, let us assume that persons A and B each receive an annual income of 1,000 consumption units, and they require only 500 consumption units to meet their BN. According to the Principle of Comparable Harm, each individual would have a moral duty to spend *all* of their disposable income in helping others meet their BN, once their own BN are satisfied (although in certain situations they may elect to deprive themselves of their own BN in order to assist others).[3] Hence persons A and B would each be obligated to give 500 consumption units annually to assist the poor according to the Principle of Comparable Harm. Let us assume that person A enthusiastically gives away the 500 consumption units required by the Principle of Comparable Harm in the first year, but then begins to feel the burden of his commitment in the second year and cuts back to 400 consumption units. By year three the discipline required to perpetuate voluntarily his minimal existence becomes overwhelming. He contemplates reducing his commitment to a mere 100 consumption units; but, upon further consideration, he dismisses this idea as tokenism and attempts to maintain the current level of 400 consumption units in year three. By the end of year three his frustration is unbearable, and he decides to give nothing in year four. By contrast, person B has no illusions about his capacity to sustain a long-term commitment of this type and decides to allocate a small amount of his income consistently over a 20-year period. Reflecting critically on his various life goals, person B decides that 100 consumption units is the maximum he can give consistently on an annual basis. Assuming that person B can maintain this commitment over a 20–year period, he would be able to provide others in need with 2,000 consumption units, in contrast to the 1,300 consumption units of person A.

Obviously the determinants of stability will vary markedly from each person or national regime (if we are considering the moral obligations of states to give assistance) to the next, depending on a host of historical, cultural, political, and psychological factors. For example, for many individuals in the industrialized world, economic and psychological stability is associated with a comfortable standard of living, some degree of job satisfaction, a modicum of personal happiness, and a reasonable degree of economic security. Insofar as governmental regimes are concerned, stability is affected by a number of factors, including various economic indicators, autonomous sources of countervailing power, social choice processes, public perceptions of leadership, internal checks and balances, political coalitions, and foreign affairs. It would be extremely difficult to identify and weight those factors that would generate a level of economic and psychological stability sufficient for sustaining the sort of long-term moral commitment envisioned by the BNM and BNI.

Given the intrinsically subjective nature of the Replication Constraint, due to the variability of the determinants of stability, each individual or national regime must decide for itself what consumption level is necessary in order for them to discharge their diachronic moral obligations over a substantial period of time. Obviously this proviso opens up a veritable Pandora's box for evading one's diachronic moral responsibilities; however, the variability of individual life plans and national priorities logically requires a wide berth for individual and collective choice at this point.

Do the subjective dimensions of the Replication Constraint make it impossible to establish minimum parameters for BN assistance from individuals or nations? The answer seems to be no. Common sense suggests that no significant aspect of an individual's life plan or a country's national priorities will be adversely affected by contributions that represent a small percentage of their economic resources.[4]

We could expect, for example, that a high-income household will not be kept from any significant individual or family aspiration by allocating 10% of its income to those experiencing BN shortfalls. Moreover, if a middle-income household gives away 5% of its income in BN assistance, this is not likely to have a pronounced effect on their collective welfare (unless they have a very large family). The same would be true of a low-income household that gives away 2.5% of its income. (The distinction between low-, middle-, and high-income households is intentionally vague, in view of the large role that perceptions of relative deprivation will inevitably play in the way that donor households conceive of their responsibilities to provide BN assistance.) In terms of the moral responsibilities of richer nations to assist poorer countries, it seems clear that any industrialized nation can afford to part with 1% of its annual GNP without compromising any of its central national objectives.

In view of the above considerations, it seems reasonable to establish, on intuitive grounds, mandatory *minimum* parameters for BN assistance at 10% for high-income households, 5% for middle-income households, 2.5% for low-income households, and 1% of the annual GNP for nation-states. Of course, charitable donations for nonbasic needs would not be counted in assessing these minimum percentages of household or national income for BN assistance, although educational programs designed to raise public awareness of global poverty would certainly qualify as BN assistance (owing to the eventual impact of such programs on aid flows). Consequently the foreign aid budgets of OECD countries would have to be higher than the 1% minimum parameter, given the fact that a large share of those budgets is currently being allocated for nonbasic needs.

As low as these percentages may seem, they appear more like bold donor targets than minimum contribution thresholds when compared to actual patterns of assistance. For instance, in 1985 the United States gave only .24% of its annual GNP for official development assistance, and most of that money, apportioned on political grounds, went to middle-income LDCs (e.g., over one-third of ODA from the United States goes to Israel and Egypt). Altogether only .04% of the U.S. annual GNP went to those countries in most dire need (in the form of bilateral aid): the low-income LDCs (World Bank, 1987). In light of these statistics, a contribution rate of 1% for ODA (targeted for BN objectives in the low-income LDCs and restructured to support the recurrent costs of BN programs) would represent over a thirtyfold increase in the rate of assistance targeted for those most in need.

Figure 5.1 graphically portrays the relationship between the Replication Constraint and levels of assistance given to those in need. The vertical axis represents the income available to a household for consumption and savings at three different budget ranges, represented by budget constraints A, B, and C. The horizontal axis represents the amount of money a household decides to allocate in assisting those outside the household to meet their BN (not including gifts to others relating to nonbasic needs). Line D represents the particular BN threshold (BNT) for this family (below which the family cannot fully meet its BN). Points E, F, and G lie on the BN threshold and represent the maximum parameter for the household's Replication Constraint for the three budget lines A, B, and C, respectively. Similarly points H, I, and J lie on the minimum mandatory Replication Constraint trajectory (RC_{min}) and represent the minimum parameters for budget lines A, B,

Figure 5.1
Parameters for a Household Replication Constraint

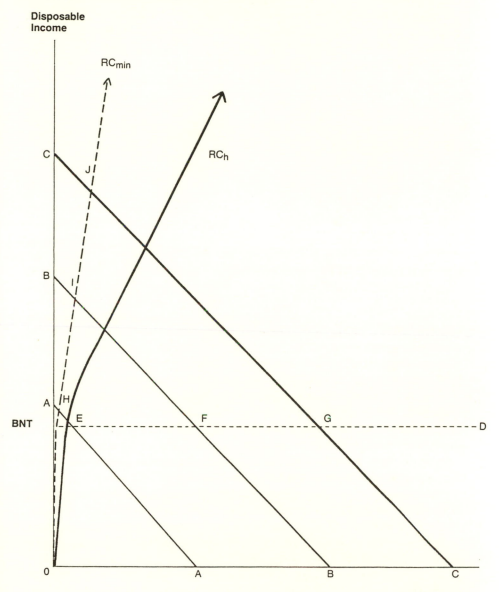

and C, respectively, based upon the reasonable minimum parameters of 2.5% for low-income households (budget line A), 5% for middle-income households (budget line B) and 10% for upper-income households (budget line C). Trajectory RC_h represents the particular Replication Constraint selected by a strongly altruistic household.

One could imagine that a number of creative things could be done in order to dovetail certain important household goals with the moral obligation to provide assistance to those suffering from BN shortfalls. For example, banks and mutual funds might encourage individuals to set up high interest "Individual Donor Accounts" (IDAs) that encourage people to select a specific savings target (e.g., $2,500, $5,000, or $10,000) and to start an additional account once that target is reached. The interest earned from these IDAs could be allocated by the bank or mutual fund directly to a relief or development agency of the individual's choice. An arrangement such as this would benefit many households by encouraging the discipline of saving and would provide a consistent flow of resources to those in need, enabling various charitable organizations to plan their projects with greater stability and precision, as well as reducing their overhead costs in soliciting contributions.[5]

5.4. THE SOCIALITY CONSTRAINT

The third and final constraint for diachronic moral obligations is the Sociality Constraint. The Sociality Constraint simply holds that BN assistance should be channelled in such a way that does not undermine the social stability of the donor household or state. In a sense, the Sociality Constraint is simply an extension of the Replication Constraint, in that both aim at optimizing the stability of aid flows by enhancing the ability of individuals and countries to perform their diachronic moral obligations over time.

Intensity and scope are two important dimensions of human sociality. Both are essential to the definition of the Sociality Constraint and its application to diachronic moral obligations to provide assistance. Intensity refers to the total amount of energy an individual is able to invest in social relationships, which presumably has some upper bound but undoubtedly varies from one person to the next, owing to varying endowments of emotional and spiritual resources. Scope refers to the extent to which individuals are able to invest their emotional resources in broad social expressions that provide limited or nonexistent degrees of feedback or response. Depending on the ethical and religious values of the individual in question, a wide range of combinations of intensity and scope can be emotionally gratifying, ranging from focused expressions of sociality that are characterized by immediate feedback to generalized social expressions that are characterized by little or no affective feedback. In this regard, it should be emphasized that forms of sociality that feature high degrees of scope typically

Figure 5.2
Two Dimensions of Human Sociality: Intensity and Scope

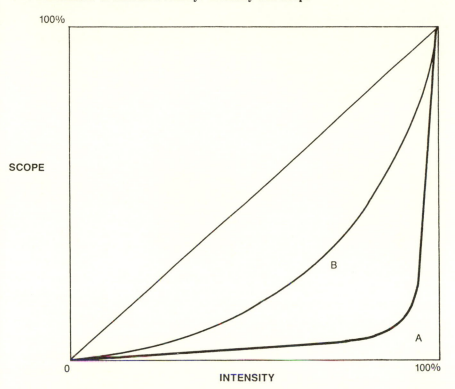

require a well-developed sense of imaginative empathy in order to sustain actions that net little or no feedback.

Figure 5.2 graphically portrays the dimensions of intensity and scope in much the same way that income inequality is represented by the Lorenz curve. Intensity and scope are represented by the horizontal and vertical axes, respectively, spanning hypothetical scales of 0–100%. The 45° diagonal cutting across the diagram represents the perfectly equal balance between the two dimensions of scope and intensity, perhaps only attained by the great religious and ethical leaders of human history, ranging from the enigmatic Egyptian Pharoah Akhenaton (Amenhotep IV) in the 14th century B.C.E. to Mother Teresa of our day, including such figures as Gautama Buddah, Lao-tse, Confucious, Zoroaster, Jesus ben Sirach, Jesus of Nazareth, Mohammed, al-Ghazzali, St. Francis of Assisi, Albert Schweitzer, Ghandi, and Pope John XXIII. Indeed most religious traditions have emphasized the essential complementarity between scope and intensity. For example, within the Christian tradition, this thought is expressed most forcefully in Jesus' command to "love thy neighbor as thyself" (Mark 12:31) in relation to his radical notion of loving one's enemy (Matthew 5:43–44) and his Parable of the Good Samaritan (Luke 10:30–36). Sociality curve *A* represents an imbalanced, narcissistic form of sociality that emphasizes intensity to the exclusion of scope. By contrast, sociality curve *B* represents a far more preferable mix between intensity and scope.

The effect of the BNI on an individual's sociality curve would be to move it closer to the 45° diagonal. We might expect that this movement toward increasing scope in conceptions of sociality will be accompanied by cultural forms that emphasize the empathetic identification of oneself and one's family with the global human community.[6] Indeed there is a tremendous need for artists, philosophers, entertainment figures, and political and religious leaders to make imaginative contributions in building a strong cultural foundation for social expressions that are characterized by increasing breadth of scope. In this regard, it should be noted that the import of the well-publicized Live Aid concert (with its theme song of "We are the World") and the Hands Across America campaign was to provide a symbolic yet concrete expression of global solidarity by emphasizing the essential complementarity between scope and intensity in our conceptualization of social life.

Of course, we could never expect most individuals to maintain sociality curves that are tangent to the 45° diagonal. In fact, if everyone were to maintain a *perfect* balance between intensity and scope, the effect would be socially destabilizing, owing to the collapse of focused loyalties, as Freud (1961) argued in his criticism of Jesus's commandment to "love your neighbor as yourself."

However, it should also be noted that sociality curve *A* is also very socially destabilizing, as this mix of intensity and scope yields highly compartmentalized and narcissistic forms of sociality (see Lasch, 1979). We know, for example, that Nazi S.S. officers were able to maintain tender social relationships within their families while coldly executing genocidal acts toward other human beings. One wonders whether historians of the 22nd century will look back upon our period of human history with the same disgust we feel toward Hitler's Third Reich, given our contemporary passion for affluent narcissism in a world in which 24 people die needlessly of malnutrition every minute...18 of whom are children under five years of age (The Hunger Project, 1985, p. 7). Indeed it is difficult to believe that any truly advanced civilization could permit such barbaric dimensions of deprivation to coexist with the unprecedented wealth enjoyed by the industrialized countries of the world.

It is likely that the Sociality Constraint will generally affect one's duties to provide BN assistance in two respects: (1) it will tend to shift an individual's Replication Constraint in a leftward direction (see Figure 5.1), as more resources will be spent on nonbasic needs within the household and throughout the surrounding community or nation; and (2) it will focus people's attention more on BN shortfalls within one's own country than upon BN shortfalls in foreign countries. In light of these probable effects, it is extremely important to clarify the limits of the Sociality Constraint.

First, while the Sociality Constraint will usually move an individual's Replication Constraint to the left, one cannot invoke the Sociality Constraint as a justification for dropping below the minimum parameters of the Replication Constraint. In other words, any conception of sociality that emphasizes intensity over scope to such a degree that it precludes giving small amounts of BN assistance to others is definitionally a deficient and unstable concept of sociality and therefore cannot be sanctioned by the Sociality Constraint.

Second, the Sociality Constraint cannot override the rank-ordering and weighting principles of the BN bundle (as presented in Chapter 2) with respect to the allocation of BN assistance. In other words, the desire to meet the BN of those within one's national boundaries must never become an excuse for not being actively concerned with the BN of those individuals in foreign countries. This is a particularly important qualification in view of the fact that absolute poverty (the most extreme manifestation of BN shortfalls) is virtually nonexistent in the developed countries of the world. In fact, most of the poor within MDCs would be middle-class citizens in most LDCs. The oft-heard maxim that "we must first help those in our backyard before we go overseas" fails to comprehend the extreme magnitude of deprivation faced by human beings in the Third World. Moreover, social expenditures from the rich countries are strongly biased in favor of their own citizens (e.g., from 1974 to 1976 the United States spent $508 per person in social expenditures for its own population and only $2 per person for those outside its borders [Cassen et al., 1986, p. 24]). Consequently the allocation of BN assistance must proceed on the basis of BN Investment Ratios and the BN Multiplier Principle, instead of being influenced by arbitrary considerations relating to geography and ethnicity. Not only is development assistance for low-income LDCs mandated from a moral point of view, but also it is a more efficient or productive use of resources in relation to BN objectives.[7]

In summary, the BNM and BNI, as species-ethics, mandate an extensive moral regime of global human rights that logically generates an array of correlative duties aimed at safeguarding those human rights. These correlative duties not only consist of synchronic and diachronic negative duties prohibiting actions that deprive others of their basic goods, but also synchronic and diachronic positive duties to assist those who are experiencing BN shortfalls. The extent of one's synchronic duties to provide BN assistance is defined by the Principle of Comparable Harm. However, owing to the special characteristics of diachronic duties to provide assistance, the Principle of Comparable Harm must be qualified by three constraints: (1) the Sphere of Influence Constraint, (2) the Replication Constraint, and (3) the Sociality Constraint. The combined effect of these three constraints on the Principle of Comparable Harm is to optimize the magnitude and stability of BN aid flows over time. Owing to the high degree of variability in the estimation of both the Replication Constraint and the Sociality Constraint, these constraints must be established subjectively by each individual or nation. Nonetheless it is reasonable, on the basis of common sense, to set minimum parameters of BN assistance for individual household incomes at the level of 2.5%, 5%, and 10% for low-, middle-, and high-income households, respectively, within the developed world. Moreover, it seems reasonable to establish an MDC minimum parameter for BN assistance (in the form of ODA) at a rate of 1% of their GNPs.

Although the mandatory minimum parameters of BN assistance have been set extremely low, it seems likely that once the habit of giving is established and conceptions of sociality take on greater scope, there will be a long-run tendency for the Replication Constraints of individuals or nations to shift to the right (see Figure 5.1). Moreover, once the issue of absolute poverty penetrates political discussion to a meaningful degree, there will be an opportunity to clarify national interests rationally without resorting to visceral xenophobia as a basis of foreign policy (e.g., in 1985 the United States spent about 150 times more on defense programs than on bilateral development assistance to low-income LDCs [calculated from World Bank, 1987,, pp. 243, 247]).

The existence of a large and efficient network of nongovernmental relief and development agencies around the world has made it possible for an ordinary individual to save more human lives than even those who invest considerable personal and financial resources to become physicians or nurses. Indeed what better pathway to happiness than the joy of making the gift of life possible for others? What better demonstration of patriotism and national pride than the confidence that our foreign policies will create a more just and stable world for our children and our children's children? What better road to self-actualization than participating in the actualization of humanity by joining the epochal movement of the expanding circle?

NOTES

1. For a discussion on BN Investment Ratios, see Chapter 2, section 2.10.

2. The Replication Constraint is closely related to the Principle of Recurrence, as presented in Chapter 2, section 2.13. However the two concepts differ in this respect: the Principle of Recurrence refers to the stability of BN programs in relation to the health of various nonbasic sectors of the economy over time, and the Replication Constraint is focused on the stability of altruistic behaviors and aid flows over time.

3. The BNI does not require self-sacrificial actions or what ethicists call "supererogatory actions." These are actions that are praiseworthy yet could never be required of a person, because they necessitate extreme self-sacrifice. For instance, medical personnel have often risked their own lives to come to the aid of victims of war or pestilence. Moreover, in time of war, one hears reports of soldiers who leap on live grenades to save the lives of their fellows.

It may be objected that the BNI would prohibit such supererogatory actions, as such actions violate the Principle of Comparable Harm. In responding to this objection we must return to the three species universals of existence, intelligence, and sociality and examine their relation to expressions of love and spirituality (see Chapter 2, section 2.4). It will be recalled that love was construed as an ideal of sociality and spirituality was interpreted as a construct of both intelligence and sociality. I would argue that the supererogatory acts exemplified by so-called saints and heroes essentially represent attempts to actualize a concept of spirituality or love (or perhaps some other ideal of sociality, e.g., loyalty) in an extreme situation. Hence the saint or hero who performs a supererogatory act displays a willingness to sacrifice his lower material BN for the sake of higher values relating to intelligence and sociality. In this regard, Maslow (1948) observed a tendency for people to place a greater value on higher needs than on lower needs "by those who have been chronically gratified in both." While the BNI establishes an interclass priority in the order of existence, intelligence, and sociality, insofar as the allocation of basic goods is concerned, this certainly does not preclude individuals from voluntarily sacrificing their BN in order to actualize a social or spiritual ideal related to a higher need. Indeed to prohibit supererogatory acts is tantamount to denying the transcendent character of our shared social existence. Moreover, such heroic behaviors are indicative of advanced notions of human sociality and, therefore, are regarded favorably by the BNI.

4. P. Singer (1977b) has taken an approach similar to this in his redefinition of his utilitarian Famine Relief Argument.

5. I am indebted to W. L. Gaines for this suggestion.

6. It is significant that several relief and development agencies have concluded that people are much more willing to give their resources in the struggle against absolute poverty if those gifts are linked with child sponsorship programs of one type or another. See Behar (1986).

7. Goldstein (1985) proposes that a "plateau curve" exists between BN satisfaction and real per capita GDP, indicating that BN investment in low-income LDCs will be more efficient or productive insofar as BN indicators are concerned.

6

The Basic Needs Mandate and the Population Explosion

6.1. THE IMPENDING CRISIS OF OVERPOPULATION

A global problem closely related to the crisis of absolute poverty is the high rate of population growth taking place within the less-developed world. It has been estimated that by the year 2000, 92% of the world's population growth will take place in LDCs (U.S. Council on Environmental Quality and Department of State, 1980). Much of this new population growth will be absorbed in squalid slums and unplanned squatter settlements, due to dramatic increases in the rate of rural to urban migration. Unfortunately the current and projected age-sex composition of LDC populations reveals that the bulk of the population is comprised of individuals in younger age groups who have their childbearing years ahead of them. Consequently continuing high rates of population growth are inevitable, and the only question facing us is how soon we can bring down the birth rates in developing countries to their approximate replacement level of fertility. Unfortunately we are in a dramatic race against time to reduce the rate of population growth, in view of the fact that each decade of delay in reaching the goal of replacement fertility will increase the world's ultimately stabilized population by 11% (McNamara, 1979). The World Bank projects that the global population will eventually stabilize at about 10.5 billion people by the end of the 21st century, assuming projected standard rates of decline in both fertility and morality for this period (Vu, 1985; World Bank, 1984, pp. 74–75). According to the National Academy of Sciences (1969, p. 5), a world population of 10 billion "is close (if not above) the maximum that an *intensively managed* world might hope to support with some degree of comfort and individual choice."

It is helpful to place the present high rates of population growth in historical context in order to get some idea of the novelty and urgency of the population crisis. Let us assume that the world's total population was somewhere in the vicinity of 300 million in A.D. 1. It took over 1,500 years for the world's population to double, reaching 600 million people. Between 1600 and 1850 the world's population doubled again, within the span of only 250 years. By 1900 the world's population reached 1.7 billion people. During the first half of the 20th century the annual increase in population growth grew from 0.5% to 1%, and after 1950 the annual rate of population growth jumped to an unprecedented 2%. As a consequence, between 1950 and 1980 the earth's human population nearly doubled in the short span of 30 years from 2.5 billion to almost 4.8 billion (World Bank, 1984, pp. 2–3). This rapid increase in population growth was not related to increases in the fertility rate, but instead was precipitated by new developments in medical technology. After World War II there were dramatic declines in the mortality rates of LDCs, owing to the introduction of antibiotics, vaccines, antimalarial spraying, and certain public health measures, which greatly reduced the incidence of mortality related to malaria, cholera, and smallpox (Cassen, 1976; Myrdal, 1970, pp. 141–143; World Bank, 1984, p. 63).

The response to the population crisis by the international community has been less than heartening. On the one hand, a small but vocal minority has taken an extremely pessimistic, neo-Malthusian approach to the population crisis, advocating a global application of the principle of "triage" or "lifeboat ethics" as the solution to the problem. On the other hand, a large segment of social scientists and policy makers has adopted overly optimistic understandings of the problem that fail to appreciate the complexities involved in reducing fertility.

6.2. LIFEBOAT ETHICS

Proponents of lifeboat ethics assert that the only responsible solution to the population crisis is a global application of the medical principle of triage. They argue that generalized sympathy for the poor will only cause the present dilemma to grow worse, turning good intentions into a recipe for disaster. Hence the "ethics of the lifeboat" dictate that we should terminate our assistance to LDC "basket cases" in order to preserve the earth's ecology. According to this view, the current outlook is so bleak that responsible people have no choice except to suspend their normal canons of social justice in preference for the higher calling of the survival of the species (Ehrlich, 1971; Hardin, 1977; Paddock and Paddock, 1967).

One need not engage in extended discussions of the morality of the "survival of the fittest" in responding to the claims of the lifeboat ethicists. First, there is no factual basis for the claim that the developed countries of the world are approaching a kind of lifeboat situation in the face of diminishing global resources. For example, the World Bank (1980b, p. 61) estimates that if only about 2% of the world's total grain output were redirected to the mouths that need it, we could wipe out malnutrition from the face of the earth. Indeed the appropriate metaphor for modeling the present situation of the developed countries in relation to the less-developed world is not a lifeboat but a luxury liner. The weighty moral decision facing the crew and passengers of this cruise ship is not ecological survival but whether or not the pool deck will be overcrowded.

Second, advocates of lifeboat ethics have incorrectly assumed that the most effective response to the population crisis is that of withdrawal, instead of involvement. In point of fact, the withdrawal of development assistance from regions of the world that need such assistance will only exacerbate the population problem, because declines in mortality no longer contribute substantially to overall population growth as they did in the 1950s and 1960s. For example, a rapid decline in the mortality rate increases the population of LDCs in 2050 by only 7% more than the standard decline in mortality; whereas a rapid decline in fertility would produce a population 25% smaller than the standard fertility decline (World Bank, 1984, pp. 73–76). Consequently it is neither morally justifiable nor pragmatically feasible to try to balance the world's population on the backs of starving infants. The only feasible way to solve the population crisis is to decrease the rate of new births, instead of maintaining or slowing the rate of decline in mortality. Obviously it will require more development assistance, not less, from the richer countries in order to achieve the objective of reduced fertility.

6.3. SIMPLE SOLUTIONS FOR A NOT SO SIMPLE PROBLEM

Unfortunately, in responding to the pessimistic position advanced by lifeboat ethicists, many social scientists and policy makers have advocated overly optimistic, simplistic solutions for the problem. Three schools of thought have exercised considerable influence in this regard: (1) the theory of demographic transition, (2) the child-survival thesis, and (3) the population-push theory of technological innovation.

The theory of demographic transition postulates that LDCs will follow a course of population growth similar to that of MDCs. Beginning with an initial situation of high fertility and high mortality rates, the theory of demographic transition holds that developing countries will pass through a disequilibrium period of high fertility rates and declining rates of mortality (due to improvements in public health and the standard of living) until the fertility rate adjusts, after a considerable lag, to the declining mortality rate. As a consequence, "development is the best contraceptive" (a sentiment echoed throughout the Third World delegations at the United Nation's first World Population Conference at Bucharest in 1974), because the increasing standard of living brought about by economic development will naturally slow the fertility rate, as it did with the industrialized countries.

The child-survival thesis attempts to understand the population crisis in terms of the economic implications of having children, particularly with respect to old-age security. In societies lacking social security systems or work-related pension plans, there is a natural tendency for parents to treat their children as a form of old-age security. The child-survival thesis holds that parents will not reduce the size of their household until they are assured that a reasonable number of their children (especially males) will be alive and in a financial position to care for them in old age. Given the high rate of infant and child mortality in LDCs, having a large family is a means of hedging one's bets against the harsh realities of poverty. Consequently the child-survival thesis holds that once the infant and child mortality rates are reduced, parents will elect to have smaller families, as they can be assured that enough of their children will be around to care for them in old age.

Finally the population-push theory of technological innovation contends that the population crisis is really no crisis at all—a position diametrically opposite to lifeboat ethics. This position, argued with considerable methodological eloquence by Julian Simon (1977), holds that population growth has a *positive* effect on technological development; and, within certain limits, moderate levels of population growth are preferable to low rates of population growth. The population-push theory claims that certain kinds of innovations require higher population densities for their implementation. These sorts of population-push innovations contrast sharply with the traditional, Malthusian invention-pull technological innovations, which occur independent of prior rates of population growth and are labor-saving at the time of their discovery. On the one hand, if technological development is dominated by invention-pull innovations, population growth will have an adverse effect on economic development (as the benefits of technology will have to be shared with more people). On the other hand, if population-push innovations are the dominant force in technological development, population growth will have a strongly positive effect on economic development (as population growth would drive the discovery and implementation of population-push innovations). Obviously advocates of the population-push theory press this latter claim, and therefore hold that moderate rates of population growth are preferable to slower rates of growth or no growth.

While each of these three positions embodies some degree of the truth, they present an overly simplistic understanding of the problem and have major shortcomings. In particular, the following difficulties are prominent: (1) the theory of demographic transition overlooks crucial discontinuities between the historical experience of the MDCs and the recent situation faced by the LDCs; (2) the child-survival thesis fails to account for the considerable lag between reduced infant and child mortality and parental decisions to limit family size, as well as the important role of educational and employment opportunities for females in stimulating fertility declines; and (3) the population-push theory of technological development lacks relevance for the sorts of innovations that have characterized technological change during the latter half of the 20th century.

The primary difficulty with the theory of demographic transition is that it overlooks some prominent discontinuities between the recent crisis faced by LDCs in relation to the historical experience of MDCs. To begin with, the rate of population growth is substantially higher in contemporary LDCs (2–4%) in comparison to MDCs during their rapid growth period (1.5%). Moreover, in contrast to the experience of 19th-century Europe, contemporary LDCs cannot channel new population growth to other regions of the world through large-scale emigration, and most developing countries no longer have large tracts of unutilized, arable land for agricultural development. More importantly, the human and physical capital within contemporary LDCs, as well as their political and social institutions, are significantly less developed in comparison with the MDCs during their period of rapid growth (see World Bank, 1984, p. 79).

The child-survival thesis represents an important contribution to our understanding of fertility inasmuch as reduced infant and child mortality is viewed as a necessary, but not sufficient, condition for fertility declines. Unfortunately advocates of the child-survival thesis tend to treat declines in infant and child mortality as a *sufficient* condition for fertility declines by presuming a causal link between increased life expectancies and parental judgments about their children's probability of survival. This strong link is unjustified for at least three reasons: (1) there is no direct evidence for an independent effect of declining infant and child mortality on declining fertility (Cassen, 1976); (2) the most immediate effect of reduced infant and child mortality will be increased population growth until a considerable time lag has passed (which could span several generations), when parents become aware of such mortality declines, are assured that the reduced mortality rate will continue, and have resisted the tendency to overinsure during the transition period; and (3) there are many reasons for parents to have a large family besides old-age security, including the perceived economic benefits of children in the short and medium terms, as well as the enhanced social status netted by both the husband and wife in many cultures.

Finally the major shortcoming of the population-push theory of technological innovations is that it is irrelevant to the pattern of technological development characteristic of the latter half of this century. Nearly all contemporary technological innovations are of the invention-pull type, in that they are labor-saving at the time of their discovery and do not require greater population densities for their implementation. Moreover, the benefits of certain contemporary population-push technologies, of which biogas technology may be an example, certainly do not outweigh the adverse consequences of increased population growth. Additionally there is no evidence that population growth itself has been influential in promoting new technologies within the latter half of this century (e.g., most of the technological advances associated with the Green Revolution originated in MDCs). Furthermore, the computer simulations that support Simon's conclusion that moderate population growth has positive feedback responses on technological development are far from credible, because his neoclassical economic model failed to account for the effect of continued population growth on scarce natural resources, as Simon (1977, p. 484) contends that "such resources are created by mankind in response to human needs."

Clearly both the extreme views of lifeboat ethicists and the simplistic understandings embodied in the theory of demographic transition, the child-survival thesis, and the population-push theory of technological development must be dismissed as inadequate in the formulation of a credible response to the population crisis. Does the BNM present us with a promising alternative?

6.4. MORALITY AND POPULATION CONTROL

As a species ethic, the BNM requires policies that promote a K-reproductive strategy (see Chapter 3, section 3.5), in that the open genetic program of human life markedly enhances the adaptive range of our species and the BNM limits intraspecific competition of the life-and-death variety. Consequently the BNM can neither ignore the population crisis nor sanction forms of ecological imperialism by Homo sapiens in the name of justice. It must be asked, though, whether the sorts of BN programs encouraged by the BNM are inconsistent with a K-reproductive strategy. In other words, is there an inherent operational conflict between meeting BN and lowering the rate of population growth in LDCs?

The available evidence indicates that no such inherent conflict between BN policies and fertility declines exists (Morawetz, 1978). Moreover, inasmuch as BN programs emphasize educational opportunities for females (beyond the third grade) and open up new employment opportunities for females, such programs constitute the most effective policy tool available for reducing fertility rates within LDCs (Cochrane, 1979; World Bank, 1984, pp. 109–111). Therefore well-crafted BN packages would be the best way to reduce fertility in the long term, instead of militating against a K-reproductive strategy.

An important aspect of any BN package for a particular community, region, or country is access to contraceptive technologies, as discussed in Chapter 2, section 2.7. If access to low-cost contraceptive technologies is denied to a population through legal, economic, or cultural restrictions, attempts to promote fertility declines will be seriously impaired and a substantial zone of uncertainty will be introduced into people's life plans (although it should never be assumed that access to contraceptives will naturally lead to fertility declines). Indeed the benefits associated with modern contraceptive technologies require no elaboration. Moreover, there is an especially promising array of "new generation" contraceptive technologies on the horizon, including improved, long-acting steroid injections, steroid implants and vaginal rings, antifertility vaccines, sperm-suppression contraceptives for men, simplified male and female sterilization techniques, reversible male and female sterilization, and pharmacological sterilization techniques. Yet, in spite of the benefits associated with modern contraceptive techniques, there are serious moral questions that must be addressed with respect to certain contraceptive practices, namely: (1) intrauterine devices (IUDs), (2) "morning-after" pills, (3) menstrual regulation techniques, and (4) abortion.[1]

The primary moral issue surrounding these four contraceptive practices revolves around the definition of human life. On the one hand, if one holds that human life begins at the moment of conception, then all four contraceptive practices would be typically deemed morally impermissible (unless conception occurred as the result of rape or incest or the mother's life is seriously threatened by the pregnancy). On the other hand, if the definition of human life is deferred until the last trimester or the actual birth of the infant, then all four contraceptive practices would be considered morally permissible.

The key issue surrounding the definition of human life concerns whether human life is defined in terms of a completed genotype or a partially manifest phenotype. In simple biological terms, there is no doubt that the genetic portrait or genotype of an individual human being is secured at the moment of conception. In the course of embryonic and fetal development the phenotypic manifestations of that genotype become increasingly prominent and continue to unfold throughout the growth and aging processes from infancy through adulthood. Consequently, those who wish to define human life in terms of phenotypic manifestations are logically constrained to identify an approximate phenotypic threshold at which the organism is deemed human—a task that is complicated by the fact that phenotypic development occurs, to varying degrees, throughout the life cycle of the organism.

Is it possible to identify a phenotypic threshold that provides a meaningful benchmark for defining human life? On the one hand, it is clear that the moment of birth is an extremely unsuitable phenotypic threshold, as the birth process is not associated with any immediate phenotypical changes but instead precipitates a critical environmental change in the organism's development (involving delinking the infant from the mother's bloodstream, breathing and vocalization, the perception of light). On the other hand, if the completed genotype is accorded all the rights and privileges of an infant or child, we are faced with the disturbing reality that the natural loss of human life *before* birth is far greater than the loss of life produced by all the wars, famines, and pestilence since the dawn of our species.

Whereas it was previously thought that only about 15% of pregnancies ended in spontaneous abortion, the use of human chorionic gonadotropin (hCG) and the pregnancy-specific protein EPF has revealed a much higher rate of silent or subclinical pregnancy loss (i.e., spontaneous abortions before the mother is aware she is pregnant). Consequently the estimated rate of spontaneous abortions as a percentage of conceptions has been placed at 43% (Miller et al., 1980), 62% (Edmonds et al., 1982), 70% (Hertig, 1967), 77% (Rolfe, 1982), and 78% (Roberts and Lowe, 1975). Most of these silent abortions take place in the first month of pregnancy (the high-risk period being shortly after implantation) and the risks decrease dramatically with gestation age (Shepard and Fantel, 1979). Approximately one-half of such spontaneous abortions can be attributed to chromosonal abnormalities with the remaining half caused by problems of implantation, defects in gametogenesis or fertilization, and developmental abnormalities after fertilization (Hafez, 1984; Lauritsen, 1976). The implication of these findings is that for every conception that goes to full term, there are two or three human embryos that do not survive the first trimester of pregnancy. If we regard those embryos as full-fledged human beings, we are forced to conclude that the natural process of conception and embryonic development is the *most* tragic dimension of human life, dwarfing a host of natural and man-made tragedies, ranging from earthquakes to genocide.

By itself, the massive loss of human embryos in the process of conception, implantation, and embryonic development offers no conclusive evidence either for or against the contention that the human zygote is a full-fledged human being. However the highly tentative nature of the first few weeks of embryonic life does diminish the force of a class of noninterventionist arguments that hold that the zygote's potential to develop into a full human being constitutes prima facie grounds for treating it with the same respect accorded to infants and children. Given the fact that the existence of the human embryo is extremely tenuous during its early development, so that the odds are stacked against the survival of any individual zygote, it would be more realistic to understand the first few weeks of embryonic development as nature's winnowing period for isolating embryos that are characterized by anomalous genotypes, deficient implantation, defective gametogenesis, and developmental abnormalities.

If the first few weeks of embryonic life are understood as a kind of winnowing phase for human reproduction, it seems inappropriate to accord the zygote with the same regard we hold for a fully developed human being. Consequently we must look for a suitable postconception phenotypic threshold. One attractive possibility in this regard has been suggested by Baruch Brody (1975). He recommends that the question—"When does human life begin?"—may be best approached by asking: "When does human life end?" Brody notes that death has been traditionally associated with the cessation of blood circulation and breathing. However, this former concept of death has been made obsolete by modern life support systems, and currently there is a consensus within the medical community that human life ceases with irreversible brain-death, usually (yet not definitively) indicated by a prolonged flat electroencephalogram (EEG). Brody argues that this contemporary definition of death provides us with a meaningful criterion for defining the onset of human life. If death is defined in terms of brain-death, then life should be defined in terms of brain-life (i.e., the presence of electrical activity in the brain or EEG waves). Since the fundamental structures of the brain are in place by the end of the third month of fetal development and sporadic EEG waves can be detected on the surface of the brain (Rose, 1973; Reinis and Goldman, 1980, pp. 234–235), it seems reasonable to regard the end of the first trimester as an adequate phenotypic threshold for defining the beginning of human life.[2] Therefore, according to the brain-life criterion, IUDs, "morning-after" pills, menstrual regulation techniques, and abortion within the first trimester are morally permissible means of birth control. However abortion in the second or third trimester is morally impermissible.

Of course, neither the BNM nor the BNI provide us with definitive criteria for establishing the beginning of human life. It is possible that new data could reveal some definitive phenotypic threshold other than the brain-life criterion.

However, in the absence of a more adequate phenotypic threshold, the brain-life criterion appears to be the best candidate for the BNM and BNI.[3]

It should be emphasized, though, that the prohibition of abortion by the BNM and BNI after the first trimester does not imply that abortion procedures are morally impermissible in all situations after the first trimester. Clearly abortion is justifiable when the life of the mother is threatened, according to the Principle of Comparable Harm, discussed in Chapter 5, section 5.1. Moreover, if amniotic data indicate serious genetic abnormalities, making it impossible for the fetus to develop fundamental physical and intellectual capabilities, abortion procedures would be sanctioned by the BNM and BNI.[4] Additionally these principles would permit second trimester abortions in the case of pregnancies resulting from incest and rape, given the involuntary character of such situations. The conflict between the fetus's right to life and the female's desire to avoid the further emotional trauma and economic hardship involved in carrying the pregnancy to term must be resolved in favor of the female, because her moral obligations to aid the fetus arose as a *direct* consequence of involuntarily suffering from the violent actions of others. In other words, the denial of the female's basic human rights generated a new set of moral obligations to a fetus who would not have existed apart from the violent imposition in the first place. To insist that she is morally responsible to aid the fetus and must alter her chosen life plan is to perpetuate her victimization beyond the bounds of reason.[5]

6.5. FERTILITY DECLINES AS A PRISONER'S DILEMMA

In crafting policy responses to the population crisis, it is helpful to model the current situation in terms of the familiar "Prisoner's Dilemma" of game theory (Luce and Raiffa, 1957, pp. 94ff.).[6] "Prisoner's Dilemma" situations are characterized by the fact that the natural outcome of the game is different than the cooperative solution. Because the equilibrium point lies outside the cooperative quadrant, there is always a temptation to defect from cooperative solution.

Figure 6.1 depicts a payoff matrix, comprised of quadrants A, B, C, and D, for a two-person society consisting of X and Y. Each person has an individual fertility preference (FP_i) and a social fertility preference (FP_s). Quadrant D is the cooperative position, representing individual fertility decisions by X and Y that are in accord with their social fertility preferences, netting each of them a payoff of 3. If either X or Y decide to defect from the cooperative position (in the hope of earning the higher payoff of 5), the society will move from the optimal situation in quadrant D to quadrants B or C, respectively (with X's payoff in the lower left corner and Y's in the upper right corner). Given the inherent instability of quadrants B or C, the defection of either person X or Y will encourage the other to pursue his or her individual fertility preferences, meaning that both parties will end up in the unfavorable situation represented by quadrant A, each netting a payoff of −3.

This analysis suggests that public policies designed to reduce the rate of

Figure 6.1
The Prisoner's Dilemma and Fertility Declines

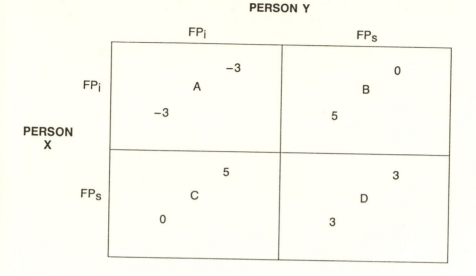

PERSON Y

population growth must aim at reducing the gap between individual and social fertility preferences by making defections from the cooperative position increasingly less attractive. This could be accomplished through the use of positive incentives (which encourage individuals to move to or remain in quadrant D) or negative incentives (which decrease the benefits of defection to quadrants B and C by increasing the costs of defection). In addition to direct incentives, fertility declines could be encouraged indirectly by the strategic design and implementation of BN programs.

Of the two kinds of incentives, positive incentives are the most acceptable, both in terms of their political feasibility and their complementary effect on BN programs. Among the most promising approaches in this regard are the deferred incentives schemes (which have been instituted to a limited extent in India and China). For example, the government of Bangladesh is considering two deferred incentive schemes for encouraging fertility declines. The first program would offer nonnegotiable bonds in the amounts of $80 to $120 to men less than 40 years of age and women under the age of 35 who have two or three living children and agree to be sterilized. The bonds would mature over 12 years, and the final value of the bonds would be between $275 and $425. At any time during the 12-year period, the bondholder could obtain a loan for the purchase of productive goods (e.g., fertilizer, fish ponds, irrigation pumps) of up to 50% of the bond's value. Obviously a deferred incentive scheme of this type also has some positive spillover benefits in terms of old-age security. The second program involves awarding three-year and five-year certificates of $20 for couples who delay the birth of their first child until at least three years after marriage and second and third births until five years after marriage (World Bank, 1984, p. 125–126). Unfortunately the available data do not permit us to draw any conclusive answers concerning the independent effect of positive incentives on fertility declines in LDCs (Simon, 1977, pp. 379–388). Moreover, incentive payments in sufficient magnitude and coverage to stimulate rapid declines in fertility would be beyond the fiscal reach of many LDCs, unless development assistance from MDCs helped subsidize the cost of the program.

Negative incentives are far more prevalent than positive incentives and are typically administered through the tax system of the country. For example, in Tanzania, Singapore, Ghana, Malaysia, and Pakistan there have been limitations placed on the allocation of tax deductions, child allowances, and maternity benefits based upon the size of the family. In China, negative incentives, varying from one province to the next, have been employed in order to promote the concept of a one-child family. In some areas, a couple may be required to pay a substantial sum for the privilege of having a second child. Some have been willing to pay twice their annual income for this privilege. Other provinces impose special taxes and deny certain paid maternity and medical benefits for families with three or more children (World Bank, 1983, pp. 103–109; 1984, p. 124).

While negative incentives are more economically feasible than positive incentives, their effectiveness is blunted by the fact that they are typically administered through tax systems that do not adequately cover the lower income groups, where the fertility rate is the highest. Moreover, disincentive programs that tax a certain percentage of household income or remove certain educational or medical benefits for large families have the effect of penalizing the children for their parents' decisions and, thereby, militate against important BN objectives. Additionally, from a strictly pragmatic point of view, an extensive system of negative incentives would be extremely difficult, if not impossible, to administer within the soft political structures of most noncommunist LDCs.

Of course, the most extreme policy instrument available for population control is compulsory sterilization after a couple has had a certain number of living children, such as the law that was briefly instituted in the Indian state of Maharashtra, which made sterilization compulsory after the birth of the third living child. Clearly such compulsory measures would be sanctioned by the BNM only as a method of last resort, if they could be implemented equitably across all social classes and if an array of well-designed incentive and disincentive policies had been tried and had failed. It is highly unlikely, though, that such compulsory measures could ever be implemented successfully and equitably within most LDCs, and it is clear that conventional incentive and disincentive schemes have not been implemented to a sufficient degree to permit the introduction of compulsory policy measures at this time.

It is likely that the best way for governments to influence fertility decisions within the household is by a judicious mix of positive, deferred incentive programs and well-integrated BN programs. For example, BN packages that provide educational opportunities for females and generate opportunities for productive employment for women have great potential to stimulate fertility declines. The effect of such targeted development policies is to increase the opportunity cost of having children. Given the considerable investment of time required in raising children, women would be more reticent to have a large family if they were able to translate their time into direct economic benefits through gainful employment inside or outside of the household. The strength of this approach is that it forges a direct link between BN policies and programs intended to reduce the rate of fertility. Moreover, this indirect approach is less likely to encounter the large number of political obstacles facing those strategies that depend on direct negative incentives.

Obviously it will be quite costly to engineer substantial fertility declines by either direct or indirect methods. Consequently most LDCs will need significant levels of development assistance from the MDCs in order to implement such policies. This consideration raises two important questions: (1) Is it morally permissible for MDCs to withdraw development assistance from countries that have not demonstrated a serious intent to control population growth?; and (2) Do MDCs have the right to grant conditional development assistance that stipulates that a substantial percentage of this assistance should be allocated for BN programs and deferred incentive programs designed to reduce fertility?

The first question must be answered in the negative on both strategic and moral grounds. From a strategic standpoint, the withdrawal of development assistance would seriously weaken the capacity of MDCs to influence the internal policies of LDCs, and this sort of approach would only leave a disagreeable residue of resentment in its wake. Moreover, the withdrawal of development assistance would have the effect of slowing declines in fertility that may be associated with existing development programs. From a moral standpoint, it hardly seems just to penalize the economically and politically disinherited citizens of a country on the basis of their national regime's policies on population control. This would be on par with imposing punishments on children for the actions of their parents.

As to the second question, the granting of conditional development assistance relating to well-integrated BN initiatives and deferred incentive programs designed to reduce fertility seems advisable on both strategic and moral grounds.[7] On a strategic plane, there is little hope for influencing many LDC regimes to take serious steps in the direction of population control apart from progressive initiatives emanating from the MDCs (due to the internal political risks associated with such policies for LDC regimes). Unfortunately, though, such MDC initiatives will be perceived as violations of state sovereignty by most LDCs. However, one way of strategically mitigating this problem is for an MDC (or, more preferably, a group of MDCs) to announce to the international community that substantial amounts of development assistance are available in regular installments to any country that is below a certain threshold of per capita GNP, provided that certain verifiable conditions are met (including measures designed to reduce fertility).[8] While a move of this type may raise protests of interference with state sovereignty, there would probably be many LDCs who would accept substantial flows of aid on these conditions. The long-term effect of such unilateral initiatives would be to establish a sense of good faith between the MDCs and LDCs, given the fact that many LDCs perceive MDC complaints about population control as a way of conveniently absolving themselves from making further commitments in development assistance and trade reforms. Moreover, the conditions attached to aid disbursements would help establish accepted international standards for the appraisal and inspection of development programs, thereby reducing the potential for such funds to fall prey to corrupt government officials.

NOTES

1. I assume that the argument that all forms of artificial birth control techniques are immoral does not raise serious moral questions, because the argument is based upon untenable conceptions of the natural world and human sexuality. The nonprocreative aspects of sexuality have played a very important role in the evolution of human sociality. Therefore any conception of morality that denies the legitimacy of the nonprocreative dimensions of human sexuality forfeits its credibility.

2. Brody (1975, p. 83) claims that EEG waves are present during the sixth week (yet does not document this) and mistakenly infers that the fetus has "the capacity for conscious experience, at least at a primitive level." In point of fact the cerebral cortex seems to be largely inactive until birth, and the newborn is primarily a subcortical being.

3. Of course, brain-life is not synonymous with neurological function, as the functional development of the brain continues through early childhood.

4. It is important to emphasize that I am referring to *gross* intellectual or physical deficits that are indicated by amniocentesis. There is no attempt here to sanction procedures that deny life to fetuses who fall below socially defined conventions of normalcy relative to physical or intellectual handicaps. Moreover, such considerations cannot be employed to justify infanticide or involuntary euthanasia on the basis of mental retardation, advanced senility, or severe physical handicaps.

5. Admittedly there are many instances in life where violent actions impose incredible burdens of care on third parties and do not cancel their moral obligations to give assistance. Yet instances of incest and rape are unique in that the female's moral obligation to aid the fetus did not exist prior to the involuntary imposition itself.

6. The real-life setting of the so-called Prisoner's Dilemma refers to a situation in which two criminals—accomplices in the same crime—are interrogated separately by the district attorney. The criminals have to decide individually whether or not they will confess to their crime (and receive a somewhat lenient sentence) or to remain silent and receive a short prison term on a trumped-up charge. However, if one prisoner confesses and the other does not, the district attorney intends to give a significantly reduced sentence to the one who confesses but plans to throw the book at the individual who chooses not to confess. Obviously the cooperative solution is for both criminals to remain silent and to get off with light sentences.

7. While most types of deferred incentive programs will indirectly have a BN component, in some cases they could be classified as nonbasic government expenditures.

Nonetheless such nonbasic expenditures would be justified, even mandated, by the BNM in light of the Principle of Recurrence (see Chapter 2, section 2.13).

8. A suggestion of this type was proposed to President Carter in an open letter by Roger Hansen (1977).

7
The Basic Needs Mandate and the Nuclear Arms Race

7.1. EVOLUTIONARILY STABLE STRATEGIES

Since the day that fire rained from the sky over Hiroshima, the world became a fundamentally different place for Homo sapiens—a world in which many of the traditional meanings and values associated with the institution of war became functionally obsolete. The values that have often been associated with war— such as heroism, friendship, patriotism, freedom, loyalty, social justice, and the expansion of civilization—lose their meaning in the context of nuclear war, where the fruits of victory are no different than the miseries of defeat. Indeed it is the foremost challenge of human cultural evolution to redefine the meaning of war and, thereby, to negotiate successfully the tenuous transition period between the prenuclear era and a stable postnuclear epoch.

How does the BNM relate to the current predicament of the nuclear arms race? In responding to this question, it should be recalled that the BNM, as a species-ethic, prohibits any policies that lead to the extinction of other species (see Chapter 3, section 3.5). Whereas any species may legitimately compete with other species over a particular ecological niche, the complete destruction of another species or their ecological niche is morally impermissible, given the fact that it would be logically inconsistent for any species-ethic to sanction courses of action that would lead to the extermination of other species. Just as the BNM mandates a K-reproductive strategy and does not permit humans to exploit their reproductive advantage by overrunning the planet, it also does not permit Homo sapiens to use their enhanced capacities of intelligence and sociality for the destruction of the ecological niche of other species. In view of the incredible magnitude of ecological destruction that would be created by a full-scale nuclear exchange, the subject of nuclear arms control is certainly a matter of preeminent importance for the BNM.

The BNM mandates nuclear arms policies that minimize the possibility of ecological destruction over an indefinite time horizon. This can be best expressed by the concept of an "evolutionarily stable strategy" (ESS), as developed by John Maynard Smith (1972, 1974, 1982, 1983). An ESS is a strategy that yields more expected utility if it is played against itself than any other alternate strategy that may be played against it. Stated formally, strategy I is an ESS if the expected utility (EU) of I is greater than any other strategy J played against strategy I, or if both strategies I and J yield an equivalent amount of expected utility when played against strategy I but the expected utility of I is greater than J when played against strategy J: $[EU_I(I) > EU_I(J)] \ V \ [EU_I(I) = EU_I(J) \cdot EU_J(I) > EU_J(J)]$, where the strategy in parentheses is played against the strategy indicated by the subscript. The evolutionary significance of strategy I as an ESS is that a population that adopts strategy I will not be overrun by mutant strategies, because those who adopt alternative strategies (e.g., J) would not increase in frequency and the population would be stable under conditions of mutation and selection.

Is it possible for us to identify an ESS for the postnuclear era that would be stable in the volatile international environment of the next two or three centuries? The question is tantalizing. We could expect that if such an ESS exists, it would permit nuclear arsenals at a level that could still pose an immense ecological danger to earth's plant and animal species. Indeed one of the singular tragedies of the nuclear era is that nuclear weapons cannot be disinvented, and therefore it is likely that humanity will always have to live under some kind of nuclear threat, presumably for at least the next few hundred years. No doubt, an ESS in an ideal world would not only minimize the probability of nuclear war, but would also reduce nuclear arsenals to the extent that large-scale devastation would be a technical impossibility. Unfortunately there is little likelihood that nuclear arsenals could be reduced to this point without opening up a Pandora's box of political instability, given the inherent payoffs for "mutant" countries who would have much to gain by defecting from the agreement (Schelling, 1963). Obviously disarmament proposals that call for complete denuclearization hardly qualify as an ESS.

If there is such a thing as an ESS for nuclear arms policy, it will probably take considerable experience and reflection for us to discover it. Presumably such an ESS will not be forged as a grand solution, but instead will develop on a piecemeal basis, comprised of an ad hoc mix of unilateral policy initiatives, superpower game rules, negotiated arms conventions, and some trial-and-error experimentation. However, it does seem clear that any ESS for nuclear arms will require at least two things: (1) the development of coordination histories among the superpowers and newly emergent nuclear powers (with the superpowers modeling the nuclear arms game rules); and (2) the development of theories of deterrence that are consistent with the objectives of an ESS.

7.2. THE DEVELOPMENT OF COORDINATION HISTORIES

While nuclear weapons policy has many symbolic implications relating to power, prestige, and loyalty in the international community, the arms race is first and foremost a highly complex set of coordination problems. The solutions to these coordination problems may be sought through both formal agreements (e.g., treaties) and informal conventions or understandings. To date most of what has taken place in arms control has been through formal agreements. Unfortunately the potential of creating durable coordination histories between the superpowers through informal conventions has often been overlooked in our preoccupation for negotiated solutions.

Formal agreements are necessary when matters of interpretation are critical for a common understanding of what is being negotiated (e.g., should NATO's nuclear warheads be counted as part of the U.S. arsenal?) or how an agreement will be implemented and verified. Yet, while negotiated settlements will inevitably play a strong role in superpower arms control, they are not always the most effective way to build a coordination history. Formal negotiations typically mirror the competitive, adversarial ethos that brought about the arms race in the first place, failing to achieve the climate of trust and cooperation on which meaningful arms limitations and reductions must be based. On balance, one would suspect that various informal means of establishing arms control conventions could be just as or more effective than formal treaty agreements (Schelling and Halperin, 1985, pp. xiii, 77–90).

Informal solutions can be effective when the parameters of a coordination problem are salient and interpretive matters are limited (e.g., the introduction of a new generation weapons system [see Axelrod, 1984; D. Lewis, 1969]). Whereas formal coordination solutions require an array of prenegotiating maneuvers (or posturing), a description of the problem, a statement of aims, and a series of compromises by each side, informal approaches attempt to establish coordinating conventions by the judicious initiation of unilateral (deescalating) actions that are designed to demonstrate good faith and will remain in force as long as the other side reciprocates accordingly (assuming that such initiatives are neither couched in language suggestive of an ultimatum nor timed for obvious propaganda purposes). The theoretical justification of this approach is that unilateral gestures of this type are psychologically powerful means of reducing mistrust and inducing reciprocity (Osgood, 1962). For example, Pilisuk (1984, p. 313) developed and tested a modified Prisoner's Dilemma disarmament game using laboratory subjects and found that "a consistent pattern of unilateral moves can alter the behavior of the other player even in the absence of power or coercive sanction." Moreover, there seems to be some evidence from the Kennedy administration, involving a series of unilateral initiatives by the United States that were promptly reciprocated by the Soviet Union, that informal conventions of this type can be remarkably successful (Etzioni, 1979).

The primary goal of both formal and informal approaches to arms control should be the development of coordination histories among the superpowers and newly emergent nuclear powers. Unfortunately our myopic preoccupation with formal or negotiated solutions does not serve this purpose well. Because informal agreements (crafted through an interplay of unilateral initiatives and reciprocation) accentuate the integrity of concrete actions over words and the demonstration of good faith over the presumption of suspicion, they possess an elegance and clarity unmatched by formal negotiating processes. Moreover, one would expect that unilateral (yet conditional) deescalating moves of this type could create a kind of coordination inertia that would have the effect of conditioning the responses of the other side. Eventually the action-feedback structure of deescalation and reciprocity would provide a strong catalyst for further arms reductions, as those who initiated arms reductions would have the distinct advantage of choosing their own terrain.

7.3.   THE THEORY OF DETERRENCE

The theory of deterrence, in one form or another, has been the mainstay of nuclear policy since the onset of the nuclear era. The theory holds that any first strike will be met with a retaliatory strike so devastating that it would deter nuclear aggression by one side or the other. In essence the theory of deterrence, in its major outlines, is nothing more than an updated version of the ancient institution of exchanging hostages to secure agreements (Schelling, 1963). As was often the custom in ancient times, cooperative agreements were secured with untrustworthy parties by the exchange of hostages as surety for the agreement. The difference is that in the nuclear age, everyone becomes everyone else's hostage.

The so-called Game of Chicken in game theory provides a helpful illustration of the theory of deterrence.[1] Like the Prisoner's Dilemma, the cooperative outcome in the Game of Chicken does not correspond to the natural equilibria of the game, and consequently both players must resist the temptation to defect from their cooperative agreement. Figure 7.1 depicts a hypothetical payoff matrix, comprised of quadrants A, B, C, and D, for two nuclear superpowers—countries X and Y. The leaders of countries X and Y can play one of two strategies: (1) a strategy of cooperation (S_c) by refraining from initiating a first strike on the other country; and (2) a strategy of defection (S_d) by initiating a first strike. In quadrant A, the cooperative solution, both countries receive a modest payoff of 5. If either X or Y elects to follow a strategy of defection, entering quadrants C or B, respectively, the gains for defection would be substantial and the losses experienced by the country following the cooperative strategy would be even more devastating (with X's payoff in the lower left corner and Y's in the upper right corner). Essentially the theory of deterrence is designed to rule out the possibility that either country X or Y can remain in quadrants C or B, threatening that defection by one side will be met by a similar response by the other. Of course, if both countries follow the strategy of defection, both countries will suffer the catastrophic outcome of quadrant D, where the payoff for each country is euphemistically represented as -100 (but whose monstrous magnitude perhaps could only be represented by -100^{100}). Therefore the effect of the theory of deterrence, if it is successful, is to rule out the possibility of either country

Figure 7.1
The Theory of Deterrence and the Game of Chicken

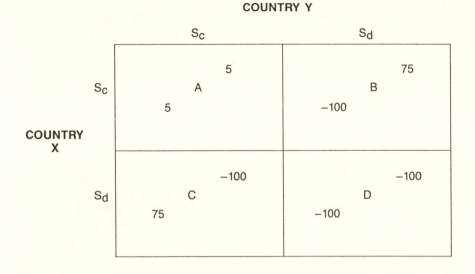

remaining in quadrants *B* or *C*, so that there are functionally only two choices: mutual cooperation or mutual devastation.

The basic problem with the theory of deterrence, as it is traditionally presented, is that once either country *X* or *Y* has launched a first strike, there is no reason, beyond sheer vengeance, why the other country should augment the gruesome magnitude of human and ecological devastation by launching a retaliatory strike. In other words, the strategy of deterrence is only effective in preventing a first strike but loses its usefulness once the missiles have been launched. Consequently nuclear powers are in the double-bind of having to assure the other side that retaliation is inevitable if a first strike is initiated and yet lack any sound rationale for carrying out the threat once such a strike is launched. Of course, this predicament of the theory of deterrence simply reflects the unique technological situation ushered in by the nuclear era with respect to our conceptualization of war. Unlike conventional warfare, where typically there are clearly defined winners and losers, in nuclear warfare there are only losers.

In spite of the above glaring weakness of the theory of deterrence, it is difficult to know whether we have any credible strategic alternative as long as a high level of mistrust persists in U.S.-Soviet relations. One would like to think that there must be some way to get away from the primitive practice of exchanging hostages, yet one is at a loss to know how that might be done, short of a complete transformation of the global order.

Of course, the proposed Strategic Defense Initiative (SDI) or "Star Wars" represents an attempt to create an alternative to the theory of deterrence through sophisticated, and largely undeveloped, computer and laser/particle beam technologies. Unfortunately this alternative to the policy of deterrence, whatever the merits of its intent, is ill-conceived on both technological and strategic grounds, having the potential to introduce a great deal of instability between the superpowers. On technological grounds, it is difficult to believe that any defense shield could be impervious to a massive salvo of MIRVed (multiple independently targeted reentry vehicle) intercontinental ballistic missiles (ICBMs), replete with decoys. Moreover, even if it were possible to create an impervious defense shield, existing or prospective antisatellite technology would be sufficient to cripple the system in a preemptive attack (which could shorten the nuclear fuse by provoking a first strike from the country relying upon their defense shield). In addition, an array of other delivery systems for nuclear warheads could be deployed in order to offset the decreased effectiveness of a country's ICBM force (e.g., cruise missiles, submarine-launched ballistic missiles [SLBMs] launched near coastal waters, stealth bombers).

Furthermore, it seems clear, on strategic grounds, that there are no clear demarcations between offensive and defensive weapons systems in the nuclear age. Consequently it is untenable to believe that defensive weapons systems will not have destabilizing implications for the arms race. Consider the following scenario. Let us assume that in January 2008 the United States is one year away from having a fully operational, debugged system of satellite-based lasers that could effectively protect U.S. cities and ICBM silos from a massive first strike. At that time the USSR is 10 to 15 years away from developing a similar system (a gratuitous assumption given the U.S. edge in computer technology). Would the Kremlin sit by idly during the remainder of 2008, waiting for the United States to render its nuclear arsenal impotent? Probably not. It seems likely that the Soviets, or any other country in that position, would take any measures necessary to prevent the defense shield from becoming operational, including launching a preemptive nuclear attack.

Certainly the most immediate danger posed by the immense nuclear arsenals of the United States and the Soviet Union is the ill-founded belief by most military authorities in both countries that it is possible to wage a limited nuclear conflict. This belief is founded on the twin assumptions that (1) there is a clear and operational distinction between the introduction of low-yield, tactical nuclear weapons in the battlefield and the use of strategic nuclear weapons in a full-scale nuclear exchange, and (2) it is possible to wage a limited nuclear war with strategic weapons systems.

The difficulty with the first assumption, stemming from game-theoretical considerations, is the absence of a clearly identified "firebreak" or the lack of salience[2] in the blurred theoretical distinction between tactical and strategic nuclear weapons. The lack of a firebreak between tactical and strategic weapons seriously complicates even well-intentioned attempts to avoid crossing the strategic weapons threshold (D. Lewis, 1969, pp. 36–37; Schelling, 1963, pp. 74–77, 257–266). Indeed, as Bundy et al. (1982, p. 757) have argued, the one clearly definable firebreak against the worldwide disaster of general nuclear war is the one that stands between all other kinds of conflict and any use whatsoever of nuclear weapons. To keep that firebreak wide and strong is in the deepest interest of mankind.

The problem with the second assumption is that C^3I systems (i.e, command, control, communications, and intelligence) are extremely vulnerable to the new generation ICBMs, whose accuracies have fallen below one-tenth of a nautical mile. As Desmond Ball (1981) has argued persuasively, the inherent vulnerability of military command and control systems poses a serious challenge to the assumption that a nuclear war, once under way, can be limited. Among the factors that Ball considers, the following are most serious.

First, there is a strong possibility that any first strike launched by the Soviets would begin by a "decapitation" strike on Washington by an SLBM. This would mean that the warning time for the president and his key advisors would be no more than ten minutes, and could even drop below five minutes. Under optimal conditions, the helicopter trip from the White House to Andrews Air Force Base is eight minutes, assuming that the helicopter is based at the White House (which is rarely the case). This, of course, does not include the time it would take to collect the president and his military aide (who carries the updated launch codes). An additional lapse of time would be required before the specially equipped Boeing 747 (designated E4-B) National Emergency Airborne Command Post (NEACP) would be safely in the air with the president. Consequently, there are strong reasons to doubt that the president would survive a dedicated first strike by the Soviets, leaving the decision as to the nature and extent of U.S. retaliation up to the political or military leaders next in the chain of command. The fact that most of these leaders are also located in the Washington area would create confusion as to who was still alive and able to assume authority in ordering a retaliatory strike, suggesting that a U.S. response would be formulated by a lower echelon political leader, who would be less than adequately prepared to understand the nuances of prevailing strategic doctrine and most likely would simply accept the recommendations of the military establishment at the time. Worse yet, the provisions of a highly classified White House contingency plan, known as "permissive action," authorizes Poseidon and Trident submarine commanders to retaliate individually, acting separately and on their own, after a decapitation strike (Catudal, 1986, pp. 333–334). The fact that each of these commanders would be acting in isolation and on their own precludes any hope for a moderate or graduated retaliatory response. Given the epithet of the Trident submarine commander as "the third most powerful man in the world" (as he controls more destructive power than that of the combined military resources of Britain, Italy, Spain, Brazil, Argentina, West Germany, Japan, the Philippines, India, and Pakistan), the prospect of an uncoordinated retaliation by Trident submarine commanders is cause for profound distress.

A second consideration against the viability of fighting a limited nuclear war concerns MOLINK or the Moscow-Washington Hot Line. Ball argues that MOLINK would probably not survive a strategic nuclear exchange—a fact that would seriously reduce the probability of terminating a nuclear war once it is initiated. Without a direct communication link intact between the two super-powers, the possibility of utilizing occasional "negotiating pauses" at certain stages of a nuclear conflict is practically nil. The fact that the cable and radio links of MOLINK were replaced in 1978 with a satellite communications system (comprising two independent, parallel circuits consisting of two satellites and four ground stations) probably increases the vulnerability of the system during a nuclear attack (even though the satellite system improves the reliability of the Hot Line during peacetime).

A third problem with limited nuclear war is related to the inherent time limitations of the most survivable component of the U.S. command and control systems: the Strategic Air Command (SAC) Airborne Command Post (known as "Looking Glass"). The SAC Airborne Command Posts consist of specially equipped Boeing 707s (designated EC–135), laden with highly sophisticated communications equipment, that are based at Offutt AFB near Omaha, Nebraska. At least one of these aircraft is airborne at all times. It is estimated that they can remain in the air for a maximum of 72 hours, assuming that the EC–135s have access to airborne refueling tankers.[3] Barring the destruction of these aircraft by nuclear detonations at or near their flight elevations, it is conceivable that the general in command of "Looking Glass" would be inclined to use all of the nuclear retaliatory forces at his disposal before endangering his craft by trying to land (assuming that a selected runway of sufficient length was still intact).

In spite of these and other difficulties relating to the inherent vulnerability of C^3I systems during a nuclear attack, strategic doctrine since the early 1970s has moved away from the traditional understanding of deterrence (which focused on being able to mount a devastating retaliatory strike after sustaining a massive first strike by the enemy) toward concepts of deterrence that presume the capacity to wage a limited and protracted nuclear war. As a result, the more recent developments in U.S. strategic doctrine such as "flexible targeting," "coun-terforce," "intrawar deterrence," "prevailing counterforce" and "nuclear uti-lization target selection" (NUTS) have increasingly emphasized the development of nuclear warfighting capabilities, representing a radical departure from the traditional understanding that the introduction of nuclear weapons into East-West hostilities would rapidly lead to "mutual assured destruction" (MAD) (see Ca-tudal, 1986, pp. 156–187).

This recent trend in the evolution of strategic doctrine is extremely disturbing. The current U.S. reliance upon a "counterforce" targeting strategy in its Single Integrated Operations Plan (SIOP) places a high priority on the destruction of hardened Soviet ICBM sites by a new generation of nuclear weapons with pinpoint accuracy, such as the MX (Missile Experimental) ICBMs, the Trident II (D–5) SLBMs, the intermediate-range Pershing II missiles (representing the first deployment of a MaRV weapon, that is, a maneuverable reentry vehicle directed by an in-flight inertial guidance system), and the Tomahawk ground-launched cruise missiles (GLCMs). The ominous implications of the counterforce doctrine and our rapidly expanding technological capability to destroy hardened ICBM sites and command and control centers are threefold.

First, it is difficult to envision any meaningful pause in the arms race when our strategic doctrine insists that ''we must somehow match everything the rocket commanders in the Soviet Union extract from their government'' (Bundy et al., 1982, p. 764). This policy of matching weapon for weapon, irrespective of their strategic significance, will neither enable us to assess our national security needs rationally nor permit us to step off the nuclear escalator at any time in the near future.

Second, the alleged morality of the counterforce doctrine over alternate targeting strategies (e.g., targeting industrial centers according to the ''countervalue'' approach or the destruction of major population centers implied by the MAD doctrine) is hardly compelling. Not only would the counterforce strategy imply a high amount of ''collateral damage'' (i.e., civilian casualties) but also there is a strong likelihood that the Kremlin would construe such counterforce measures as a veiled attempt to achieve a first-strike capability (e.g., why devote one's nuclear weapons to missile silos that would be empty after a first strike if one is really interested only in using nuclear weapons to retaliate after a first strike?).

Third, with the progressive enhancement of counterforce capabilities, the temptation to institute ''launch on warning'' policies will be almost irresistible, in an effort to guarantee the viability of one's nuclear forces. Obviously this would create a highly dangerous situation, exponentially increasing the possibility that a full-scale nuclear exchange could be initiated by a computer malfunction or some other type of accident.

In view of these considerations, it is imperative for U.S. strategic planners to formulate a strategic doctrine that will permit the United States to pursue an approach to deterrence that is consistent with an ESS for nuclear weapons. Clearly the present emphasis on counterforce targeting of hardened ICBM silos and command and control centers is inconsistent with any conceivable version of an ESS for nuclear weapons. Not only does the counterforce doctrine institutionalize a never-ending arms race that insists on matching weapon for weapon, but also it is predicated on the illusion that it is possible to wage a controlled and protracted nuclear war with existing or prospective C^3I systems. As we have discussed, a sudden SLBM decapitation strike on Washington that killed the president and dedicated nuclear strikes at alternate hardened control and command centers as well as major airfields would mean that the U.S. National Command Authority (NCA) would have a maximum of 72 hours in which to fashion a retaliatory response from a Boeing 707 SAC Airborne Command Post. It is hoped that the general in charge of ''Looking Glass'' would refrain from deploying all surviving U.S. nuclear forces in one final, coordinated retaliatory strike against the Soviet Union before the plane landed or crashed. However, even if nuclear restraint became the order of the day for the "Looking Glass" commander, millions of humans would still be at risk by the independent, uncoordinated, and uncontrolled retaliatory powers accorded to the Poseidon and Trident submarine commanders by the decentralized policy of "permissive action." Hence the cherished illusion that nuclear war can be limited and controlled would become a collective nightmare for all human generations to follow—if there were any human beings left to dream at all.

7.4. STRATEGIC TRIAD OPERATIONAL PHASING (STOP): A PROPOSAL

Is it possible to formulate a strategic nuclear doctrine that would be consistent with an ESS for nuclear arms control and could provide the West with a credible nuclear deterrent? In responding to this question, two considerations should be noted at the outset.

First, the departure from MAD during the 1970s was inspired, in part, by the belief that the United States could not credibly threaten to destroy major population centers in the Soviet Union in a retaliatory strike after a first strike had been launched by the Kremlin. Clearly the value of any military deterrent is directly related to the enemy's perception that the deterrent will actually be employed if circumstances warrant it. The inflexible, "all or nothing at all" character of MAD hardly enhances the credibility of a nuclear deterrent. The only way to resolve this problem would be very unacceptable—the retaliatory strike could be automatically triggered by some type of "doomsday machine" and, therefore, placed beyond human control. Additionally U.S. strategists felt that a highly authoritarian regime that lost 20 million people in World War II may not be genuinely deterred by a nuclear strategy that targeted only population centers. Consequently the emphasis on "counterforce" and "countervalue" (e.g., urban-industrial centers, oil refineries, ports) targeting emerged partly as a response to the U.S. perception that the Soviets would be deterred by any retaliatory strike that threatened to destroy its primary military installations and industrial infrastructure. While it is ridiculous to believe that major counterforce and countervalue objectives could be achieved without excessively high civilian casualties, it is readily apparent that attacks on most counterforce and countervalue targets are preferable to direct attacks on population centers, unless such targeting strategies dramatically increase the probability of a full-scale nuclear war (e.g., by forcing the other side to adopt a launch on warning policy).

Second, the foremost challenge for contemporary strategic nuclear planning is to fashion a phased deterrence strategy that *unilaterally* structures substantial time lags between attack and retaliation in the midst of a full-scale nuclear conflict. Such institutionalized time lags are critical for two reasons. First, assuming that measures are taken to harden the Washington-Moscow Hot Line and that a first strike did not include a decapitating strike against either Washington or Moscow, such time lags would provide precious opportunities for negotiating pauses, which could lead to the termination of a nuclear war. Second, there appears to be a strong tendency for humans to confuse low-probability/low-consequence events with low-probability/high-consequence events (Lumsden and Wilson, 1981, p. 88). Because humans seem to lack the intuitive skills necessary for generating integrated probability judgments, they tend to underestimate the gravity of potential disasters until such disasters have actually occurred. It is hoped that such significant time lags would permit moments for reflection and remorse for the existing leadership of both superpowers. This factor becomes all the more critical in light of the profuse manifestations of the psychological defense mechanism of isolation in strategic jargon, and the unprecedented degree of "personal distance" (Becker, 1975) that exists between the small number of people involved in the actual execution of a nuclear strike and the millions who must suffer the consequences of their actions.

In light of these considerations, any new alternative to the current assortment of strategic doctrines must represent a credible deterrent that is staged, in a predetermined fashion, over a period of time substantially longer than the current worst-case threshold of 72 hours. I recommend that such an alternative would build upon the existing strengths of the strategic triad of land-based missiles, strategic bombers, and submarines, particularly emphasizing our extensive submarine leg of the triad (e.g., 50% of all U.S. nuclear warheads are based on submarines). I call this alternative strategic doctrine "Strategic Triad Operational Phasing" (STOP).

The essence of STOP is that it would give the United States and NATO (North Atlantic Treaty Organization) the ability to activate its nuclear deterrent according to a preset, graduated formula (which could be terminated at any point) consisting of three retaliatory phases over a period of at least four months. As such, STOP represents a move away from the traditional U.S. understanding of deterrence as punishment, toward the Soviet view of deterrence as a denial of military and political objectives. Moreover, the phased deterrent approach differs markedly from the notion of waging a controlled and limited nuclear war, in that STOP is concerned only with the ability of U.S. forces to execute three retaliatory strikes over a lengthy period of time and does not entertain any illusions about the possibility of winning a nuclear conflict.

The first phase of STOP would be initiated shortly after the United States sustained a major first strike by the Soviet Union. Those ICBMs and strategic bombers with air launched cruise missiles (ALCMs) that survived the first strike would be employed selectively (in proportion to the magnitude of the initial attack) against *soft* military targets (including submarine ports, isolated oil refineries, power facilities, etc.) within the Soviet Union, excluding both hardened ICBM silos and command and control centers. The fact that this first-phase retaliation would not include the targeting of any urban-industrial centers or cities would have the effect of making the threat of deterrence far more credible. Moreover, the inherent dangers involved in targeting hardened ICBM silos or command and control centers would be avoided by the focus on *soft* military targets—a factor that would also remove the need to insure even the partial survival of our ICBM force, as all of the soft military targets could be easily handled by ALCMs mounted on strategic bombers or through direct interception by B-2 stealth bombers.

Phases two and three of STOP would be handled exclusively by the submarine leg of the strategic triad, assuming the worst-case scenario that both the airborne and underground command and control centers have been destroyed. Both of these phases would be executed by one of two designated Alternative Submarine National Command Posts (ASNCP)—the underwater equivalent of "Looking Glass." There would be no need to build a special submarine for this purpose, as six of the large Trident submarines could be equipped with the special communications gear that such ASNCPs would require. At any time, at least two of the six ASNCPs would be out to sea, designated ASNCP–1 and ASNCP–2. Each underwater command post would be staffed by one of eight well-compensated, high-level civilian experts, specially appointed by the president, who would serve for three months out of the year. In the event of a first strike and the destruction of the underground and airborne command and control centers, the U.S. NCA would revert to the civilian designated by the president in ASNCP–1. In the highly improbable event that ASNCP–1 was detected and destroyed, the NCA would automatically revert to ASNCP–2.

In the event of a dedicated first strike by the Kremlin that threatened the integrity of hardened C^3I systems and U.S. communications/surveillance satellites, the Trident fleet could be alerted immediately by (1) the extremely low frequency (ELF) communications system based in Michigan's Upper Peninsula, (2) the TACAMO (for Take Charge and Move Out) fleet of submarine communications aircraft (only two of the TACAMO aircraft would need to be airborne at all times), or (3) the blue-laser satellite, called the SLCSAT (Submarine Laser Communications Satellite), which is presently being constructed by the Lockheed Missiles and Space Company. Once the submarines received the coded alert message, they would follow a complex, prearranged timetable, identified from a menu of operational plans by the coded ELF, TACAMO, or SLCSAT signals. This operational plan would disperse the Trident fleet across the Pacific and would configure the fleet (according to a preset timetable) so that each submarine could establish intermittent, underwater, intersubmarine communications with ASNCP–1 by means of blue lasers, without either concentrating the fleet or running the risk of detection.[4] After regular communications were established with all members of the Trident fleet across the Pacific, ASNCP–1 would be in a position to monitor the extent of nuclear devastation, the disposition of U.S. and Soviet forces, the radiation and smoke/dust levels in the atmosphere, and any indications of deterioration in the ozone layer. Given the current level of uncertainty about the magnitude of the secondary effects accompanying a large-scale nuclear exchange concerning the extent of radioactive fallout, the impact on the earth's fragile ozone layer, and the devastating prospect of a "nuclear winter" created by soot and dust in the atmosphere, the monitoring function of

ASNCP–1 would be of critical importance in assuring that retaliatory strikes did not exceed certain environmental thresholds. This monitoring function could be accomplished by launching two or three satellites from one of the Trident submarines or another class of submarines designed for this purpose. (There are indications that the Trident D–1 missile may already have the capacity to launch a communications satellite [Dalgleish and Schweikart, 1984, p. 262].) In the event that U.S. military experts believed that the launching of reconnaissance satellites would pose undue risks to the Trident fleet, it would be possible to design a small fleet of satellite reconnaissance submarines (SRSs), which would be fitted with an array of communications and surveillance satellites yet would not carry any nuclear weapons. Obviously, given the high-risk nature of their assignment, such SRSs would be staffed with a minimum number of personnel, as their position would be exposed once their satellites were launched.

If it became necessary, phase two of STOP could be activated several weeks after the initial first strike. Once ASNCP–1 had positively determined that the atmosphere was not at risk by further nuclear detonations and that the Soviets were beginning to exploit the melee following the first strike (as evidenced by Soviet troop movements in Western Europe or the Persian Gulf), phase two could be initiated. Phase two would consist of extensive "countervalue" targeting throughout the Soviet Union, including its urban-industrial centers (which should be evacuated by this time), oil refineries, ports (but excluding the hardened command and control centers around Moscow).

In the unlikely event that phase two did not succeed in obstructing the Kremlin's military objectives, phase three would be initiated three or four months after the first strike.[5] Phase three would consist of a dedicated attack by a salvo of Trident II (D–5) missiles on all the hardened, underground command and control centers surrounding Moscow and elsewhere in the Soviet Union, as well as any hardened ICBM silos that have not been fired and/or military sites that show activity. The Trident II missiles have a hard-target kill capability at 6,000 nautical miles or more with a circular error probability (CEP) of only 30 meters (Dalgleish and Schweikart, 1984, p. 34). Presumably there would be no need to target urban population centers during phase three, although the collateral damage to human populations still could be very great during this period, particularly if people began to repopulate the environs of Moscow and if the ICBM silos are located in the proximity of population centers (as is often the case).

The striking feature of STOP is that it would provide the United States and NATO with an exceptionally strong nuclear deterrent, building on the inherent strengths of the strategic triad concept, with a substantially reduced number of total nuclear warheads and a small investment in new C^3I systems. As such, STOP would permit the United States to work on the development of an ESS in its arms control policies with the Soviet Union. Not only would STOP allay fears within the United States about its ability to mount an effective retaliation in the highly unlikely, worst-case scenario of a dedicated first strike by the Kremlin, but also this strategic doctrine would help alleviate Soviet suspicions that the United States may be seeking to achieve a first-strike capability through its new generation of highly accurate weapons in conjunction with the defensive capabilities developed under the SDI program.

The fact that the Soviet Union has been unable to track even one submarine in the over 2,000 U.S. submarine patrols since 1960 makes STOP a remarkably promising approach to nuclear deterrence. Moreover, the remarkable evasive and defensive capabilities of the Trident class submarines make this deterrent nearly impervious to either current or foreseeable developments in antisubmarine warfare (ASW) (Dalgleish and Schweikart, 1984, pp. 206–246). The unofficial speed and diving depth of the Trident alone assures it of a high degree of survivability. Since the Trident can cruise at underwater speeds of 40 knots and can dive in excess of 2,000 feet, it is able to outrun most of its ASW combatants (excluding the Soviet Alpha submarine; however, there are substantive doubts about the reliability of the Alpha and its capacity to exceed Trident's cruise speed for more than brief intervals). Additionally, each Trident submarine is fitted with elaborate decoys known as mobile submarine simulators (MOSS), which emit sonar signatures nearly identical to the Trident submarine and can be deployed to confuse Soviet attack submarines. Moreover, the deployment of the SIAM (self-initiated antiaircraft missile) technology in Trident submarines will give it the capability of destroying ASW airplanes or helicopters while remaining submerged (after the missile breaks the water, it hovers momentarily before locking on to its target). Of course, the Trident fleet would be operating in a relatively friendly environment after phase one of the retaliation, presuming the SIOP of phase one would target critical elements of the Soviet ASW capabilities, making it impossible for the Kremlin to engage in extensive ASW.

In addition to the Trident's evasive and defensive capabilities, the range of the Trident II (D–5) missiles will give it a formidable missile-firing operational range of 42.5 million square miles (which would be increased by the erratic cruising patterns specified by the STOP timetable). It would take at least 850,000 nuclear warheads (i.e., over 15 times the total inventory of nuclear weapons in the world today) in order to destroy most of these submarines across this operational range. Even then, the Trident has the structural capability to withstand the underwater nuclear shock waves from a near hit on the surface of the ocean.

Of course, there are a number of measures besides STOP that NATO and the United States could take unilaterally to lessen the possibility of nuclear war. Among the most important of these is the removal of tactical nuclear weapons from forward-based positions in Western Europe, and the establishment of tank obstacles, field fortifications, substantial stockpiles of combat supplies, and other conventional defensive measures along the borders of the NATO and Warsaw Pact countries, but especially along the border of the Federal Republic of Germany. One of the most promising technological developments in this regard is the expanding repertoire of highly accurate, "smart weapons" or precision guided munitions (PGM), armed with conventional warheads, which are particularly effective antitank weapons.

One comprehensive analysis of NATO and Warsaw Pact troop strengths and military capabilities concluded that a moderate increase in NATO troop strengths, along with a series of defensive improvements in the military posture of NATO's conventional forces, would enable NATO to defend Western Europe far more effectively than its present military posture (which relies on the early introduction of tactical nuclear weapons in a major invasion by Warsaw Pact forces) (Gottfried et al., 1984). Excluding the recurrent costs associated with the increased troop strength, the study calculated that the necessary conventional improvements would cost less than $100 billion over a six-year period. The upshot of this analysis is that NATO could eventually move toward a no-first-use policy insofar as nuclear weapons are concerned with a limited financial investment and a far more effective military deterrent.

Additionally, a number of cooperative efforts could be undertaken between the United States and the Soviet Union in order to reduce the possibility of an accidental nuclear war and to facilitate the termination of a nuclear war once it has begun. These cooperative efforts could include the creation of a joint, standing commission of U.S. and Soviet experts at both ends of the Hot Line to interpret data relevant to a nuclear alarm (Stone, 1984, p. 148). Moreover, joint efforts to harden the Washington-Moscow Hot Line and to provide several backup ground circuits in the event of a nuclear exchange would be very helpful as well.

In conclusion, it seems reasonable to expect that there will be discussions and debates going on about nuclear arms control for at least the next few hundred years, if not the next millenium or so. To think that the problem can be solved once and for all by some gigantic leap of faith by the superpowers is just as deceptive as the facile belief that nuclear weapons are so devastating that they will automatically put an end to large-scale global conflict. There are no political or technological quick fixes to this problem. Instead the global human community must proceed with vigilance in the establishment of coordination histories among Earth's nuclear powers. Indeed this task represents the greatest evolutionary challenge to date of the adaptive capabilities that constitute the open genetic program of human life. Most of the aggressive skills and out-group suspicions that we utilized so effectively during our prolonged existence as hunters and gatherers are no longer functional in the Nuclear Age. The question facing us is whether Homo sapiens will be able to graduate quickly enough into the Nuclear Age, through rapid cultural evolution, in order to negotiate this transition successfully. The outcome of this evolutionary challenge has yet to be determined by history, and indeed the continuation of human history itself may depend on the outcome.

NOTES

1. The Game of Chicken gets its name from the "game" played by teenagers in the 1950s, in which two drivers would test their strength of will by speeding toward one

another from opposite directions on a deserted road, and the driver who was the first to veer away lost the game. For more on the Game of Chicken, see Rapoport et al. (1976, pp. 151–158, 241–245).

2. Salience refers to conspicuous features of a coordinating problem that provide clues for a coordination equilibrium where there is no communication between the players.

3. Strategic Air Command, Public Affairs, Offutt Air Force Base, Omaha, Nebraska.

4. In an interview by the author on November 6, 1986, with D. Douglas Dalgleish, co-author of *Trident* (1984), he indicated that blue laser technology has developed to a point that makes intersubmarine underwater communication possible. At this time research on blue lasers is cloaked in a great deal of secrecy, and I have been unable to find unclassified technical literature on the subject. However, for a helpful nontechnical discussion, see Heppenheimer (1987).

5. The normal patrol time for a Trident submarine at sea is 70 days. According to Dalgleish (November 6, 1986 interview), this period could be extended to a maximum of 120 days with an austerity food menu for the crew. Presumably this 120-day maximum could be increased further by the provision of emergency food rations.

8
The Basic Needs Mandate and Political Systems

8.1. THE PROBLEM OF POLITICAL LEGITIMATION

Since the emergence of large-scale political systems in ancient Egypt and Mesopotamia, the problem of political legitimacy has figured prominently in political life in one way or another. Whether the right to rule was legitimated by divine fiat, hereditary succession, military or administrative competency, the defeat of a dreaded enemy, class warfare, or the consent of the governed, the claim to legitimate authority has been an essential precondition for the acquisition and maintenance of power.

The BNM provides us with a powerful normative framework from which to resolve the long-standing problem of political legitimacy. That normative framework is simply this: Political systems retain their legitimacy inasmuch as they are making significant inroads in meeting the BN of their relevant populations. Conversely, any political regime that systematically denies basic human rights to its citizenry tacitly forfeits its right to rule.

The implications of the BNM's understanding of political legitimacy are sweeping and obviously raise a number of critical issues germane to political theory. However, for the purposes of this discussion, I will limit the examination of the BNM in relation to political systems to the following three topics: (1) alternate ways of structuring the political order, (2) legitimate uses of violence by citizens against the state, and (3) the right of foreign states to intervene in the domestic affairs of another state. The first two topics will be addressed in this chapter and the latter issue will be taken up in the context of a discussion on international law in Chapter 10, section 10.4.

8.2. THE BASIC NEEDS MANDATE AND SELECTED POLITICAL CONFIGURATIONS

What sorts of political systems would be sanctioned by the BNM? In addressing this question, it is necessary to evaluate an array of political configurations in terms of their potential for meeting the BN of their citizens. Figure 8.1 presents a rough graphic depiction of nine selected political configurations, ranging from the most centralized to the most decentralized. The relative power of the respective components of each political configuration is represented by placing the ultimate or decisive source of power in the uppermost portion of the diagram.

Configurations A, B, C, and D depict four variants of a dictatorial form of government, signified by the prominence of the central government at the top of the diagram. Configuration A portrays a pure dictatorship where the central regime wields power over its citizenry with impunity. Configuration B represents dictatorships whose power is significantly qualified by an autonomous social/religious institution (e.g., 12th century Europe, some Islamic societies). Configurations C and D represent decentralized variants of dictatorships that strengthen the decision-making power of regional governmental organizations while still retaining ultimate control. In configuration C, the regional governmental organization is merely a conduit whereby the central regime articulates and implements its policies at the local level and monitors the compliance of the population. Configuration D differs from C in that there is a genuine sense of political participation in regional governmental organizations; however, the limits of such local participation are clearly delineated by the central regime and neither circumscribes nor weakens its sphere of influence. In fact, configuration D could be a very effective way to enhance the power of the central government and to diffuse pockets of dissention by creating the illusion of political participation.

Configuration E depicts an interesting political arrangement that could function as a transition configuration between dictatorial political structures and representative forms of government. In this political configuration the influence and autonomy of regional government organizations (treated only as instruments to enhance and sustain the power base of the central regime in configuration D) have matured to such a degree that they place serious limitations on the power and autonomy of the central government. As a consequence a nascent form of representative government inadvertently emerges from the dictatorial configuration D, and the general population is able to exercise indirect power over the central regime through their regional governmental organizations.

Configurations F, G, H, and I are marked by the prominent and decisive role of the individual citizen in shaping national policy through an array of social choice processes. Of these four configurations, H and I are obviously not suitable for large-scale political organization, given the impossibility of administering the day-to-day affairs of government through direct social choice processes. Consequently there is a need to design representative structures of government

Figure 8.1
Selected Political Configurations

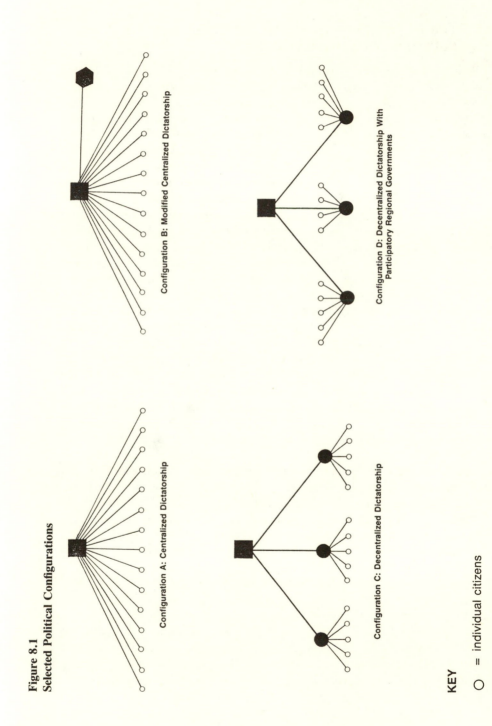

Configuration A: Centralized Dictatorship

Configuration B: Modified Centralized Dictatorship

Configuration C: Decentralized Dictatorship

Configuration D: Decentralized Dictatorship With
Participatory Regional Governments

KEY

○ = individual citizens

■ = central regime

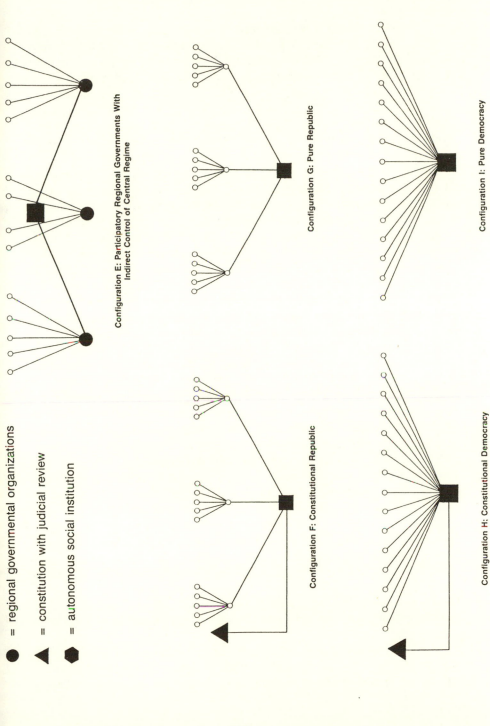

= regional governmental organizations

= constitution with judicial review

= autonomous social institution

Configuration E: Participatory Regional Governments With
Indirect Control of Central Regime

Configuration F: Constitutional Republic

Configuration G: Pure Republic

Configuration H: Constitutional Democracy

Configuration I: Pure Democracy

that are responsive to their respective constituencies, as reflected by configurations F and G.

A distinctive feature of configurations F and H is the presence of a written constitution that provides for the independent judicial review of government policies. Because the constitution and the central judiciary are neither directly influenced by the central regime nor by immediate social choice processes, the constitutional structure is able to create a remarkably high degree of stability in government affairs, as well as safeguarding the rights of minorities against the preferences of the majority. Presumably any constitutional structure (with or without judicial review) that appears in dictatorial configurations is a constitution in name only, being responsive only to the wishes of the central regime.

In examining each of these political configurations in terms of their potential for meeting the BN of their populations, it is clear that both configurations A and C are very unsuitable, given the fact that it seems quite improbable that even enlightened dictators could maintain their power without resorting to political repression, thereby violating the BNM at the X_3 level (see Table 2.1). Moreover, even if an enlightened dictator were able to implement successful BN policies at the X_1 level (e.g., food, shelter, safe water) in the short term, the inherent instabilities in a dictatorial framework would seriously undermine the prospect of continuing those policies in the middle and long terms.

At the other end of the spectrum, there is no doubt that configurations F and H (and to a lesser extent configurations G and I) would be consistent, on a theoretical level, with BN policies at the X_1, X_2, and X_3 levels in middle- to high-income countries, notwithstanding the theoretical problems associated with the so-called paradox of voting that Kenneth Arrow (1963) has identified in his famous "Impossibility Theorem." Unfortunately, though, these political frameworks may be too decentralized to promote effective BN programs at the X_1 and X_2 levels in countries characterized by low levels of per capita GNP, a highly unequal and rigidly stratified distribution of productive resources, or in countries where prevalent attitudes concerning the subordination of females to males have impeded the education of females. There are three reasons for this reservation.

First, if the entire population votes on BN programs, there is a very strong likelihood that they will prefer general BN subsidies that benefit all of the population (irrespective of income level) instead of voting for BN programs targeted for especially vulnerable populations (e.g., children, pregnant and lactating females, the poorest half of the population). In the case of low-income LDCs, such as Sri Lanka, the democratic preference for general subsidies poses a real threat to the fiscal stability of BN programs that perhaps can be overcome only by exceptionally strong political leadership or indigenous cultural/religious traditions that emphasize the priority of helping the most needy members of society first.

Second, it is very clear that the education of females is a critical component of effective BN programs, as well as efforts to reduce the rate of fertility. Given the strong likelihood that democratic social choice processes would reflect traditional attitudes concerning the subordination of females to males, democratic systems may have great difficulty in securing adequate provisions/safeguards for the education of females. These traditional attitudes could be transformed through public education and cultural change in the long term; however, the exigencies of absolute poverty and the population crisis do not allow the human community the luxury of relying on gradual cultural transformation to resolve this problem. Consequently there are strong reasons to doubt that decentralized means of governance will adequately address the critical problem of female education in the short to middle terms.

Third, it is quite improbable that decentralized political configurations can adequately rectify entitlement patterns and stimulate rapid economic growth in LDCs where there is a highly unequal and rigidly stratified distribution of productive resources (particularly land) and an abundance of surplus labor. There are several reasons for this, including the following: (1) it is not clear that land reform schemes can be effectively implemented on a large scale without a fairly high degree of political centralization (although see Prosterman and Riedinger [1987] for land reform strategies designed for decentralized political systems); (2) there is probably an inverse correlation between the economic success of nationalization programs and the degree to which nationalization decisions emerge from revolutionary fervor or social choice processes; (3) the combination of a wealthy elite with an impoverished, illiterate, and politically segmented peasantry heightens the probability that a small and well-organized elite could effectively subvert social choice processes through legal means in order to protect their vested interests; and (4) centralized regimes are in a much better position to achieve high rates of capital accumulation and to invest these resources strategically within the economy.[1] While none or all of these points can be adduced as conclusive support for the belief that decentralized political configurations are incompatible with the redistribution of productive resources on a large scale, it does suggest that democratic institutions are hardly a panacea for such entitlement transformations and indeed face immense obstacles.

Although the evidence is somewhat mixed and open to interpretation, it seems that centralized socialist regimes have fared better than their decentralized capitalist counterparts in the education of females and the provision of basic goods and services, and to a lesser degree in terms of redistribution of productive resources (Jameson and Wilber, 1981; Molyneux, 1981; Morawetz, 1980; White, 1983). This raises the interesting question as to whether centralized socialist regimes could function as a temporary transition configuration in the economic and political development of certain LDCs.[2] The fact that nearly all instances of indigenous socialism in the world today are within LDCs (excluding the USSR and Yugoslavia) makes the question all the more tantalizing.

This question brings us to a consideration of configurations D and E. As previously mentioned, the extent of political participation permitted by configuration D is extremely limited and may be instituted by the central regime in order to create the illusion of grass-roots participation in the government and thereby to extend its sphere of control. However the possibility exists that an embryonic nexus of political and economic forces could be unintentionally nurtured by the central regime in such a way that configuration D gave way to configuration E. While configuration E is not democratic in the sense of providing for direct social choice procedures to regulate the central regime, it ultimately places the affairs of government in the hands of individual citizens through their participation in mediating regional governmental organizations. As such, configuration E would be consistent, on a theoretical level, with the requirements of the BNM and could ultimately be the harbinger of democratic political configurations. One would imagine that socialist reforms in the way of economic decentralization would be among the political and economic forces gestating in configuration D that could give birth to configuration E. In this regard, the political and economic development of the People's Republic of China will be especially interesting to watch during the next 50 years or so (see Lockett, 1983).

The crux of the matter concerning the possible transition from configuration D to configuration E consists of a judgment call as to whether centralized regimes will eventually yield to the democratic impulse and reconcile themselves to the inherent risks of participatory government. If power, once acquired, is rarely voluntarily relinquished, as human history provides ample confirmation, then the prospects of a peaceful transition from configuration D to E seems incredibly dim. Moreover, there are important regions of instability in configuration E that could lead to a reversion to configuration D. The most important of these instabilities is the ability of the central regime to dispense government subsidies and services in a manner that segments the power of regional governmental organizations, offering the moral equivalent of bribes to selected regional organizations and their respective constituencies. These and other considerations cast substantial doubt on the feasibility of engineering a successful transition from D to E; however, they do not make such a transition impossible.

As a rule of thumb, it seems clear that there is a far greater degree of probability that decentralized regimes could meet the BN of their respective populations at the X_1 and X_2 levels than the probability that centralized regimes will eventually make the transition from the dictatorial configurations A, C, or D to the indirect, participatory structure of configuration E or the fully representative configurations of F, G, H, and I. Let us assume, for example, that over a 40-year time horizon the probability that a particular centralized regime will meet the BN of its population at the X_1 and X_2 levels is .90 and the probability that it will make the transition from configuration D to E is .05. On the basis of these figures, there would be only a 4.5% chance that the BN of the citizens would be met at the X_1, X_2, and X_3 levels. It seems clear that most decentralized political configurations would have no difficulty in exceeding this low probability of BN satisfaction over a 40-year period. It may be objected that such overall probability judgments of BN satisfaction should be weighted to reflect the disproportionate importance of needs at the X_1 and X_2 levels. Yet, even if we were to place four times more emphasis upon needs satisfaction at the X_1 and X_2 levels than upon needs satisfaction at the X_3 level, there still would only be an 18% chance that the BN of the citizens would be met at all three levels.

This analysis suggests that in spite of the structural weaknesses of democratic regimes with respect to certain BN objectives, these political configurations are far more preferable in terms of overall BN satisfaction than centralized regimes. Consequently the BNM would endorse political configurations E-I and, accordingly, would rule out configurations A, C, and D. Configuration B represents a borderline case insofar as the BNM is concerned, as everything hinges on the operational ideology of the autonomous social/religious institution. On the one hand, if the autonomous social/religious institution helps to safeguard individual rights and provides avenues for meaningful forms of political participation, then configuration B would not be inconsistent with the BNM. On the other hand, if the autonomous social/religious institution sanctions oppressive policies by the central regime, configuration B would obviously fail to meet the BNM's requirements.

The BNM's bias for representative forms of government should not be construed as a carte blanche approval of democratic political systems. Unfortunately the most devastating scandal in the historical development of democratic ideologies and institutions in the West has been the complacency that is often attached to meeting the material dimensions of human need. Indeed true friends of democracy will be just as concerned about material deprivation as the most ardent socialist. The failure of Western democracies to respond decisively to the problem of global poverty either proceeds from outright greed or the sheer lack of insight.

8.3. THE BASIC NEEDS MANDATE AND JUST REVOLUTIONS

The BNM not only provides a framework whereby an array of political configurations can be evaluated, but also establishes parameters for the legitimate use of violence by citizens against the state.

According to the BNM, the legitimate authority of the state ultimately derives from its role as guarantor of the BN of its population. Since these BN include the rights to municipal protection and national defense, the state has the prerogative to threaten and employ selected applications of violent force insofar as this is necessary to safeguard the BN of its citizens. With respect to municipal protection, the state's mandate to exercise its role of BN guarantor will entail the establishment of sufficiently differentiated yet clear law codes and a criminal justice system that minimizes the arbitrary application of law and enacts an array of graded sanctions through judicial procedures and safeguards. In terms of national defense, the state has an obligation to provide for the collective defense of its citizens to the extent that such military preparations are warranted by potential threats to the territorial integrity of the country. Obviously, though, a state's national security mandate does not sanction the use of military power to sustain a dictatorial political regime against the aspirations of the country's citizens, where national security becomes synonymous with the preservation of a particular regime.

To what extent may the state exercise violent force in the discharge of its obligations to make provision for municipal protection and national defense? The question raises a number of subtle issues that extend beyond the scope of this discussion and the conceptual range of the BNM. Nonetheless the BNM provides us with two general criteria that set limits on the state's prerogative to exercise violent force.

The first of these criteria is that public investment in municipal protection and national defense should be allocated in a cost-effective manner that minimizes the actual weighted probability of violence (V_{awp}) and the actual probability of invasion (I_{ap}) in relation to other BN objectives, in accordance with BN Investment Ratios and the BN Multiplier Principle (see Chapter 2, sections 2.6.e, 2.10, and 2.12). Therefore a regime cannot abuse its mandate to provide appropriate levels of internal and external security by pursuing self-serving measures of police or military security to the exclusion of other BN objectives.

The second criterion is that a state is only permitted to exercise the minimal amount of violent force necessary in order to achieve its BN objectives. In matters of municipal protection, this would mean that the state is empowered by the BNM to deny individuals of their BN at the X_3 level in order to reduce the actual weighted probability of violence (V_{awp}); however, the state and the officials it empowers do not have the prerogative to transgress the BN of individuals at the X_1 and X_2 levels, unless such acts of violence are committed in self-defense or would immediately save the lives of innocent victims. In other words, the state has the prerogative to imprison criminals (thereby preventing them from doing further harm to its citizens), but the state does not have the right to torture, starve, alter the mental capacities, or destroy individuals under the care of the criminal justice system. Similarly the state may strategically apply violent force against the military representatives of other states insofar as this is necessary for the state to preserve its territorial integrity (as long as collateral damage to noncombatants is minimized); however, the state can neither mistreat nor execute its prisoners of war.

Of course, the state retains its legitimate prerogative to threaten and employ the use of violence only inasmuch as it respects the BN of its citizens. Conversely the state forfeits its privilege of using coercive force if it uses that power in such a way that denies its citizens their BN. This brings us directly to a consideration of just revolutions or the legitimate use of individual or collective violence by citizens against the state.[3]

When do citizens have the right to assert themselves violently against the state? The question can be addressed only through a case-by-case analysis that calculates a coefficient of revolution on the basis of the compound probability of three independent outcomes: (1) the success factor—the probability that the revolution will succeed if it is launched; (2) the BN factor—the probability that the satisfaction of BN at the X_1, X_2, and X_3 levels will be realized to a significantly greater degree following the revolution; and (3) the noncombatant factor—the probability that the revolution will not entail the extensive loss of life by noncombatants. Obviously the noncombatant factor should not be weighted equally with the other factors if the state is already conducting mass executions in order to intimidate and demoralize its population.

Once the rough probabilities of each one of these factors have been calculated, we are in a position to calculate the coefficient of revolution and to assess whether or not a particular revolution would be sanctioned by the BNM. For example, let us assume that a revolutionary movement within country A has a success factor of .85, a BN factor of .20, and a noncombatant factor of .75. This would mean that the compound probability of the three factors, or coefficient of revolution, is only .13, indicating that even though a revolution had a very high chance of success, its coefficient of revolution was too low to be sanctioned by the BNM. However, if a particular revolutionary movement in country B has a success factor of .65 but a BN factor of .95 and a noncombatant factor of .85, the coefficient of revolution is a fairly respectable .52. Presumably this coefficient would be sufficiently high in order to receive the approval of the BNM. Therefore the BNM would sanction the revolution in country B, even though it had less of a chance of success than the revolution in country A.

Obviously the BNM cannot specify *definitive* thresholds separating just revolutions from unjust revolutions on the basis of a rough measure like the coefficient of revolution. Nonetheless, one would imagine that any revolution with a coefficient above .50 can be reasonably assumed to be a just revolution. Of course, a revolution that has a coefficient in the .25 to .50 range (or perhaps even under .25) may also be a just revolution, if and only if the low coefficient of revolution is due to a low success factor. Under certain extreme circumstances, it may be appropriate to initiate a revolution with only a dismal chance of success for the express purpose of making a political statement about extremely oppressive conditions, thereby mobilizing either world public opinion or major segments of the population in preparation for a subsequent revolutionary movement through the so-called demonstration effect (Greene, 1984, pp. 174–175). In addition, there is some evidence that strategies of nonresistance may, in fact, help aggravate the level of oppression instead of reducing it, suggesting that resistance, even in the most dismal of circumstances, may be the best strategy for decreasing the scope of oppression (Shure et al., 1965).

Now that we have examined some of the implications of the BNM for political systems, we are ready to consider the BNM in relation to economic systems.

NOTES

1. For example, Malenbaum (1982, p. 59) notes that "none of the Third World lands now aspiring to progress has achieved so rapid an expansion of industry as is recorded in China. Similarly, the records of Western development a century or more back offer no comparable rates of industrial expansion over a 3-decade interval."

2. I do not mean to suggest that socialist regimes *cannot* be governed by truly democratic social choice processes. Admittedly, though, most socialist regimes to date have depended on high concentrations of economic and political power in order to secure their existence, placing them squarely within the class of dictatorial political configurations.

3. Throughout the discussion I assume a meaningful distinction between revolutionaries and terrorists. A terrorist, unlike a revolutionary, is concerned about social destabilization, not social transformation. Consequently the terrorist's use of violence is neither strategic nor redemptive. It is violence for the sake of demoralizing the public and undermining their confidence in the government's ability to protect them. Such an arbitrary and unqualified use of violence, irrespective of the ends to which it is ultimately directed, is prohibited by the BNM, in contrast to permissible forms of revolutionary violence.

9
The Basic Needs Mandate and Economic Systems

9.1. ECONOMIC ARRANGEMENTS AND CULTURE UNIVERSALS

Economic arrangements for resource allocation, production, and distribution play a major, and sometimes predominant, role in shaping the structure of any human society. Indeed the enduring contribution of Karl Marx was his recognition of the immense influence of economic structures upon the formation and reproduction of social systems. Unfortunately, though, Marx's theory of dialectical materialism overstated the significance of economic structures in relation to cultural systems and, accordingly, replaced the deterministic ideologies that he branded as "false consciousness" with a new determinism of his own.

Obviously there is a wide range of diversity in the structure of economic arrangements within human societies. Such diversity not only reflects the marked cultural differences among historical societies ranging from nonliterate cultures to modern industrial societies, but also suggests that economic arrangements are intrinsically characterized by a high degree of plasticity in both their form and content. Consequently it is extremely difficult to identify a set of culture universals, insofar as economic arrangements are concerned, from the patchwork quilt of human cultural evolution.

In spite of the inherent pitfalls involved in the identification of culture universals concerning human economic arrangements, it seems reasonable to draw the following bare generalizations on the basis of the available evidence. First, some degree of private property entitlement (or the privileged use and disposition of resources), however limited, is a universal trait of human societies and appears to be a logical extension of human territoriality (D. Miller, 1976, pp. 258–261; Sahlins, 1972, pp. 92–94; E. O. Wilson, 1978, pp. 109–110). Even relatively successful, yet short-lived, attempts to construct small communities that have relinquished nearly all entitlement claims, such as John Humphrey Noyes' Oneida

Community, require an extraordinary amount of religious imagination and a congenial cultural milieu. Second, since the advent of the hunting and gathering way of life, some division of labor has been regularly manifest in human societies (Sahlins, 1972, pp. 78–79). Third, a strong sense of reciprocity (diminished to varying degrees by structures of exploitation) seems to be characteristic of all human communities. This trait is commonly manifest in an array of socially determined rules and mechanisms for assessing value and facilitating exchange, even though the precise meanings and motivations surrounding these patterns of exchange are not easily ascertained (Ekeh, 1974; Mauss, 1967). Fourth, it appears that human economic behavior displays a "satisficing" or "maximin" strategy in resource allocation decisions. In marked contrast to the profit-maximizing, risk-taking image of Homo oeconomicus of neoclassical economic theory, humans appear to make decisions that assure them of a minimal level of security and optimize their nonpecuniary social dividends (Galbraith, 1978, pp. 102–118; Lumsden and Wilson, 1981, p. 90).

9.2. FOUR NORMATIVE PRINCIPLES FOR ECONOMIC ARRANGEMENTS

On the basis of these four descriptive culture universals (i.e., private property entitlements as an extension of human territoriality, a division of labor, reciprocity, and satisficing behavior), it is possible to formulate the following four corresponding normative principles that should guide the arrangement of economic rules and resources.

Principle 1 (P_1):   Economic structures should permit some degree of private property entitlement (territoriality).

Principle 2 (P_2):   Economic structures should permit some opportunity for labor specialization (division of labor).

Principle 3 (P_3):   Economic structures should safeguard conditions of fair exchange (reciprocity).

Principle 4 (P_4):   Economic structures should minimize the probability of BN shortfalls (satisficing).

It should be emphasized that P_4 derives its force not only from the widespread phenomenon of satisficing behavior, but also because P_4 conforms to the requirements of the BNM and its corollary principles (e.g., BN investment ratios, the BN Multiplier Principle, the Principle of Recurrence).

Of course, any of the above principles, taken to its extreme, will necessarily conflict with the other principles. The most obvious conflict appears between P_1 and P_4 in the case of economic systems that absolutize rights to private property (i.e., emphasizing P_1 to the exclusion of P_4) or economic systems that insist on the extensive denial of private property entitlements (i.e., emphasizing P_4 to the exclusion of P_1). Other potential conflicts among the principles include the conflict between P_2 and P_4, which emerges as a by-product of economic specialization, because highly specialized economies allow individuals to pursue widely divergent concepts of happiness in developing their individual talents and skills, at the price of increased economic dependence and interdependence, thereby reducing the individual's sphere of economic self-reliance. Another conflict occurs between P_3 and P_4 insofar as the definition of fair exchange in P_3 precludes tax and redistribution policies designed to actualize P_4 (e.g., Nozick's [1974] entitlement theory of distributive justice).[1]

By using these four economic principles as normative criteria for economic systems that are consistent with the open genetic program of human life, it is possible to infer several mechanisms and objectives for economic policy that presumably should be relevant for all economic systems (see Table 9.1). For example, it is obvious that economic arrangements consistent with P_4 would require some sort of taxation and guaranteed entitlement schemas (manifest in traditional societies by elementary food sharing practices [D. Miller, 1976, pp. 264–266]). Moreover, it would be necessary for the society to establish a social discount rate that optimizes the value of present saving and consumption in relation to the anticipated rates of economic growth and consumption values for future generations. (Given the high rates of population growth in LDCs and the strong correlation between investment in human capital and fertility declines, it can be presumed that the social discount rate will be very low for most LDCs.) Additionally, P_4 would require macroeconomic policies that lead to reasonably stable levels of employment (yet not necessarily full employment). Similarly, economic arrangements conforming to P_1 would seem to imply the following mechanisms/objectives: (1) some provision for the use of material incentives for stimulating productivity and rewarding innovation/risk-taking; (2) the establishment of optimal rates of taxation that avoid significant disincentive effects with respect to economic productivity; and (3) the implementation of judicious macroeconomic policies that strive to limit the deleterious effects of inflation on household incomes. In like manner, P_2 implies some degree of labor mobility, accompanied by structured opportunities for creativity and innovation. Finally P_3 obviously requires some means for determining economic value and facilitating exchange. While the use of competitive markets is probably the most elegant mechanism for assigning economic value and facilitating voluntary exchange, it is certainly not the only mechanism available for this purpose (see Kornai, 1983; Lange and Taylor, 1938; Lerner, 1946).

9.3. PRIMARY CONTRADICTIONS IN CAPITALISM AND SOCIALISM

The areas of conflict among principles P_1-P_4, which were briefly noted above, betray more fundamental contradictions that are present, to some degree, in any economic system. While it was the genius of Marx to illuminate the structural

Table 9.1
Universal Mechanisms/Objectives for Economic Policy

Policy Mechanisms/Objectives	Normative Principle
1. Mechanisms for assessing economic value and facilitating voluntary exchange	P_3
2. Labor mobility	P_2
3. Optimal tax schemas	P_1, P_4
4. Macroeconomic stability	P_1, P_4
5. Optimal social discount rate	P_4
6. Structured opportunities for innovation	P_2
7. Use of material incentives to stimulate productivity and reward innovation/risk-taking	P_1
8. Entitlement to a certain portion of the net social product through (a) social welfare provisions and/or (b) ownership of the means of production.	P_4

contradictions of the capitalist system that prevent the attainment of the golden age equilibrium states envisioned by Adam Smith and others, Marx's concept of human nature led him to the erroneous belief that the socialist system (and the communist utopia that would flower from it) was exempt from similar contradictions. Marx (1964, pp. 113, 138) held that man is a "species-being" who realizes his humanity by (1) consciously "creating a world of objects by his practical activity," and (2) actively recognizing that individual life is "an expression and confirmation of social life," such that "man's individual and species-life are not different." According to Marx, the capitalist mode of production alienates man from his "species-life" in that he no longer has control over the means of production. Because "labor is external to the worker," the worker "only feels himself outside his work, and in his work feels outside himself" (p. 110). This pervasive sense of self-alienation translates into "the estrangement of man from man" (p. 114), and the life of the individual is divorced from one's shared social existence.

The weaknesses inherent in Marx's theory of dialectical materialism (and evidenced in the historical manifestations of state socialism) stem primarily from the oversimplified and distorted image of man embodied in Marx's understanding of Homo faber. By defining man's species-being in terms of his capacity to create worlds of his own choosing, so that "nature appears as *his* work and his reality" (p. 114), Marx indulged in an elaborate anthropocentric fantasy that envisioned boundless possibilities for human cultural evolution. Marx believed that the historical triumph of the communist movement would issue a perfect union between the individual and the collectivity (manifest, in Engels' [1972] words, by the "withering away" of the state), providing human individuality with its true ground and expression.

A broader understanding of the inherent contradictions of human life reveals the shortcomings of both Marxian and capitalist prescriptions for economic and social well-being. Anthony Giddens' (1979, p. 143; 1984, pp. 193–199) illuminating concepts of primary and secondary contradictions provide us with a helpful point of departure in this regard. Primary and secondary contradictions refer to the inherent incongruities among the structural principles of society, as distinguished from simple conflict (which refers to struggles between social actors or collectivities). Primary contradictions refer to those structural contradictions that inhabit the constitution of social totalities, and secondary contradictions represent dependent manifestations of these primary contradictions.

By combining Giddens' notion of primary contradictions with David Stenhouse's (1974) four-factored understanding of intelligence (see Chapter 1, section 1.5.c.), I suggest that there are four primary contradictions that are rooted in the development of human intelligence and, accordingly, are evidenced in human social behavior. It will be recalled that with increased brain size and cortical sophistication, hominids developed markedly enhanced capabilities to conceive and execute courses of intelligent behavior. This enhanced capability for intelligent behavior or "sapientization" was directly related to the maturation of four primary factors that contribute to the occurrence of intelligent behavior: (1) the P factor—an ability to pause before automatically responding to a situation; (2) the C factor—a memory store for the long-term storage of information; (3) the A factor—the capacity to abstract, to generalize, to compare and contrast events; and (4) the D factor—the sensorimotor capability to execute a patterned response. While the development of these factors dramatically expanded the adaptive range of hominids over their primate counterparts, the cost of attaining this new adaptive plateau was a landscape pocked with dissonance-producing realities—revealed by the onset of human consciousness and subjectively experienced as "predicament," "contradiction," or, perhaps, "self-alienation." Table 9.2 presents a suggestive outline of four primary contradictions in relation to each of Stenhouse's four factors of intelligence. I suggest that all religious and secular utopias promise to resolve most, if not all, of these primary contradictions in social life, despite the fact that it is likely that historical man will always have to cope with these and other primary contradictions.

With the maturation of the P factor among hominids, much of human experience has been marked by an increased tension between instinctual or nonreflective responses to environmental/social stimuli and responses that are reflectively formulated and executed (i.e., the conflict between id and ego in Freudian terms). Because the suppression of instinctual responses (P factor) was accompanied by an enhanced repertoire of responses due the maturation of the A and C factors, the complexion of human choice became increasing complex, as the intricacies of individual choice were complicated by social mores (ego versus superego).

While the maturation of the P factor among hominids constituted an essential precondition for the development of human sociality, the C factor (in conjunction with the enhancement of the A and D factors, which made symbolic communication possible) has been perhaps the single most influential aspect of intelligence in shaping human social behavior. The development of a long-term memory store, along with the cognitive and motor abilities to conduct regular and effortless symbolic communication, were necessary requirements in the elaboration of reciprocal altruism and empathetic sensibilities. However, while the C factor has contributed to the distinctive social capabilities that have significantly mitigated the individualistic bent of our mammalian heritage, the C factor has also diminished the possibility that humans will surrender their individuality for the sake of social totalities. On the one hand, the evolution of individual and collective memories has enshrined and stimulated acts of heroism, profound self-sacrificial behavior, and the intense devotion to the well-being of others that we call "love." For individuals, memories associated with early childhood and acute crises in adolescence are clearly the most formative influences in the development of social behavior; and, for collectivities, the memories that are mediated through storytelling and religious traditions are principal factors in the evolution of social values. On the other hand, the bitter individual and collective memories of investing too much trust in others or being overly de-

Table 9.2
Primary Contradictions in Human Social Life

Factor of Intelligence	Contradiction
1. P factor	instinct vs. reflection
2. C factor	dependence vs. independence
3. A factor	finite individual existence vs. the apparent infinity of time-space
4. D factor	engagement vs. boredom

pendent on others have naturally tempered human social sensibilities, except in those cases where humans temporarily cling, for one reason or another, to expansive and sometimes alluring utopian ideologies that use devotion to the social totality as a pretense for self-actualization. This primary contradiction between dependence and independence is experienced by individuals and collectivities in a variety of emotional dyads such as "trust versus mistrust," "gratitude versus vengeance," "loyalty versus betrayal," "love versus hate" and "patriotism versus treason." The familiar interplay of individualism versus organicism in political arrangements and autarky versus interdependence in economic arrangements is little more than a reflection of the more fundamental tension between dependence and independence that has accompanied the development of the C factor in human sociality.

The maturation of the A factor among hominids, in conjunction with the development of self-consciousness, led to the contradiction between individual finitude in contrast to the apparent infinity of time and space. As Giddens (1979, p. 161) suggests, this contradiction probably lies at the heart of all religions, perhaps being first evidenced in Neanderthal burial rituals in the Upper Pleistocene.[2] One of the earliest attempted resolutions of this contradiction was the ancient phenomenon that the late Mircea Eliade (1954, 1959) identified as "the myth of the eternal return," referring to the attempt by ancient or nonliterate peoples to mythically reverse time by the repeated ritual recreation of the world. In essence, the myth of the eternal return represents an attempt to deny the infinity of time and space by giving humans the prerogative to recreate or repeat historical processes whenever they choose.

Finally, with the extraordinary expansion of the neocortex in the brief transition between Homo habilis and Homo sapiens and the development of a three-dimensional array of synaptic circuits (Shepherd, 1983, pp. 575–577), humans experienced a quantum leap in neurological circuitry that outdistanced their relatively modest achievements in the evolution of psychomotor capabilities (i.e., the D factor). As a consequence, humans have far more intellectual capabilities than they could ever utilize in the course of everyday life. The striking disparity between the phenomenal intellectual capabilities of humans and their comparatively modest psychomotor requirements has introduced the unsettling contradiction between engagement and boredom in human experience. Humans have attempted to resolve the gap between intellectual capabilities and psychomotor requirements through a variety of ingenious means, including the use of drugs (i.e., depressants to reduce intellectual capabilities and stimulants to augment perceived psychomotor capabilities), the management of mystical and ecstatic experiences, and the execution of physical activities that require intense concentration—where the subject feels as if his body and mind are one (e.g., rock climbing, professional dancing, playing a musical instrument, painting a picture) (Crook, 1980). This primary contradiction between engagement and boredom suggests that Marx's glorification of Homo faber is quite unsatisfactory, as some degree of self-alienation will always be present in the life of the worker, presuming that only a small percentage of the productive tasks in any society will genuinely utilize an individual's intellectual potential.

Of the four primary contradictions mentioned above, the contradiction between independence and dependence (factor C) is clearly the most important in our analysis of the capitalist and socialist economic systems. On the one hand, capitalism thrives on individualistic behavior (i.e., independence); and, on the other hand, socialism is predicated on cooperative behavior (i.e., dependence). The individualistic bias of capitalist systems gains expression in economic and social values that encourage self-interest and competition; and the cooperative bias of socialist systems is expressed in terms of economic and social values that encourage solidarity and collaboration. Table 9.3 presents a partial and admittedly oversimplified typology of some of the more prominent differences between the two systems, and Table 9.4 presents a fourfold typology of the historical variants of both systems. I assume that the principal difference between capitalist and socialist systems concerns the magnitude of public-sector involvement in production, with capitalist systems having minimal public-sector involvement and socialist regimes allocating a large role to the public sector in the ownership and control of the means of production.

In spite of the notable differences between capitalism and socialism, there is one major assumption that is shared by both systems, at least in their pure forms: If you solve the problem of production, you have solved the problem of distribution. For capitalists, the problem of distribution is resolved by the so-called invisible hand of the market, which automatically optimizes the use of resources and unerringly pays the factors of production their marginal product. For Marxists, the problems of distribution are automatically solved by placing the means of production into "the hands of the workers" (which typically becomes a synonym for "the hands of the state").

There are good reasons to think that both the capitalist and socialist modes of production must be supplemented by *countervailing* modes of distribution if either economic system is to survive in the long term. In this respect, John Stuart Mill (1965, pp. 299–301) was quite correct in insisting that the principles of production should be kept analytically distinct from socially determined principles of distribution.

In my estimation, the chief weakness of both the capitalist and socialist systems is their failure to acknowledge the necessity of regulating territorial/dominance aggression in human societies (see Chapter 4, section 4.1.c). Capitalism monetizes dominance/territorial aggression and socialism bureaucratizes the same. In capitalism, the monetization of territorial/dominance aggression takes the form of the so-called paradox of competition: Competitive states over time produce noncompetitive states (due to the detrimental impact of the concentration of income, wealth, and power on competition). In socialism, the bureaucratization of territorial/dominance aggression takes the form of the assertion of bureaucratic/state privilege over and against the rights of individuals.

An interpretation of the primary and secondary contradictions of the capitalist

Table 9.3
Distinguishing Features of Capitalism and Socialism

Concept/Characteristic	Capitalism	Socialism
1. Theory of Sociality	Atomistic	Organic
2. Structure of Economic Decision Making	Decentralized	Centralized
3. Structure of Production	Private	Public
4. Entitlement Structure	Private Ownership	Communal Ownership
5. Incentive Structure	Material	Nonmaterial
6. Concept of Freedom	Negative (freedom from)	Positive (freedom to)
7. Dominant Ethical Value	Competition	Solidarity

Table 9.4
Typology of Historical Variants of the Capitalist and Socialist Systems

System	Examples
Pure Capitalism	England and the U.S. in the 19th century; Chile after 1973; South Africa
Mixed (or Welfare) Capitalism	U.S., England, India, Sweden, France, Canada, Japan, Federal Republic of Germany, Sri Lanka
Command Socialism	U.S.S.R., North Korea, Vietnam, Cuba, China (1958-78)
Mixed (or Market) Socialism	Yugoslavia, China (after 1978), Hungary, Tanzania

183

Figure 9.1
Primary and Secondary Contradictions in Capitalism and Socialism

	Capitalism	Socialism
Primary Contra-diction	Private Appropriation vs. Socialized Production	Socialized Ownership vs. Bureaucratic Control
Secondary Contra-diction	Hegemony of the Nation-State vs. the Internationalization of Capital	State Privilege vs. Ideologies of Equality

and socialist systems appears in Figure 9.1.[3] The primary contradiction of the capitalist system is between the private appropriation and socialized production, as Engels (1972) suggested. The secondary contradiction of the capitalist system is the global manifestation of the paradox of competition: the hegemony of the nation-state versus the internationalization of capital. This secondary contradiction gains expression not only in terms of hot and cold forms of imperialism, but also in oligopolistic/oligopsonistic market power that gives the rich and privileged a comparative advantage. The primary contradiction of socialist systems is between the socialized ownership of economic resources and the necessary role of bureaucratic/state authorities in exercising control over the use and disposition of those resources (see E. Friedman, 1984; Van Ness and Raichur, 1983). The secondary contradiction of the socialist system is the contradiction between state privilege and the socialist ideals of equality, manifest in "étatism" and monopolistic managerial behavior that conforms to the institutional aims of bureaucratic territoriality and aggrandizement.

It seems reasonable to assume that any economic system that hopes to survive the test of time must come to terms with the realities of human territorial/dominance aggression. For capitalist systems, this will mean linking decentralized schemes of resource allocation and production with centralized schemes of distribution or redistribution (i.e., welfare capitalism). For socialist systems, this will mean linking centralized schemes of resource allocation and production with decentralized schemes of distribution (i.e., market socialism). Moreover, it seems self-evident that any mixed form of capitalism or socialism will always exhibit some manifestations of the primary contradiction associated with the pure form of the system. In mixed capitalist systems, the primary contradiction between private appropriation and socialized production is manifest in the familiar trade-off between economic growth and the disincentive effects and deadweight costs associated with policies aimed at redistributing the national product (Arrow, 1979; Okun, 1975). In mixed socialist systems, the primary contradiction between socialized ownership and bureaucratic control gains expression in the trade-off between inefficiencies in production (due chiefly to the "soft budget constraint" of the socialist firm and oligopolistic bargaining among the organs of management) and the minimization of economic inequality/insecurity (Hussain, 1983; Kornai, 1980; Nove, 1983).

It is difficult to know whether or how the primary and secondary contradictions of both the capitalist and socialist systems can be structurally balanced in a workable fashion. One would suspect, though, that the meager yet promising instances of worker-owned and managed firms may point us in the direction of an answer (see Jones, 1980; Oakeshott, 1978; Vanek, 1975). For example, the Mondragon cooperatives in the Basque region of Spain have demonstrated that the twin goals of worker productivity and economic equity/security can be achieved simultaneously in a capitalist environment (Thomas and Logan, 1982). The Mondragon cooperatives have succeeded in narrowing income differentials without discouraging individual productivity, in assuring workers of a high degree of security while maintaining a high level of discipline in the workplace, and in instituting a mix of decentralized and centralized mechanisms for decision making that permit the cooperatives to either match or exceed the rates of investment, innovation, and profitability of their capitalist counterparts.

Certainly the most extensive application of the concept of workers' management has taken place in Yugoslavia, beginning in 1950 (see Estrin, 1983; Horvat, 1976; Pašić et al., 1982; Prout, 1985; Sacks, 1983; Schrenk et al., 1979; Tyson, 1980). Unfortunately, though, it is difficult to draw any firm conclusions about the viability of self-managed enterprises on the basis of the Yugoslavian experience. On the one hand, it appears that self-management has increased the overall level of productivity, as evidenced by the attainment of very high rates of economic growth and a decidedly improved standard of living, without sacrificing the income equality characteristic of its East European counterparts. On the other hand, it is clear that a decentralized regime of self-managed enterprises is no substitute for coordinated macroeconomic policies and some degree of centralized economic planning, at least for a small, open economy like Yugoslavia. In spite of high rates of capital accumulation and its excellent growth record, the Yugoslavian economy suffers from extremely high rates of inflation, fairly high levels of persistent unemployment, a deteriorating balance of payments, substantial constraints on the mobility of capital and labor, artificially low interest rates, imbalances in sectoral and regional growth, and the unhappy coincidence of a high degree of economic intervention at the regional (republican) level with the lack of effective macroeconomic coordination at the federal level.

Obviously one must be very careful not to ascribe Yugoslavia's macroeconomic problems to its system of workers' self-management. The determination of the Yugoslavian people to improve and refine their self-managed economic system and the country's impressive growth performance suggest that while the experiment may not be an unqualified success, it is certainly not a failure. (For example, 75% of the strikes in Yugoslavia last one day or less and only 5% go for more than four days. Nearly two-thirds of work stoppages in Yugoslavia involve less than 100 persons [Prout, 1985, pp. 50–52].) Moreover, it is difficult to generalize upon the experience of Yugoslavian self-managed enterprises for other types of producer cooperatives, because individual workers do not actually own shares in the enterprise, as most producer cooperatives. Because the enterprise is "social property," according to the Yugoslavian Communist Party, the enterprise is "owned" by the whole of society and only "used" by the enterprise. Consequently there is a tendency in Yugoslavian enterprises for workers to allocate profits for increased wages instead of investment, as they have no financial stake in the long-term success of the enterprise. Even so, the investment rate in Yugoslavia is still very high.

Perhaps the most significant drawback of producer cooperatives is their inherent bias toward capital-intensive production techniques, as it will always make more sense for producer cooperatives to augment the productivity of individual workers through increasing the ratio of capital to labor instead of adding new workers to the cooperative. This is certainly no small concern in light of the desirability of labor-intensive technologies in economies with a large surplus of labor. Presumably, though, producer cooperatives operating in competitive markets, which are relatively accessible to new entrants, will be forced to respond to factor-price relationships in their choice of production techniques, thereby mitigating the capital-intensive bias of such cooperative ventures.

Of course, it is also possible to replicate some of the positive dimensions of worker-owned and managed firms by introducing various forms of industrial democracy in the workplace, ranging from participatory management styles in Japan and profit-sharing schemes in the United States to the West German policy of codetermination. Obviously the time has long passed when we can think of economic systems in terms of canonical iron laws and permit ideological or methodological variants of determinism to stifle human creativity. It is time for us to celebrate the tremendous plasticity and diversity of economic organization by encouraging experimentation and flexibility in the search for more effective and humane forms of economic organization.

NOTES

1. Standing firmly within the libertarian tradition, Robert Nozick (1974) regards freedom as a preeminent human good. Nozick's strong preference for individual freedom (and his corresponding absolutist theory of private property) is born from the conviction that people's life plans are so vastly different that it is not possible to find a common denominator other than the fact that different people have different preferences (p. 310). Hence he would affirm the premise that (1) "freedom is integral to human life." However, because Nozick's concept of human inviolability (which he refers to as "side-constraints") is derived strictly from the ability of humans to freely select and reflectively pursue different courses of action (including the freedom to sell oneself into slavery), he is logically constrained to restate premise 1 in stronger terms: (2) "freedom is the *only* good integral to human life." At first blush premise 2 looks ridiculous, and I assume that Nozick would agree with this assessment. Perhaps, then, a step or two has been missed in understanding Nozick's theory of the good.

Let us assume, for the sake of argument, that Nozick accepts that some goods are necessary for physical survival, even though he is unwilling to articulate this formally in some concept of human need (p. 169, fn.). Hence he could argue that premise 2 assumes that persons in a libertarian society have sufficient food, shelter, medical care, and such in a particular time period (t). This assumption could be based on one of two grounds: (1) the principle of rectification (i.e., past injustices have been rectified) has been judiciously and consistently applied to correct for previous instances of coercive exploitation; or (2) a perfectly competitive market system will never permit Pareto violations (i.e., making one person better off at another's expense). Because Nozick's principle of rectification is clearly a "historical" (and not an "end-state") principle of justice, it is not a sufficient ground for the libertarian assumption that freedom operates against a backdrop of other essential human goods. Hence only the theory of perfect competition (with its welfare outcome of Pareto optimality) can sustain this crucial libertarian assumption. Consequently premise 2 must be expanded to the following: (3)

"freedom is the only good integral to human life in time period t if and only if there have been no significant Pareto violations in market transactions during $t-1, t-2, \ldots t-n$."

The obvious crux of premise 3 is determining what constitutes a "significant" Pareto violation. Clearly Nozick's libertarian economy could, at best, only approximate the theoretical ideal of perfect competition. It is only reasonable to expect that some market failures (e.g., monopolistic and oligopolistic pricing) or external diseconomies will take place in the Nozickean minimal state, thereby generating distributions that are not Pareto optimal, creating random inequalities in income and wealth. The cumulative effect of these predictable Pareto violations could be gaping economic inequalities, producing high rates of unwarranted mortality, morbidity, and so on.

Let us assume that "significant" Pareto violations are defined in terms of violations that show up as contributing causes of such undesirable outcomes as unwarranted mortality or morbidity. Given this understanding, we may expand premise 3 to the following: (4) "freedom is the only good integral to human life in time period t if and only if there have been no Pareto violations in market transactions during $t-1, t-2, \ldots, t-n$ which are contributing causes of a set of undesirable outcomes."

Clearly premise 4 (which makes explicit the background assumptions of premise 2) is an "end-state" axiom that aims at the minimization of a particular set of undesirable outcomes in a market economy. Because it is an end-state axiom, premise 4 would be patently unacceptable in Nozick's system. Yet, curiously, premise 4 rescues Nozick from the absurdity of premise 2.

2. In the Shanidar cave of the Zagros Mountains of Iraq, a Neanderthal man was laid to rest on a bed of flowers (c. 60,000 years ago). See Leakey and Lewin (1977, p. 177).

3. The primary and secondary contradictions of capitalism are drawn from Giddens (1979, p. 143). Giddens (1981, p. 248) also suggests that the primary contradiction of socialist society "is between the planned organization of production, mediated through the state, and the mass participation of the population in decisions and policies that affect the course of their lives." I question, though, whether an essential and prominent contradiction exists between planning and participation, particularly in the case of participatory market socialist economies like Yugoslavia. To some extent, the tension between planning and participation will exist in any large-scale bureaucracy, whether it is capitalist or socialist.

10
The Basic Needs Mandate and International Law

10.1. PRIMARY AND SECONDARY RULES OF LAW

The normative prescriptions of the BNM for public policy extend well beyond the political and economic systems of contemporary nation-states to include the realm of international law as well—a logical consequence of the character of the BNM as a species-ethic. The impact of the BNM on the state-centric paradigm of contemporary international law would be to enhance significantly the scope and regulatory machinery of *jus cogens* norms (see section 10.5) in the international order, with the concomitant effects of a strengthened role for human rights norms in international law and the increased prominence of intergovernmental organizations (IGOs), international nongovernmental organizations (INGOs), and global issues regimes within the international system. The effect of these changes on the international order would be to modify markedly (yet not dismantle) the concept of state sovereignty as it emerged from the Peace of Westphalia in 1648.

While there is much skepticism that anything like an international law exists in the current structure of international relations, due to the notable absence of a central judiciary with compulsory jurisdiction and an empowered sanctioning authority designed to enforce international conventions, there are strong reasons to believe that not all forms of law necessarily require a centralized sanctioning authority. H. L. A. Hart's (1961) distinction between primary and secondary rules of law is especially illuminating in this regard.

Hart argues that all legal systems can be analyzed in terms of (1) primary rules of obligation that specify impermissible modes of behavior for the members of a society, and (2) secondary rules of recognition, change, and adjudication that govern the implementation of primary rules. Using this distinction, Hart understands the international legal system as a collection of primary rules, similar in structure to the institution of law in primitive societies, "even though the content of its often elaborate rules are very unlike those of a primitive society, and many of its concepts, methods, and techniques are the same as those of modern municipal law'' (p. 222). In spite of the fact that the secondary rules of recognition, change, and adjudication are largely absent from the international order, the presence of primary rules of obligation (conceptually distinct from moral rules) is sufficient to warrant the use of the term ''law'' when referring to the customary and conventional norms that coordinate the actions of states and ''codify regularities'' within the international system (see D. Lewis, 1969, p. 103). To deny legal status to such primary rules of obligation, according to Hart,

is tacitly to accept the analysis of obligation contained in the theory that law is essentially a matter of orders backed by threats. This theory . . . identifies ''having an obligation'' or ''being bound'' with ''likely to suffer the sanction or punishment threatened for disobedience.'' Yet this identification distorts the role played in all legal thought and discourse of the ideas of obligation and duty. Even in municipal law, where there are effective organized sanctions, we must distinguish . . . the meaning of the external predictive statement ''I (you) are likely to suffer for disobedience,'' from the internal normative statement ''I (you) have an obligation to act thus'' which assesses a particular person's situation from the point of view of rules accepted as guiding standards of behavior (pp. 212–213).

Significantly, even when states opt to disregard such primary rules of obligation, ''it is not on the footing that they are not binding; instead efforts are made to conceal the facts'' (p. 215).

10.2. STATE-BOUND VERSUS STATE-TRANSCENDENT INTERNATIONAL NORMS

Assuming that we may credibly attribute legal status to the assortment of coordinating norms that, by force of precedent, achieve the authoritative status of international law, we are in a position to assess whether or not the BNM could inform the content and justification of international law. On the one hand, if international law consists solely of state-bound norms, finding its ultimate source of content and justification in the explicit consent of individual states, then international law is neither a pliable nor promising medium for the BNM. On the other hand, if a substantial portion of international law is informed by state-transcendent norms, which derive their authority from shared values that transcend state borders, then the BNM could find a ''normative niche'' within the current structure of international law.

Tables 10.1 and 10.2 detail some of the manifestations of state-bound and state-transcendent norms within the current structure of positive international law, along with selected political/economic factors that help undergird each of the respective norms. At the outset, though, it should be noted that despite the rather lengthy list of legal manifestations of state-transcendent norms, state-

Table 10.1
International Law as State-Bound Norms

Legal Manifestations

— U.N. Charter (Preamble, articles 1.2, 2.1, 2.7, 95).

— Statute of the International Court of Justice (articles 38, 59).

— Past decisions by the International Court of Justice.

— Declaration on Principles of International Law Concerning Friendly Relations and Cooperation Among States in Accordance with the Charter of the United Nations (1970).

— The presence of denunciation clauses in all multilateral conventions.

— The absence of legal sanctions for self-help or coordinated 'humanitarian intervention' against states which are implementing genocidal policies.

— The virtual sanctity of the principles of territorial sovereignty and nonintervention as the foundation of international law, as reflected in both custom and convention.

Underlying Economic/Political Factors

— The rapid proliferation of newly independent states.

— The near universal rejection of recent colonial experience.

— The prominence of nationalism as a strategy of statecraft.

— The difficulty of achieving coordinated economic or military sanctions and their relative ineffectiveness.

— The economic and political isolation of a number of powerful states (e.g., the Soviet bloc, China)

Table 10.2
International Law as State-Transcendent Norms

Legal Manifestations

— Slavery Convention (1926, amended 1953): 77 ratifications

— Convention Concerning Forced or Compulsory Labor (1930)

— Charters of the Nuremberg and Tokyo War Crimes Tribunals

— U. N. Charter (Preamble, articles 1.2, 1.3, 2.6, 13.1, 55-57, 62, 73, 76)

— Freedom of Association and Protection of the Right to Organize Convention (1948)

— Convention on the Prevention and Punishment of the Crime of Genocide (1948): 89 ratifications

— Universal Declaration of Human Rights (1948)

— The four Geneva Conventions on the treatment of war victims (1949)

— European Convention for the Protection of Human Rights and Fundamental Freedoms, and the establishment of the European Commission on Human Rights (1950)

— Convention Relating to the Status of Refugees (1951): 90 ratifications

— Convention on the Political Rights of Women (1953): 90 ratifications

— Convention Relating to the Status of Stateless Persons (1954): 32 ratifications

— Supplementary Convention on the Abolition of Slavery, the Slave Trade, and Institutions and Practices Similar to Slavery (1956): 96 ratifications

— International Convention on the Elimination of All Forms of Racial Discrimination (1966): 115 ratifications

— International Covenant on Economic, Social and Cultural Rights (1966): 73 ratifications

— International Covenant on Civil and Political Rights (1966): 70 ratifications

— The Concept of *Jus Cogens* in the Vienna Convention on the Law of Treaties (1969)

— American Convention on Human Rights (1969)

— Declaration on Principles of International Law Concerning Friendly Relations and Cooperation Among States in Accordance with the Charter of the United Nations (1970)

— The trend from consent to consensus in international quasi-legal fora

— The ascendency of the principle of self-determination in international law

— The presumption of common good norms in the use of international rivers and regions of the ocean beyond the territorial or economic jurisdiction of states (e.g., U.N. Convention on the Law of the Sea, 1982, articles 136, 137, 140, 150)

— Convention on the Elimination of all forms of Discrimination Against Women (1979): 70 ratifications

Underlying Political/Economic Factors

— Regionalism (e.g., ASEAN, the EEC, the Andean Group)

— Economic Interdependence

— The rapid proliferation of IGOs and INGOs since 1945.

— The prominence of certain global issue regimes and the ascendancy of technological values

— The development of international public opinion as a recognizable entity in world affairs

bound norms currently enjoy a significantly greater degree of legal authority, due largely to the virtual sanctity of the principles of territorial sovereignty, sovereign equality, and nonintervention in both the customary and conventional evidences of international law. Nonetheless one cannot help but be impressed by the ascendancy of state-transcendent norms within the international order. However, while presumably the momentum is in the favor of state-transcendent norms, this trend is by no means conclusive. For instance, Navari (1982, p. 22) contends that the 20th-century norms of modernization have not diminished the authority of the state, but instead have made the state "more extensive and more powerful," given the perceived role of the state as "an engine of modernisation."

The conceptualization of international law as an authoritative collection of state-bound norms (particularly the norms of territorial sovereignty, sovereign equality, and nonintervention) finds its origin in the progressive development of the distinct yet related notions of state sovereignty and the moral personality of the state, as reflected in the thoughts of Machiavelli, Bodin, Grotius, Hobbes, Rousseau, Vattel, Hegel, and Mazzini (Klein, 1974). In terms of international law, the work of Emmerich de Vattel (1863) represents an especially significant synthesis between the dual notions of the state's sovereignty and moral personality. Vattel's analogy of states as persons significantly exceeded Grotius' notion of the "will of all nations" (which referred to the will of individual agents of the state instead of the reification of the state [Edwards, 1981]), and the analogy has since exercised great influence in the development of international law. Only recently has the philosophical cogency of the analogy of states as persons been challenged on grounds other than natural law—a challenge that has demonstrated the philosophical bankruptcy of the analogy (Beitz, 1979).

Vattel's concept of a reified, personified nation-state endowed with inalienable rights has been enshrined in both word and deed in the current structure of international law (see Brownlie, 1979, pp. 294–295, 595; R. Higgins, 1963, pp. 38–130; Luard, 1984; UN Charter, Art. 2.7). Moreover the state-bound conception of international law finds an exceptionally strong affirmation within the voluntaristic framework of the International Court of Justice (or World Court), which may only render a judgment on disputes that the contending states have voluntarily submitted to the court's jurisdiction. Since the *Fisheries Jurisdiction* cases of 1971, the recent trend of nonappearance by respondent states has provided vivid evidence of the functional limitations of the court's jurisdiction (Thirlway, 1985).

Additional manifestations of the state-bound conception of international law can be discerned from the traditional enumeration of the sources of international law as set forth in Article 38.1 of the Statute of the International Court of Justice. While Article 38.1 is quite remarkable in that it grants the court a limited lawmaking function in terms of its appropriation of (1) "the general principles of law recognized by civilized nations," (2) its own judicial precedent, and (3) "the teachings of the most highly qualified publicists of the various nations" (the latter two sources designated as "subsidiary means for the determination of rules of law''), there is little doubt that the framers of the article intended state conventions and custom to be the primary determinants of international law. In accordance with this original intention, the court has maintained a very conservative posture in terms of understanding its own judicial competence in relation to the prerogatives of sovereign states. This conservative interpretation of judicial competence seems to have eroded the moral authority of the court, as witnessed by the decline of the court's influence since the controversial second phase of the *South West Africa* cases in 1966 (see Partan, 1985).

The state-bound conception of international law is further sanctioned by the routine practice of permitting any party to a multilateral treaty, such as the Genocide Convention of 1948, the option of withdrawing from the convention after serving due notice. The presence of these denunciation clauses in multilateral treaties, along with the notable absence of effective machinery to sanction treaty violations, underscores the importance of *voluntary* state compliance within the current structure of international law. Consequently there is ample support for the interpretation of international law as an authoritative collection of state-bound norms.

However, there is growing evidence that certain state-transcendent norms—primarily related to the notion of individual human rights—are playing an ascendant role in the definition of international legal norms. The various legal manifestations of such state-transcendent international norms can be found in a variety of multilateral conventions, including the Charter of the United Nations, which advocates the protection of basic human rights and the advancement of human material and social well-being. In this regard, it should be noted that the U.N. Charter was the first multilateral treaty that included a general commitment on the part of its signatories to look after the welfare of their own citizens by promoting "universal respect for, and observance of, human rights and fundamental freedoms for all without distinction as to race, sex, language, or religion" (Art. 55.c) (see Carey, 1972).

Moreover, in addition to state-transcendent human rights norms, notions of the common good have figured prominently in international legal instruments concerning the utilization of international rivers (Livingston, 1972). However the most explicit manifestation of such common good norms to date was evidenced in the 15 years of negotiations leading up to the U.N. Convention on the Law of the Sea (1982). A major point of debate between LDCs and MDCs during the negotiations concerned the establishment of an International Seabed Authority that would redistribute a portion of the profits from the deep seabed mining of polymetallic nodules in regions of the oceans beyond the 200-mile "exclusive economic zone" for living resources and the continental shelf for mineral resources. Significantly, this "undeclared" area of the world's oceans was identified by Article 136 of the convention as "the common heritage of mankind" (see Sebenius, 1984). Additionally, common good norms underlie the general trend from consent to consensus in the conceptualization of international legal obligations, or what Richard Falk (1972) has aptly termed the movement from a "Westphalia conception" of the international order to a "Charter conception." A most significant manifestation in this regard is Article 2.6 of the U.N. Charter, which presumes that the charter's principles should even apply to nations who have not given their consent to the charter, insofar as this "may be necessary for the maintenance of international peace and security."

Certainly the most dramatic manifestation of state-transcendent norms in our day is the ill-defined yet persuasive principle of "self-determination." While there is much controversy as to the legal status of this principle, there is little doubt that the Wilsonian norm of self-determination has been an exceedingly powerful political principle in shaping the affairs of states during the latter half of the 20th century. Whereas there were only 51 members of the United Nations in 1945 and much of the world was dominated by a few colonial powers, today there are three times as many members and only a few colonial territories still dot the earth. Whereas the U.N. Charter makes only passing mention of the principle of "the self-determination of peoples" (articles 1.2, 55) and nowhere speaks of the "right" of self-determination, the nonbinding yet influential Declaration on Principles of International Law Concerning Friendly Relations and Cooperation Among States in Accordance with the Charter of the United Nations (1970) devotes considerable attention to the principle of self-determination (see Pomerance, 1982).

Unfortunately there are numerous conceptual ambiguities surrounding the principle of self-determination, primarily focused on the definition of "self" in self-determination and the adjudication of claims of self-determination against competing claims by other relevant parties (see Beitz, 1979, pp. 92–115; Paust, 1980). Because of these conceptual ambiguities, claims of self-determination have evidenced considerable variance in moral authority, as the principle has been invoked by political leaders as diverse as Mahatma Gandhi and Adolf Hitler (Friedlander, 1980). To some extent the UN's Declaration on Principles of International Law (1970) has tried to qualify the principle of self-determination in order to prevent its use by repressive governments (who understand the self in self-determination to refer to their particular regime). For instance, the declaration states the following:

Nothing in the foregoing paragraphs shall be construed as authorizing or encouraging any action which would dismember or impair, totally or in part, the territorial integrity or political unity of sovereign and independent States conducting themselves in compliance with the principle of equal rights and self-determination of peoples as described above and *thus possessed of a government representing the whole people belonging to the territory without distinction as to race, creed or color* [emphasis added].

However, in point of fact, claims for self-determination are only seriously entertained within the United Nations when directed against a traditional colonial power. By contrast, claims directed against noncolonial regimes are ignored by the General Assembly (e.g., Biafra, Kurdistan, the southern Sudan, Eritrea, Formosa, Tibet) (Finger and Singh, 1980; Klein, 1974, pp. 143–155). In practice, claims for self-determination have only been effective against colonial regimes (with East Pakistan and the Palestine Liberation Organization as notable exceptions); and, once a colonial power has been expelled, there is little hope for successionist movements within the newly independent country. Consequently the principle of self-determination has been invoked more as a political principle that served the interests of rapid decolonization, instead of functioning as a moral or legal principle that actually guides the conduct of states. Presumably the principle of self-determination has seen its heyday, and its functional influence will steadily decline, irrespective of the rhetorical power of the principle in forays against the remnants of colonialism and economic neo-colonialism. If this observation is correct, the recent history of the principle of self-determination provides us with a poignant example of how powerful state-transcendent norms can be co-opted and absorbed within the predominant state-bound conception of international law.

10.3. POLITICAL AND ECONOMIC FACTORS ASSOCIATED WITH STATE-BOUND AND STATE-TRANSCENDENT NORMS

Since international law gradually reflects structural changes within the global political and economic landscape (by virtue of the prominent role of custom in the definition of international law), it stands to reason that both the state-bound and state-transcendent conceptions of international law have been influenced and supported by certain political/institutional developments. A brief listing of some selected underlying political factors appears in Tables 10.1 and 10.2.

Certainly the most prominent political factor that supports the state-bound conception of international law is the rapid proliferation of newly independent states within the Third World. In most cases, these states face immense political and economic obstacles in consolidating their national identity, due to the prevalence of illiteracy, poor communication systems, inadequate or deteriorating transportation infrastructures, a pronounced degree of cultural and social segmentation (e.g., colonial borders that crosscut tribal allegiances), and the absence of strong nongovernmental institutions that limit the power of central regimes. Given the formidable obstacles that hinder the formation of a national identity, it should not surprise us that 125 of the 130 wars that have been fought since 1945 have taken place in the Third World and over 100 of these have been tribal, religious, separatist, or antiregime wars (Navari, 1982, p. 28). In the face of these challenges to national development, most Third World regimes have resorted to cult-like nationalistic ideologies that legitimate the expansion of state power through modernization strategies of either a capitalist or socialist genre. Consequently, it only stands to reason that when LDC representatives converge at international fora, the doctrines of territorial sovereignty, nonintervention, and sovereign equality figure prominently in joint resolutions and legal instruments emanating from such gatherings.

Beyond the self-serving interests of nationalism, an additional affirmation of the state-bound conceptualization of international law is related to the doctrine of the sovereign equality of states and its role in accelerating the demise of colonialism. While the state-transcendent norm of self-determination has provided the immediate inspiration of decolonialization since 1945, the seeds of decolonialization were already planted, at a conceptual level, by the European doctrine of the sovereign equality of states. With the development of the European society of states, the notion of the sovereign equality of states was applied, albeit unevenly, to non-European and non-Christian peoples. Unfortunately, though, the doctrine of constitutive recognition (i.e., states attain sovereignty by recognition from other states) and the prevalence of racist ideologies permitted European colonial powers the luxury of avoiding the revolutionary implications of their doctrine of the sovereign equality of states. However, with the unmasking of the self-serving notion of constitutive recognition (and the corresponding ascendancy of claims of self-determination) and the debunking of racist ideologies, the doctrine of sovereign equality provided an important theoretical underpinning for the dissolution of colonial territories (see Bull, 1984). Given the near universal rejection of colonialism and our close temporal proximity to the era of European colonialism, it only stands to reason that the doctrine of the sovereign equality of states has received a cherished status by the international community (and the related yet noncorrelative norms of territorial sovereignty and nonintervention have benefited by association).

Another powerful locus of support for the state-bound conception of international law is communist states and their client regimes. The so-called Group D countries (i.e., the Soviet voting bloc) and China are consistently among the strongest supporters of absolute state sovereignty, and it is not immediately apparent that this posture will be modified at any time in the foreseeable future, given the relative political and economic isolation of these countries and the tendency in Marxist-Leninist ideology to subordinate notions of morality, law, and human rights under the higher calling of proletarian revolution (e.g., the view that human rights cannot be violated in a communist state). Consequently any attempt to assert state-transcendent, humanitarian norms over and against the prerogatives of national sovereignty is bound to encounter strong resistance from the communist states.

Obviously none of these political factors bode well for the development of state-transcendent norms within the international legal order. Nonetheless there are several recent political trends that could eventually provide strong footholds for state-transcendent norms.

Certainly the most notable political development in the formation and dissemination of state-transcendent norms consists of the rapid proliferation of intergovernmental organizations and international nongovernmental organizations (see Taylor, 1984). Whereas there were only 25 IGOs in 1820, by 1960 their number grew to over 175—more than doubling during the brief 20-year period between 1940 and 1960. In Asia alone, IGOs multiplied from 1 organization in 1950 to 25 in 1975 (Sullivan, 1982). Currently there are approximately 300 IGOs, and there is a strong likelihood that they will stabilize at that number (Archer, 1983, p. 171). An even greater magnitude of growth has been experienced by INGOs. In 1850 there was only one organization that met the Union of International Associations' criteria for an INGO. By 1950 there were over 300 INGOs, and from 1954 to 1968 the growth rate of active INGOs averaged 4.7% each year (Skjelsback, 1971). There are now approximately 3,000 INGOs. With a modest rate of growth, the number of INGOs could grow to 9,600 by the year 2000 (Archer, 1983, p. 171). Moreover, the Nonstate Actor Project (NOSTAC), using event data, discovered that from 1948 to 1972, 56% of the international interactions involved a nonstate organization as either an actor or target, and over 11% of the international interactions involved nonstate actors exclusively (Mansbach et al., 1976, pp. 275–276).

An increasingly prominent yet ambiguous manifestation of the ascendancy of nonstate actors in global politics is the emergence of large transnational corporations (TNCs). Table 10.3 attempts to capture the magnitude of these nonstate actors in the global arena by combining the 100 largest GDPs of nation-states with the largest gross annual revenues of TNCs for 1984. While this mode of comparison is deficient in some respects, it provides us with an overall picture of the relative magnitude of TNCs in relation to contemporary nation-states in terms of annual income. According to the 1984 data, the top 21 income producers were states, ranging from the United States in first place to Switzerland, ranked 21st. However, beginning with Exxon, ranked 22nd, TNCs play a predominant role as sources of global income. In this regard, Royal Dutch/Shell is ranked ahead of Belgium and Czechoslovakia, General Motors ahead of Nigeria and South Africa, Mobil ahead of Denmark and Finland, Ford ahead of Thailand, and so forth. Altogether 40 out of the 100 top global income producers are TNCs, and less than 40% of the world's countries made the list.

If power follows wealth, one would expect that the emergence of the large TNC heralds a dramatic transformation in the international order—a transformation viewed by some as hopeful and others as ominous. However neither the hopes nor fears that have attended the emergence of TNCs seem justified. On the one hand, TNCs can make a positive contribution to global development by creating jobs, facilitating the transfer of technology, stimulating investment and employment in other industries (through backward and forward linkages), and by modeling better working standards for indigenous firms (e.g., higher wages, employee benefit packages). On the other hand, these corporations can have a negative effect by diverting domestic capital resources away from indigenous firms/industries, by concentrating land ownership in the hands of the wealthy, and by lobbying governments to formulate policies that increase the corporation's profitability but diminish the country's development prospects. On balance, the positive and negative effects of multinational corporations probably cancel each

Table 10.3

The 100 Largest GDPs and Gross Annual Revenues for Countries and Transnational Corporations in 1984

Country/Corporation	GDP/Gross Annual Revenue (in millions of U.S. $)
1. United States	3,634,600
2. Japan	1,255,006
3. U.S.S.R.	1,213,660a
4. Federal Republic of Germany	613,160
5. France	489,380
6. United Kingdom	425,370
7. Italy	348,380
8. Canada	334,110
9. China	281,250
10. Brazil	187,130b
11. Australia	182,170
12. Mexico	171,300
13. India	162,280
14. Spain	160,930
15. Islamic Republic of Iran	157,630b
16. Netherlands	132,600b
17. Poland	130,820a
18. Saudi Arabia	109,380
19. German Democratic Republic	105,500a
20. Sweden	91,880b
21. Switzerland	91,110
22. Exxon	88,561
23. Republic of Korea	83,220
24. Indonesia	80,590

Country/Corporation	GDP/Gross Annual Revenue (in millions of U.S. $)
51. Philippines	32,840
52. Hong Kong	30,620
53. Libya	30,570
54. Egypt	30,060
55. Greece	29,550
56. Malaysia	29,280b
57. United Arab Emirates	28,840
58. Pakistan	27,730
59. Standard Oil (Indiana)	27,635
60. Standard Oil of California	27,342
61. General Electric	26,797
62. Gulf Oil	26,581
63. Atlantic Richfield	25,147
64. ENI	25,022
65. IRI	24,518
66. New Zealand	23,340b
67. Israel	22,350
68. Kuwait	21,710
69. Unilever	20,292
70. Chile	19,760b
71. Toyota Motor	19,741
72. Shell Oil (Houston)	19,678
73. North Korea	19,500a
74. Occidental Petroleum	19,116
75. Portugal	19,060

25.	Royal Dutch/Shell Group	80,551
26.	Belgium	77,630
27.	Czechoslovakia	76,430a
28.	Argentina	76,210
29.	General Motors	74,582
30.	Nigeria	73,450
31.	South Africa	73,390b
32.	Austria	64,460
33.	Romania	64,250a
34.	Yugoslavia	60,150a
35.	Norway	54,720
36.	Mobil	54,720
37.	Denmark	54,640
38.	Finland	51,230
39.	Algeria	50,690
40.	Hungary	49,920a
41.	British Petroleum	49,195
42.	Venezuela	47,500
43.	Turkey	47,460
44.	Ford Motor	44,455
45.	Thailand	41,960
46.	IBM	40,180
47.	Texaco	40,068
48.	E. I. du Pont de Nemours	35,378
49.	Columbia	34,400
50.	Bulgaria	33,730a

76.	Peru	18,790
77.	Francaise des Petroles	18,350
78.	Ireland	18,270b
79.	Singapore	18,220
80.	Elf-Aquitaine	18,188
81.	U.S. Steel	16,869
82.	Matsushita Electric Industrial	16,719
83.	Petrobras	16,258
84.	Philips' Gloeilampenfabrieken	16,177
85.	Pemex	16,140
86.	Syrian Arab Republic	15,930
87.	Hitachi	15,804
88.	Siemens	15,724
89.	Nissan Motor	15,698
90.	Volkswagenwerk	15,693
91.	Daimler-Benz	15,660
92.	Cuba	15,418a
93.	Phillips Petroleum	15,249
94.	Sun	14,730
95.	United Technologies	14,669
96.	Bayer	14,616
97.	Hoechst	14,558
98.	Renault	14,468
99.	Fiat	14,467
100.	Tenneco	14,353

a = GDP estimates for 1984 at 1980 prices (figures for N. Korea and Cuba are 1980)—Source: The WEFA Group (Wharton Econometric Forecasting Associates)

b = Gross Domestic Product, 1983

Sources: ''The Fortune International 500,'' *Fortune*, August 20, 1984; the WEFA Group (Bala Cynwyd, PA); World Bank, *World Development Report, 1986* (Washington, D.C.: World Bank, 1986).

other out (although this neutral assessment could be easily contested in many parts of the world).

Potentially, though, multinational corporations could play a very positive role in economic development if the governments of the host countries are able to regulate effectively the activities of such corporations. The fact that TNCs are often perceived either as agents of neocolonialism or as profit-seeking ogres without community loyalties lends political strength to attempts by LDCs and MDCs to regulate their activities. Eventually one would expect that the growth of TNCs will strengthen the individual investor rights against the state powers of expropriation, although the trend is going in the other direction at the present time, as exemplified by the 1974 U.N. Charter of Economic Rights and Duties of States. Moreover, one would anticipate that TNCs will encourage the development of global norms of professionalism and facilitate the uninhibited transfer of technology.

While it is unclear how IGOs, INGOs, an TNCs will ultimately fare in the struggle for power and prestige within the society of states, there is little doubt that the twin engines of economic interdependence and regionalism significantly augment the capabilities of such nonstate actors. Considered in isolation, neither economic interdependence nor regionalism provide a sufficient foundation for global integration. For example, interdependence could intensify global tensions due to increasing perceptions of vulnerability and ballooning conceptions of national interests. Similarly, regionalism could conceivably lead to further economic and political segmentation within the global system. Yet where these two powerful forces are associated with IGOs or INGOs that have the ability (1) to regulate effectively the frequent sorts of interstate interventions that are inevitable in interdependent relations (O. Young, 1982) and (2) to facilitate the development of nonisolationist and inclusive concepts of political identity (Lasswell, 1972), then economic interdependence and regionalism can contribute significantly to global integration and the development of state-transcendent norms.

It is significant, for example, that the agreements concluded by the European Economic Community (EEC) and the Commission of Euratom are binding on member states, and that the EEC exercises "quasi-legislative powers over matters normally within the sphere of a national legislature, for example in regard to customs tariffs" (Brownlie, 1979, p. 689). Moreover, both the Court of Justice of the European Communities and the High Authority of the European Coal and Steel Community enjoy direct jurisdiction in their respective economic sectors within member states of the EEC. Coincidentally, it should be noted that the European Court of Human Rights—mandated by the European Convention for the Protection of Human Rights and Fundamental Freedoms of 1950 but ultimately established in 1959—is the only international tribunal that grants access to complaints from private citizens against member states (Brownlie, 1979, pp. 584–588).

The phenomenal growth and dissemination of IGOs and INGOs can only partly be attributed to the twin forces of economic interdependence and region-alism. In most instances, such organizations were spawned from collective at-tempts, on the part of states or individuals, to address specific global problems that require cooperative (and often highly technical) initiatives for their resolu-tion. These global issue areas, or what Coate (1982) has aptly termed "Global Issue Regimes," are located at the margins of individual state power. They include issue areas such as nuclear proliferation, arms control, economic de-velopment, international public health measures, population control, seabed ex-ploitation, trade reforms, and so forth. Significantly, it appears that there is a positive correlation between the magnitude of INGO participation by a country and the degree of global consciousness attained within the country (Angell, 1973). Examples of existing IGOs and INGOs that play leading roles within their respective issue areas include the World Health Organization (WHO), the U.N. Conference on Trade and Development (UNCTAD), the World Bank Group, the International Air Transport Association (IATA), the Food and Ag-riculture Organization (FAO), the International Telecommunication Union (ITU), the International Olympic Committee, the General Agreement on Tariffs and Trade (GATT), Amnesty International, the Universal Postal Union (UPU), and the International Labor Office (ILO). With the steady encroachment of "low politics" (e.g., trade and economic development) upon "high politics" (e.g., peace and security issues), one would expect that IGOs and INGOs that concern themselves with global issue areas within the purview of social and economic areas will grow in scope and influence, as Keohane and Nye (1972, p. 377) have suggested. This is not to suggest, though, that the effectiveness of nonstate actors in the global arena is confined to "low politics." For example, it is noteworthy that the first mutual on-site verification of nuclear weapons tests between the United States and the Soviet Union was privately negotiated by two nongovernmental organizations: the Natural Resources Defense Council, based in New York City, and the Soviet Academy of Sciences in Moscow (Duffy, 1986).

Finally, the development of the amorphous yet discernible entity known as "international public opinion," a by-product of the communications revolution, is destined to play an increasingly prominent role in the development of state-transcendent international legal norms. While it is certainly inadvisable to make facile inferences concerning the erosion of state power and the evolution of "central guidance systems" on the basis of an expanding "planetary conscious-ness," due to the highly uneven global distribution of participatory governments (Stone, 1984) and the notable lack of awareness about international affairs among the mass publics of LDCs (Dominguez, 1981), international public opinion does play a critical role in providing diffuse social pressure against the violation of integral humanitarian norms. Presumably the establishment of the long-proposed U.N. High Commissioner for Human Rights would strengthen the role of in-ternational public opinion in this respect. It seems clear that until international law develops a reasonably effective system of coordinated sanctions against the violation of international legal norms, international public opinion will function as an important constraint on the exercise of state power against human beings— in many cases it will be the only constraint.

10.4. THE BASIC NEEDS MANDATE AND HUMANITARIAN INTERVENTION

International public opinion functions as an important trend-setter for international law, particularly in the area of human rights. For example, on the one hand, there currently is a strong conviction within international public opinion that no state has the right to commit acts of genocide (e.g., Hitler's final solution, the systematic slaughter of the Hutu by the Tutsi in Burundi) and related atrocities (i.e., systematic massacre or enslavement that is not necessarily directed against any identifiable ethnic religious or political group, such as Amin's Uganda or Pol Pot's Kampuchea) against members of its own population. Yet, on the other hand, within the current structure of international law there are no legal sanctions whatsoever for individual "self-help" or collective "humanitarian intervention" by concerned states for the purposes of obstructing the genocidal policies of a state regime (Harff, 1984; Kuper, 1981). In fact, there is overwhelming evidence that humanitarian justifications for military interventions designed to obstruct genocidal policies carry little or no weight in the international legal order, being expressly forbidden by the sacred taboo of nonintervention (Akehurst, 1984). Hence the concept of the inviolable personhood of the state becomes a perverse legal permission for states to raze the personhood of its own citizens.

One would anticipate that the growing influence of international public opinion on world affairs will have the effect of extending the notion of the sovereign equality of states to include the equal rights of all human beings. An important conceptual requisite in facilitating the movement from sovereign equality to the equality of basic human rights will be the reformulation of the notion of sovereign equality on grounds other than the imputed personhood of the state. Without such a conceptual reformulation, the norm of nonintervention will certainly continue to enjoy its cherished status within the community of states. The question facing us is: How can we rescue the valuable notion of the sovereign equality of states from the ill-defined and indefensible notion that state regimes should be regarded as inviolable persons?

This question brings us back to the discussion of the BNM and political systems in Chapter 8, section 8.1. It was argued that political legitimacy is derived from a regime's ability and willingness to make significant inroads in meeting the BN of its population. In light of this understanding of political legitimacy, regimes that systematically deny basic human rights to their citizens tacitly forfeit their right to rule. The immediate effect of such systematic deprivation is that the coefficient of revolution would increase, depending upon the (1) extent of deprivation, (2) the availability and desirability of alternate political leadership,

(3) the potential of securing a broad base of support among political constituencies, and (4) strategic military considerations. However, it may take decades for the coefficient of revolution to increase to such an extent that intolerable conditions spawn a major revolutionary effort against the central regime.

Does the discussion of political legitimacy in section 8.1 imply that any state that is not making significant inroads in BN satisfaction tacitly forfeits its right to be recognized as a sovereign state by other states? If so, this would interject a great deal of instability into the international order, making the right of foreign state intervention symmetrical with the right of domestic revolution. Clearly such a move would be unacceptable in terms of actual international practice. Yet how are we to reconcile the decisive role of BN satisfaction in terms of domestic political legitimacy with the BNM's more restrictive scope in applications involving interstate relations?

In addressing this question, two considerations should be noted at the outset. First, there is typically a significant degree of parallelism between the intended goals of popular revolutionary movements and the best interests of the state, particularly in the case of revolutions that are sanctioned by the BNM. By contrast, most foreign interventions lack any such parallelism of interests. Consequently there is extremely high probability that most military interventions by foreign states will be primarily motivated by the geopolitical interests of the invading state (with humanitarian justifications being employed as one of the grounds for intervention). A recent example of this lack of parallelism of interest would be the invasion of Kampuchea by Vietnam. Moreover, both Japan and Germany invoked humanitarian reasons to justify their respective interventions into Manchuria in 1931 and Czechoslovakia in 1938 (Sztucki, 1974, p. 51). In fact, a survey of military interventions between 1827 and 1972, in which the intervening state justified its actions on humanitarian grounds, concluded the following: "History shows that when humanitarian justification has been invoked, it has mostly been under circumstances in which there is at least a strong suspicion that the facts and usually the motive, were not as alleged" (Franck and Rodley, 1973). Second, as Michael Walzer (1980) has emphasized, the right to revolution is a permission that may be exercised by the populace when necessary, but it is not a mandatory obligation. Individual citizens are still free to choose whether or not they wish to join the revolution, but no such sphere of choice exists in external military intervention.

Both of these considerations suggest that the right to revolution cannot be placed on a par with the right of intervention. Yet neither consideration provides us with a decisive reason as to why the BNM might sanction a revolution while, at the same time, proscribe intervention by foreign states that would achieve the very same BN outcome as the revolution (a theoretical possibility, although quite improbable in practice). In order to justify an asymmetry between the right of revolution and the right of intervention, we must return to the notion of territorial aggression.

It was argued in Chapter 3, section 3.1.c that territorial aggression is an enduring fact of human life and presumably has some basis in the human genetic code. Certainly the most obvious manifestation of territorial aggression is that humans routinely defend their immediate advertised territory and, by extension, their community and nation against outside intruders. Presumably most forms of foreign intervention, even those motivated by beneficent humanitarian considerations, would incite resentment and invite defensive modes of territorial aggression. To expect otherwise is to deny the reality of human territoriality and the *prima facie* human mistrust of outgroups. Just as a police officer intercedes in a hostile family conflict only to find that both parties suddenly turn their energies against the benevolent outsider, one would expect that, in most instances, a military intervention will be perceived as a hostile invasion in the eyes of the country's citizens, irrespective of the BN improvements that such an intervention may bring about.

Obviously, though, if the state commits gross human rights violations through genocidal policies or related atrocities (i.e., systematic massacre or enslavement) any military intervention by a foreign state will be perceived by the affected population more as liberation than as an occasion for despair (unless there are long-standing tribal or racial antipathies between the two states). This suggests that military intervention is justified in the extreme cases of genocide or related atrocities, where the mistreatment of a citizenry by foreign occupying troops definitionally *cannot* exceed the suffering they experience at the hands of their own government. However the same would not be true in the case of less acute violations of human rights—violations that may justify domestic revolution but would not justify foreign intervention.

Hence the BNM's understanding of political legitimacy must necessarily make some concession to the facts of human territoriality when it comes to the recognition of a state by other states. To argue otherwise is to deny the existence of a recurrent feature of human behavior. Yet to endow the state with absolute territorial sovereignty is to deny the very existence of *individual* human territoriality—a state of affairs suited to social insects but hardly appropriate for advanced mammalian species. In short, the asymmetry between the right to revolution and the right to intervention is required by human territoriality and, accordingly, must be respected by the BNM. The very same human characteristic that ultimately grounds a right of revolution similarly grounds a presumption against outgroup intervention (which would include covert intervention as well).

In view of the foregoing considerations, it would appear that the valuable notion of the sovereign equality of states can be transplanted with relative ease from its original conceptual foundation in the analogy of "states as persons" to the moral framework provided by the BNM and its understanding of human territoriality. As a consequence, one state has the same rights and prerogatives as other states in the international order—rights and prerogatives that are grounded in the assumption that states represent a collective extension of the individual territorial rights of the citizens who comprise it. However, this understanding of sovereign equality does not entail the absolute norm of nonintervention that logically followed from the analogy of states as persons. Instead it calls for a *qualified* norm of nonintervention that is revoked when a state's claim of territorial sovereignty involves the blatant disregard of the territorial claims of individual citizens for basic survival. Presumably the ultimate impact of the delinking of absolute territorial sovereignty from the notion of sovereign equality within the international legal order will be to safeguard the notion of the sovereign equality of states by placing it on a sound conceptual foundation and to accelerate the extension of the notion of equal rights from the realm of states to persons.

10.5. JUS COGENS NORMS AND THE INTERNATIONAL ORDER

Perhaps the most significant development of the concept of state-transcendent legal norms in recent times was the introduction of the concept of jus cogens ("compelling law") into the realm of positive international law through the Vienna Convention on the Law of Treaties of 1969 (see Brownlie, 1979, pp. 512–515; Rosakis, 1976; Sinclair, 1984; Sztucki, 1974). The Law of Treaties was the product of years of hard work by the International Law Commission, which began work on the treaty soon after its founding in 1949. On January 27, 1980, the convention came into force with the deposit of the thirty-fifth instrument of ratification or accession. By mid–1988, 57 states have either ratified or acceded to the convention.

The concept of jus cogens, drawn from the realm of municipal law, refers to norms that have a peremptory or overriding character, such that individual states (or a small group of states) do not have the prerogative of contracting out of these fundamental legal obligations (presuming that the violation of these fundamental norms would undermine the social fabric of the international system). Consequently the introduction of the jus cogens concept to international law could accelerate the development of the concept of objective illegality within international law (Rozakis, 1976, p. 27), perhaps eventually paving the way for the development of secondary rules of adjudication within the international legal order (i.e., effective machinery for sanctioning international law).

Article 53 of the Vienna Convention on the Law of Treaties (which was adopted by 87 votes to 8, with 12 abstentions) understands the concept of jus cogens norms in this way:

A treaty is void if, at the time of its conclusion, it conflicts with a peremptory norm of general international law. For the purposes of the present Convention, a peremptory norm of general international law is a norm accepted and recognized by the international community of States as a whole as a norm from which no derogation is permitted and which can be modified only by a subsequent norm of general international law having the same character.

Thus, while the category of jus cogens norms is state-transcendent (once the parties to the convention have given their consent), the identification of those norms of general international law that have achieved the jus cogens status must still be determined by "the international community of States as a whole" (i.e., the so-called test of double consent). The words "as a whole" were inserted by the Drafting Committee as a safeguard against the misuse of the jus cogens concept by states who may desire to invalidate unilaterally existing treaty obligations on spurious grounds. The phrase was not meant to suggest that any state or small group of states had veto power over jus cogens norms (Rosakis, 1976, p. 77).

Of course, insofar as the Vienna Convention is concerned, jus cogens norms refer only to the invalidation of newly concluded treaties (Article 53) or the termination of existing treaties (Article 64). As such, the concept of jus cogens does not yet extend to the unilateral actions or policies of states that do not entail treaty obligations of one kind or another. Moreover, the inadequate procedures for the sanctioning of jus cogens norms, established under the Vienna Convention, suggest that we are a long way from the day the jus cogens norms will be applied to the unilateral actions of states and be backed by some sanctioning machinery. For example, while the convention establishes a procedure for the invalidation or termination of treaty obligations in Articles 65 and 66 (primarily to discourage the arbitrary misuse of the jus cogens concept), these provisions ultimately leave the enforcement of jus cogens norms up to the states who themselves were parties (presumably knowingly) to the treaty that violated a peremptory norm of international law. Consequently the international community lacks direct and effective means of recourse for the enforcement of jus cogens norms beyond the traditional means of diplomacy or exerting pressure through international public opinion.

Beyond the practical difficulties involved in the extension of the jus cogens concept to include the unilateral actions of states and the design of effective sanctioning machinery, there is the important practical problem of identifying jus cogens norms according to the flexible yet tautological definition employed by the drafters of the convention (which places a considerable burden of proof upon those who wish to invoke the jus cogens norms [see Sztucki, 1974, pp. 119–120]). The candidates for jus cogens norms that drew the most support from the participating delegations included the prohibition of aggressive war (13 delegations), the prohibition of genocide (13 delegations), the prohibition of slavery or slave-trade (13 delegations), human rights (7 delegations), the sovereignty of states (7 delegations), the principle of self-determination (6 delegations), and nonintervention in the domestic affairs of other states (5 delegations). Moreover, occasionally the principle *pacta sunt servanda* (i.e., states should enter treaty obligations in good faith and observe agreements) has been designated as a jus cogens norm; however, the logical consequence of this move would be to imbue all of the rules of the law of treaties with the special jus cogens status (Rosakis, 1976, p. 47, n. 3).

The contribution of the BNM to the emergent notion of jus cogens in international law would be to provide clarity in the definition and justification of jus cogens norms. Given the consensual definition of jus cogens norms in Article 53 of the Vienna Convention, it is clear that the BNM's formulation of jus cogens norms must be sensitive to the realities of the international order, avoiding the temptation to proffer a laundry list of commendable moral objectives that significantly exceed the accepted principles of general international law. One would expect that the development and crystallization of the jus cogens concept would significantly heighten the behavioral expectations that states have toward one another, thereby playing a role similar to that of human rights norms in heightening the expectations of international public opinion about the conduct of states.

A logical way of drafting jus cogens norms that both proceeds from the BNM and meets the criteria established in Article 53 of the Vienna Convention would be to identify well-established norms of international law that *must* be respected if the provisions of the BNM are to be realized in the international system. Clearly such necessary conditions for the actualization of the BNM include legal norms prohibiting genocide and related atrocities, aggressive war, state-sponsored terrorism, racial discrimination, slavery, colonization (i.e., the violation of the sovereign equality of states), and the denial of fundamental human rights. With the exception of the final category, there is little doubt that these norms have achieved the jus cogens status, in spite of the fact that we currently lack effective machinery for sanctioning *any* of the above norms.

Presumably it will be some time before the human rights concept gains sufficient definitional clarity and acceptance to graduate to the status of jus cogens norms. Nonetheless, one would anticipate that the historical acceptance of the human rights concept by states will proceed roughly along the lines of the three-tiered schema of the BNM. In other words, human rights norms that prohibit the violation of the biological integrity of the human being (i.e., BN at the X_1 level) will be among the first to be widely received as jus cogens norms. These legal norms would include prohibitions against torture, the mistreatment of prisoners, the denial of basic goods and services, and state-sanctioned forms of murder (e.g., paramilitary death squads). Certainly it will be far more difficult to win agreement concerning human rights norms protecting BN at the X_2 and X_3 levels, including equal access to basic education, access to uncensored information media, and freedoms of expression and association. Consequently, instead of treating human rights as an ill-defined umbrella concept that means different things to different people, it would be better to differentiate the human rights concept into a graduated array of legal norms, encouraging the international community to secure agreement first on the more fundamental of these norms (e.g., prohibition of torture, state-sanctioned forms of murder) in moving up the BN ladder. To insist on an all-or-nothing strategy for human rights would ultimately lead to the denigration of the human rights concept and widen the gulf between political rhetoric and state practice.

Certainly the most conspicuous omissions from the above listing of jus cogens norms are the principle of nonintervention and the principle of self-determination. The principle of nonintervention does not qualify as a jus cogens norm because it contradicts the BNM by valuing the territorial integrity of the state over the territorial integrity of human beings, and it creates a logical inconsistency between the observance of the principle of nonintervention and future attempts to develop international machinery for sanctioning jus cogens norms. To regard nonintervention as a jus cogens norm is to insist that the peremptory norms of international law are *logically* incapable of being sanctioned by force—a doctrine that would subvert the fundamental legal character of the principles of international law.

The omission of the principle of self-determination from the BNM's list of jus cogens norms is not related to decisive reasons arguing against its inclusion but rather proceeds from the absence of strong arguments that favor its elevation from a norm of international law to a peremptory norm. As previously noted, the principle of self-determination is fraught with conceptual ambiguities and, therefore, has been pressed into the service of a variety of less-than-noble causes. In light of these inherent ambiguities, any proposal to bestow the special jus cogens status on self-determination warrants considerable reflection and certainly a more precise understanding of self-determination than is currently available. Moreover, the fact that all of the manifestations of colonialism can be addressed by the conceptual apparatus of the sovereign equality of states suggests that the addition of the principle of self-determination neither advances nor clarifies our understanding of the peremptory norms of international law. In a more practical vein, it is not apparent, on the basis of state practice, that the principle of self-determination is even an accepted norm of international law, insofar as the principle has been invoked by secessionist movements within newly independent states.

In effect, the introduction of the jus cogens concept into positive international law provides the BNM with a kind of normative niche by establishing, on a conceptual plane, a mechanism that may facilitate the development of direct links among moral theory, international public policy, and international law. Without such a linkage, the conceptual integration of the BNM with international law would be extremely difficult, if not impossible, This is not to suggest, though, that the practical integration of the BNM with international law will be easy—with or without the jus cogens concept. Instead one imagines that the actual conduct of states will be affected by conceptual breakthroughs in international law only after a considerable lapse of time, meaning that patience and discernment will be among the cardinal virtues of those who anticipate that international legal concepts and practices will one day approximate the widely shared moral intuitions that the BNM supports and clarifies.

10.6. A DEVELOPMENTAL SCHEMATIC OF INTERNATIONAL LAW, 1648–2110 AD

Despite the fact that we have a very long way to go before the fundamental precepts of the BNM are mirrored in actual state practice, past historical experience is quite encouraging. Figure 10.1 presents a conjectural schematic of the development of international law from 1648 to 2110 AD.[1] Undoubtedly the most striking feature of this schematic sketch of international law concerns the dramatic advances that have taken place in the historical periods t_1 through t_5, spanning less than 350 years. We have moved from a highly decentralized and fragmented collection of states to a decentralized yet moderately integrated international system. In t_1 we lacked established mechanisms for diplomatic relations and treaty-making, legal proscriptions against the use of aggressive force (except breaches of neutrality), and universal norms beyond the prohibition of piracy. By t_5 we have achieved a standing international court, an elaborate multilateral treaty governing the access to and use of the sea and its resources, a well-established (albeit ineffective) concept of illegal aggressive force, and a universal organization of states established to preserve peaceful relations among nations and to promote fundamental human rights. While these achievements are inadequate to meet the global challenges ahead, one cannot help but be impressed by the striking progress that has been made to date.

Although the task of predicting the future is probably best reserved for either prophets or fools, the temptation to extrapolate a plausible scenario for the future development of international law is almost irresistible. From our present vantage point, one could imagine that historians of the 22nd century will view the brief 15-year period of t_4 as a decisive period in the formation of international law. However, there are good reasons to believe that the critical period in the development of international law—if there is a single crucial moment—lies in the near future, perhaps during the latter half of t_6.

During t_6 the twin forces of rapid population growth in LDCs and dwindling nonrenewable energy sources available to MDCs will place incredible strains on the international system, either leading to self-destructive forms of protectionism or stimulating the development of global issues regimes concerned with the rational utilization of the earth's resources. With the convergence of these two factors, along with the increased probability of nuclear terrorism, states will have a strong vested interest in validating the viability of the state-centric system.

It is likely that a coalition of the more powerful states will respond to this situation by forming an array of ad hoc international crisis management teams that would probably operate outside of the United Nations Organization. These crisis management teams could be granted temporary emergency powers by the coalition of states in order to resolve critical resource allocation problems within the international system. Assuming that the power base of many LDC regimes will be consolidated and relatively secure by this time and that the influence of state socialist regimes will be declining, it is likely that the claims for absolute territorial sovereignty will be attenuated in the face of the glaring need for strong international cooperation.

Presumably the patterns of cooperation that emerge from the critical period of t_6 will experience significant elaboration and intensification during the course of t_7. One would imagine that a high degree of regional and international inte-

Figure 10.1
Conjectural Schematic of the Development of International Law, 1648–2110 AD

	t₁		t₂		t₃
	1750		1850		1945
1648 Peace of Westphalia					

	t₄		t₅		t₆		t₇	
1945		1960		2010		2060		2110

t₁ = Development of the notion of state sovereignty based upon a minimalist concept of statehood (i.e., "organized states"); no clear test of "civilization" yet for membership in the society of states; no conceptual limitations of diplomatic relations on religious grounds; emergence of the concept of the balance of power

t₂ = Expansion of the international system with European exploration and colonization; the specific rules of international law are not differentiated along cultural lines; conceptual preoccupation with the definition of the state and the legal status of its appendages (e.g., territorial sea); mechanisms established for the creation and maintenance of diplomatic relations and treaties; the emergence of the law of war and neutrality (although nations were free to go to war, they could not violate breaches of neutrality); the only universally condemned behavior was piracy (to which slave-trade was later added)

t₃ = Development of the notion of the personhood of the state; the notion of statehood became increasingly important (with states defined in terms of unified social structures with a territorial base) and was ultimately dependent on European recognition; the test of 'civilization' was highly Euro-centric, however diplomatic structures were extended to non-European states (which began to exercise their influence on the international system); the creation of a code of war; the emergence of international organizations of states with the development of procedures for arbitration and conciliation; the establishment of the first standing international court (1922); a substantial reconceptualization of the legitimate use of force in international law

t_4 = Transition from a Westphalia conception of international law to a Charter conception; establishment of first universal organization of states devoted to the maintenance of peace; the onset of rapid decolonization; the increasing influence of non-European states in the international system; the creation of the International Law Commission with the increased codification of international law; the development of the concept of the exclusive rights of coastal states over resources of the continental shelf; the emergence of human rights norms as quasi-legal standards in the international order

t_5 = Development and intensification of bloc politics, especially centered upon the formation of the Group of 77 as a distinct bargaining entity; the ascendancy of the principle of self-determination and the acceleration of decolonization; the increasing prominence of "low politics" in international relations; the development of global issues regimes and the enhanced proliferation and prominence of IGOs, INGOs and TNCs; development of the notion of permanent sovereignty over natural resources and new attitudes toward expropriation; the continued elaboration of the human rights concept; the introduction of the jus cogens concept to international law

t_6 = Development of the jus cogens concept to include the unilateral actions of states; the crystallization of the human rights concept; the increased prominence of global issues regimes in international relations (particularly in the fields of population control, anti-terrorism, economic development and trade reforms); a significantly enhanced role for IGOs and INGOs; increased support for the use of military force in humanitarian interventions when situations warrant it; the attenuation of claims for absolute territorial sovereignty (related, in part, to the decline of state socialism and the consolidation of governmental power in LDCs)

t_7 = Attainment of a high degree of regional and international integration at both the economic and political levels; the establishment of resource management agencies (that begin as ad hoc crisis management teams in t_6, comprised primarily of the most powerful states) which have restricted yet compulsory jurisdiction over certain economic and natural resource areas; a gradual easing of East-West and North-South tensions; a gradual increase in the appearance of representative governments; the nascent formation of formalized and effective sanctioning machinery against state-sponsored terrorism, later extended to include genocide.

213

gration could be achieved during this period, accompanied by the establishment of permanent international resource management agencies (i.e., institutionalized versions of the ad hoc crisis management teams of t_6) that could be given restricted yet compulsory jurisdiction over certain economic and natural resource areas. Moreover, the possibility exists that t_7 will witness the appearance of formalized and relatively effective sanctioning machinery for genocide and state-sponsored terrorism. Presumably much of this sanctioning machinery will only be established in the wake of some commonly perceived international threat; and, unfortunately, the most likely candidate in this regard is the use of low-yield nuclear weapons in terrorist actions. Presumably the specter of nuclear terrorism will haunt international relations throughout much of the 21st century, and the possibility exists that either t_6 or the early half of t_7 will witness at least one incident of nuclear terrorism. One could imagine that after the first or second incident of nuclear terrorism, an intense backlash will develop among nation-states, provoking the formation of effective sanctioning machinery against terrorist actions and the states that harbor terrorist groups. Once this sanctioning machinery is in place, it could be extended to include military sanctions against states that have instituted policies leading to genocide and related atrocities (assuming that the jus cogens concept continues to mature). Eventually it is conceivable that such effective international machinery could sanction the initiation of aggressive wars, although it is highly unlikely that this will take place in t_7. Instead one would imagine that this development will not take place until we are well into the 22nd century or later.

Two prominent conclusions emerge from this conjectural scenario of the development of international organization and international law. The first is that the establishment of centralized spheres of authority within the international system will come about neither by the abnegation of state power nor the abrogation of the consent of states, but instead will proceed from the self-interested desire of states to demonstrate the viability of the state-centric international system. However the concerted attempt by states to address critical resource management issues (precipitated by the earth's burgeoning population and the depletion and increasing cost of nonrenewable energy sources) will most likely set in motion a pattern of cooperation that leaves the major outlines of the state-centric system fundamentally intact but ultimately dooms the notion of absolute state sovereignty, rendering it an ideological relic of the past. Therefore a kind of paradoxical situation obtains in which states will be forced to accept limitations on their own power in their frantic efforts to preserve the essential structure of the state-centric system. Obviously none of this will take place overnight; however, change could occur very rapidly. For example, one would hope that the early patterns of interstate cooperation that emerge from the ad hoc international crisis management teams will have a kind of wildfire effect, spreading rapidly throughout the international system (D. Lewis, 1969, p. 88).

The second conclusion is that we must consciously dismiss the hope (or, for some, dread) of achieving a world government or a Falkian "central guidance system'' at any time in the conceivable future. The hope that the human community will be able to attain such a level of political and economic unity through an expanding planetary consciousness or in the aftermath of nuclear holocaust (as many science fiction accounts suggest) is illusory. Such wishful thinking only reaffirms the pervasive sense of powerlessness that currently characterizes the present human predicament. The notable paucity of representative national governments in the world today, combined with the apparent lack of global awareness among the mass publics of LDCs and the frequency of culturally determined xenophobia within human communities, suggests that one cannot readily draw inferences about dramatic structural changes in the international system on the basis of an expanding planetary consciousness. This is to say nothing of the structural features of the nation-state that militate against the process of globalization (see Giddens, 1985). Moreover, the hope that world unity will emerge in the aftermath of a global disaster, such as nuclear holocaust, reflects far more about the nature of the apocalyptic mind-set (which usually presumes that meaningful change comes only in the aftermath of disaster) than the realities of our present situation. There is no basis whatsoever for the hope that Homo sapiens would emerge from a nuclear holocaust as more enlightened creatures (if they would survive at all), and there are many reasons for believing that such an ecological disaster would set back human cultural evolution decades, if not centuries, or, perhaps, millennia.

Probably the best we can hope for by the mid–22nd century is a level of global economic and political integration that approaches the degree of regional integration that currently exists in the EEC. One wonders whether this is too little too late in view of the pressing global issues bearing down upon the human community. Yet, against those who insist that the survival of the human species is predicated on a dramatic restructuring of the international order, it seems far more advisable to pursue a series of piecemeal coping strategies, investing confidence in human adaptive capacities to weather the crises ahead. Not only are we unable to achieve fundamental structural change in the international system by harping upon dire and dreadful scenarios of the future, but also it is possible that doomsday predictions could exacerbate an already critical situation. Even if Robert Bigelow's (1975, p. 255) assertion that ''humans resort to violence only when faced with social problems too complex for their intelligence'' may be only partly correct, it seems quite apparent that we should strive for political and economic solutions that clearly belong to the realm of the plausible, trusting that such interim measures will be sufficient to carry us through the critical period ahead.

It is difficult to overstate the importance of the maturing human rights concept and the emergent jus cogens concept in helping to lay the groundwork for the structural changes that must take place in t_6. Both the human rights and jus cogens concepts impact the international system by raising the expectations of the citizenry of the world concerning the conduct of states and their responsibilities to their respective population. States, in turn, will be anxious to validate these expectations as a means of extending their own sphere of authority. Yet, as I have suggested, states will be able to live up to these expectations only by engaging in widespread and intensive international cooperation (which will necessarily limit their individual prerogatives), given the special political and economic problems that will converge upon humanity during most of the 21st century.

It should be emphasized that much can be done at this time to limit significantly the trauma of the t_6 transition period through a conscious effort by MDCs to promote the BNA through their foreign assistance policies. The plausible scenario sketched above is not a preferred scenario. By way of contrast, Chapter 11, section 11.2 presents a preferred *and* plausible scenario for the early 21st century, involving a "Global Marshall Plan" as a kind of political incubator for international cooperation.

Through a judicious mix of BN policies, the human community may buy itself time against the deleterious effects of the population crisis, while simultaneously reducing the threat of widespread social instability in both intrastate and interstate contexts. Moreover, the extent of international cooperation required by the implementation of the BNA on a large scale would bring about a degree of global integration that could enable the global human community to negotiate the dangerous shoals of the 21st century successfully.

NOTE

1. The material for the historical segment of the timeline was drawn from Brownlie (1984).

11
Entering the 21st Century

11.1. CONVERGENT CRISES AND THE K-TRANSITION

The specters of nuclear holocaust, overpopulation, widespread ecological destruction, absolute poverty, and political totalitarianism cast a dark, ominous shadow over the future of humankind. Each of these converging crises signals the need for a dramatic shift in the cultural evolution of earth's human communities. The threat of nuclear holocaust no longer permits us to rationalize large-scale war as an adaptive means of conflict resolution and cultural diffusion. The ominous rate of human population growth is a sobering reminder of the need for K-reproductive trajectories that achieve a long-run equilibrium between the size and consumptive habits of human communities and the physical limitations of our planet's resources. The rape and obliteration of many of earth's plant and animal species through environmental pollution, the destruction of fragile habitats, and the senseless hunting of endangered species poignantly attest to the need for the human community to cultivate respect for all life forms. The crisis of absolute poverty is a tragic manifestation of our apathy and indifference toward members of our own species. Finally, the varieties of political totalitarianism—one of the 20th century's gruesome innovations—profess solutions to human predicaments that subordinate the rights and interests of individuals to the prerogatives of wealthy elites or well-entrenched bureaucracies through sophisticated methods of surveillance and control.

Taken individually or collectively, these crises are symptomatic of the precarious phase of human history upon which we have entered—what I call the K-transition. The K-transition refers to the passage between cultural forms that evolved in circumstances of expanding and variable habitats (r-cultures) and cultural systems that are suited to stable habitats at or near their ecological carrying capacity (K-cultures) (see Chapter 3, section 3.5). Table 11.1 presents

Table 11.1
r-Cultures versus K-Cultures for Humans

r-Cultures	K-Cultures
uncontrolled population growth	controlled population growth
poorly integrated social groupings	well integrated social groupings
unmanaged economies	managed economies
altruism rare	altruism common
weak or nonexistent regulatory mechanisms for governing intra- and inter-specific competition for resources	strong regulatory mechanisms for governing intra- and inter-specific competition for resources
energy utilization extensive	energy utilization intensive

a suggestive list of the traits associated with r-cultures and K-cultures in human communities.[1]

The most prominent feature of K-cultures is their moderate to high degree of regulation. The laissez-faire character of r-cultures and their social institutions is conspicuously absent. The regulatory landscape of K-cultures is explained, in part, by the keen competition for resources that usually attends K-selection. In the case of human beings, such competition for scarce resources could yield socially sanctioned forms of unmitigated narcissism (as in the case of the Ik culture in Northern Uganda [Turnbull, 1972]) or culturally acceptable forms of regulation. Since it is highly improbable that humans could optimize their adaptive capabilities in social contexts characterized by unmitigated egoism, we are left with some form of regulation for governing the competition over scarce resources. In essence, the evolutionary pressure of human intelligence and sociality takes over where natural selection leaves off. Hence some degree of regulation will be necessary if human communities are to achieve social stability in highly competitive contexts.

In this regard, it is interesting to note that r-culture fantasies about the colonization of space or earth's oceans (as a response to K-conditions) represent both the denial and affirmation of the inevitability of increasingly regulated environments. On the one hand, such fantasies represent the denial of K-conditions by perpetuating the myth of expanding habitats and geographic frontiers. On the other hand, the technological requirements of such exotic habitats presume a high degree of regulation and intragroup coordination, signaling a new set of constraints upon human freedom and behavior.

The troubling dimension of the greater degree of regulatory mechanisms within K-cultures concerns the extent to which such cultures will be able to preserve a genuine sense of individual freedom within the inherent constraints of bureaucratic oversight and management. Certainly totalitarian forms of socialism represent both inadequate and illegitimate attempts to negotiate the K-transition because of their failure to institute an effective system of checks and balances within the social structure. It is to be hoped that imaginative solutions can be devised for structuring mechanisms of checks and balances within K-cultures that temper the exigencies of environmental regulation with a meaningful sphere of individual choice.

The K-transition represents an especially tenuous and unstable phase of human cultural evolution. Figures 11.1 and 11.2 depict two understandings of the passage from r-cultures to K-cultures. In both figures the K-transition is characterized by a high probability of setbacks or reversals in the evolutionary trajectory from r-cultures to K-cultures. Figure 11.1 understands the K-transition in terms of an uneven yet linear period of instability that is marked by occasional derailment in the form of trapdoors or runaway trajectories that revert the process back to the r-culture origin. By contrast, Figure 11.2 understands the K-transition as a curvilinear trajectory that is characterized by the perceived interchange of prog-

Figure 11.1
Linear Interpretation of the K-Transition

K-Transition

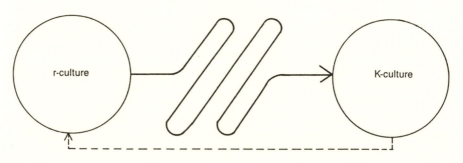

Figure 11.2
Curvilinear Interpretation of the K-Transition

K-Transition

ress and setback that ultimately achieves a stable K-culture. In both the linear and curvilinear interpretations of the K-transition, it is assumed that once a K-culture has been achieved and stabilized, there is always the possibility that a cataclysmic disaster will provoke a lengthy (and adaptive) reversal to an r-culture situation, as signified by the broken line.

Technological and sociological innovations play a critical role in the passage from r-cultures to K-cultures. Without such innovations it would be impossible to negotiate the K-transition; however, the innovations themselves are no guarantee that the transition period will be successful. Table 11.2 presents a rough chronology of selected technological innovations that have enhanced the growth and diffusion of human communities across the planet's diverse habitats:

r-amplification technologies. Table 11.3 represents a suggestive (and admittedly incomplete) list of innovations that have opened up the technological possibility of achieving stable K-cultures. Tables 11.4 and 11.5 apply the concepts of r-amplification and K-amplification to sociological innovations, respectively.

Certainly the bifurcation of key technological and sociological innovations under the r- and K-amplification headings entails some oversimplification and misrepresentation at points, as many r-amplification technological or sociological innovations would also contribute to the achievement of stable K-cultures and vice versa. Nonetheless the classification of technological and sociological innovations into the r- and K-amplification categories is instructive.

The most pronounced difference between r- and K-amplification technologies is the sheer weight of technological innovations that have contributed to the intrinsic rate of population growth (r) among the human species. By contrast, K-amplification technologies consist of very recent innovations, dating from 1838, and are confined primarily to the fields of communication, information management, contraceptive technologies, and transportation. Of particular interest is the way that nuclear and space technologies have played a prominent role as K-amplification technologies. Both technologies have compelled large segments of the human community to recognize the fragility and limits of our planet's resources, as well as the impending K-conditions that will characterize much of the 21st century.

Like K-amplification technologies, K-amplification sociological innovations are of recent vintage, and those that are of particular importance include official development assistance, the intergovernmental organization, the modern bureaucracy, the multilateral treaty, the women's rights movement, nonformal education, and the development project/program. In light of the fact that most of these sociological innovations have come into being only after World War II, one would expect that it will take some time for them to mature. Consequently a generous degree of patience with these K-amplification innovations is warranted.

Ultimately the degree to which individual societies or the global human community is able to negotiate the K-transition and the social tensions it creates will depend upon our ability to evolve rapidly a mature form of species consciousness. If sociobiologists have correctly identified kin altruism and reciprocal altruism as the primary building blocks of human societies to date (see Chapter 3, section 3.1.d), then it could be said that a third kind of altruism must carry us through the K-transition: species altruism. This variant of altruism is manifest in beneficient actions that are directed toward the survival and flourishing of one's own species and respect the habitats and genetic heritage of all life forms. It is based on the identification of the individual with his or her species. Just as kin altruism is related to the identification of the individual with the family/clan and reciprocal altruism emerges from one's identification with the tribe or society, the altruistic concerns and feelings that individuals hold for members of their own species will be ultimately determined by the maturing of their species consciousness.

Table 11.2
r-Amplification Technologies

- pebble tools (2.51 mya)
- hand axes (1.4 mya)
- discovery of fire (600,000 ya)
- the Levallois technique (for the production of stone tools, 200,000 ya)
- the Mousterian technique (for the production of stone tools, 40,000 ya)
- the invention of firing clay (25,000 ya)
- the double-barbed spear (15,000 BC)
- the spear thrower (15,000 BC)
- the bone needle (15,000 BC)
- the arrowhead (15,000 BC)
- pottery (10,500 BC)
- the invention of agriculture (10,000 BC)
- the sickle blade (10,000 BC)
- fortified city (8000 BC)
- the log boat (6400 BC but perhaps developed as early as 50,000 ya)
- the production of textiles (6000 BC)
- the sled (5000 BC)
- the slow potter's wheel (5000 BC)
- copper smelting and smithing (3800 BC)
- Sumerian picto-graphic writing (3600 BC, later evolving into cuneiform)
- bronze production (Thailand, 3500 BC)
- iron production (Thailand, 3500 BC)
- the wheel (3500 BC)
- irrigation system (Egypt, 3400 BC)
- drainage and sewer system (India, 3000 BC)
- the scratch plow (3000 BC)
- dams and canals (Sumer, 3000 BC)
- the shaduf (a water lifting device, 2300 BC)
- clay maps (2200 BC)
- the Babylonian calendar (2200 BC)
- the chariot (2000 BC)
- the miner's pick (2000 BC)
- alphabetic writing (1700 BC)
- network of roads (Babylon, 1700 BC)
- the fast potter's wheel (1500 BC)
- the Egyptian shadow clock (1450 BC)
- Eratosthenes' map (200 BC)

- mass produced cast-iron farm implements (1780)
- power loom (1784)
- steamboat (1787)
- gasoline engine (1791)
- cotton gin (1793)
- food canning (1795)
- carding machine (1797)
- introduction of vaccination (1798)
- voltaic cells (1800)
- macadam roads (1800)
- first practical submarine (1801)
- steam locomotive (1814)
- stethoscope (1815)
- milling machine (1818)
- water-filtration plant (London, 1829)
- sewing machine (1830)
- reaper (1833)
- harvester (1836)
- electric motor (1837)
- first metal ship (1837)
- first postage system (England, 1839)
- brick-making machinery (1839)
- superphosphate fertilizers (1842)
- the telegraph (1844)
- Portland cement (1845)
- pneumatic tire (1845)
- gas-stove burner (1855)
- steel (1856)
- first oil well (1859)
- steamroller (1859)
- ammonia refrigerator (1860)
- asphalt paving (1860)
- germ theory of disease (1861)
- pasteurization (1862)
- dynamite (1866)
- railroad refrigerator car (1868)
- discovery of chromosomes (1873)

- papermaking (China, 100 BC)
- the vertical water wheel (25 BC)
- the crane (25 BC)
- the compass (China, 300 AD)
- printing (China, 800 AD)
- Al-Khwarizmi's treatise on the function of zero (800 AD)
- the heavy plow (900 AD)
- the windmill (950 AD)
- gunpowder (China, 1000 AD)
- moveable type (China, 1050 AD)
- hot-air balloons (China, 1230 AD)
- the use of water mills in silk manufacture (1272 AD)
- ship's compass (1300)
- dissection of the human body, De Luzzi (1310)
- water-driven blast furnace (1320)
- water-driven saw mill (1320)
- Columbus discovers America (1492)
- portable watch (1500)
- Magellan's voyage round the world (1522)
- water pumping works (1548)
- suspension bridge (1550)
- iron-rolling machine (1552)
- lead pencil (1565)
- decimal system (1585)
- knitting frame (1589)
- bituminous coal smelting (1612)
- Harvey's discovery of blood circulation (1628)
- threshing machine (1635)
- cotton manufacture (England, 1640)
- wet sand iron casting (1708)
- lightning jar (1751)
- spinning jenny (1763)
- steam engine (1765)
- cast-iron rails (1767)
- screw-cutting lathe (1770)
- vitamin cure for scurvy (1772)
- reciprocating engine with flywheel (1775)
- circular wood saw (1777)
- steam hammer (1777)

- cure for anthrax (1877)
- electric welding (1877)
- reinforced-concrete beams (1877)
- incandescent lamp (1878)
- ball bearings (1880)
- tuberculosis bacillus isolated (1882)
- first central electric power station (1882)
- hydroelectric plant (1882)
- steam turbine (1883)
- skyscraper with steel frame (1884)
- discovery of micro-organisms responsible for cholera, tetanus, and diphtheria (1884)
- A.C. electric motor (1892)
- automobile (1895)
- diesel oil engine (1895)
- X ray (1895)
- vitamin cure for beri-beri (1897)
- Caterpillar tractor (1900)
- discovery of yellow fever transmission (1901)
- reinforced concrete (1904)
- first assembly-line production of automobiles (Ford Model T, 1907)
- helicopter (1916)
- sonar (1918)
- insulin (1922)
- radar (1922)
- bulldozer (1923)
- vitamin cure for anemia (1924)
- electric refrigerator (1926)
- discovery of penicillin (1928)
- DDT (1939)
- cure for meningitis (1940)
- DNA discovered (1944)
- streptomycin developed (1945)
- cholortetracycline developed (1948)
- neomycine developed (1949)
- polio vaccine (1953)
- open-heart surgery (1955)
- first containerized cargo ships (1957)
- DNA genetic code deciphered (1961)

Source: Compiled from Carlo M. Cipolla and Derek Birdsall, *The Technology of Man* (New York: Holt, Rinehart and Winston, 1979); and R. Buckminster Fuller, *Critical Path* (New York: St. Martin's Press, 1981), pp. 348–377.

Table 11.3
K-Amplification Technologies

— photography (1838)
— first successful transatlantic telegraph cable (1866)
— telephone (1875)
— motion picture machine (1893)
— wireless telegraphy (1895)
— photos by wire (1902)
— completion of the Pacific cable (around the world message in 12 minutes, 1903)
— Wright brothers' engine-propelled airplane flight (1903)
— radio telephone (1915)
— first transatlantic wireless phone two-way conversation (1919)
— first commercial radio broadcast (1920)
— transatlantic telephone service (1921)
— air mail (New York to San Francisco, 1924)
— first commercial airline on regular schedule (1925)
— television (laboratory only, 1927)
— Lindbergh flies nonstop across the Atlantic (1927)
— teletype (1928)
— rocket engine (1929)
— around the world airplane flight (1931)
— first trans-Pacific airplane passenger service (1935)
— portable shortwave beam radio transceiver (1935)
— jet engine (1937)
— first sustained atomic fission (1942)
— first atomic bomb (1945)
— first general-purpose, all-electronic digital computer (1946)
— supersonic air flight (1947)
— transitor invented (1948)
— photo-voltaic cell (1954)
— microwave communication (1955)
— first satellite (Sputnik, 1957)
— birth control pills (1960)
— Telstar communications satellite (1962)
— first use of satellites in T.V. transmission (1965)
— first humans on the moon (1969)
— Boeing 747 jumbo jet (1970)
— oral rehydration therapy (1971)
— gene-splitting technique discovered (1971)
— satellite hookup brings educational TV to 2400 villages in India (1975)
— smallpox completely eliminated from the planet (1978)
— high temperature superconductors (1986)

Source: Compiled from R. Buckminster Fuller, *Critical Path* (New York: St. Martin's Press, 1981), pp. 348–377.

At present, the primary manifestations of species altruism are mediated by religious symbols and counterculture movements. Those who view acts of species altruism from the ideological backdrop of r-cultures tend to interpret them as covert forms of reciprocal altruism (i.e., "there must be something in it for you") or as simply naive manifestations of "do-goodism." Ironically that which looks like sublimated egoism or foolishness from the standpoint of r-cultures becomes a foundational insight for K-cultures.

The BNM, along with other conceptualizations of human rights, represents

Table 11.4
r-Amplification Sociological Innovations

— the hunting and gathering way of life   — 'high god' religious systems

— the clan/tribe   — the empire

— polygamy   — money

— sedentary agriculture   — the market

— the city   — the gymnasium/university

— the king/court   — the nation-state

— war   — the factory

— trade

Table 11.5
K-Amplification Sociological Innovations

— monogamy

— the bureaucracy

— constitutional democracies

— free public education

— the multilateral treaty

— the intergovernmental organization

— official development assistance

— the development project/program

— the multinational corporation

— nonformal educational programs

— women's rights

one facet of the expanding species consciousness that is beginning to sweep the planet. Because the BNM provides us with a nonanthropocentric framework for thinking about human responsibility, we hope it will facilitate the development of a balanced humanism that reconciles claims about human uniqueness with an affirming and noninstrumentalist view of earth's ecosystems. As such, the BNM provides us with a meaningful conceptual foundation for the K-transition. Indeed the ultimate significance of the BNM does not lie in the modest program of sociopolitical change it prescribes, but instead concerns its potential in redefining the self-concept of our species. Presumably real-world sociopolitical change will come very slowly; however, the paradigm shift that underlies glacial progress in the sociopolitical landscape could be of epochal significance in the full sweep of human history.

11.2   A PREFERRED AND PLAUSIBLE FUTURE?

Is it conceivable that a historian from the 22nd century could write the following?

"The year 2000 came and went—neither apocalypse nor millennium occurred. While there was a growing sense throughout the world that significant political and economic changes must take place, no one knew for sure how this would be accomplished or whether makeshift solutions would suffice. For the most part, the attention of the world was riveted on superpower summits, the worldwide AIDS epidemic, global inflation, and a tragic series of famines in sub-Saharan Africa.

"It was not until 2007 that a grass-roots momentum for long-term solutions to the crisis began to gain expression. Numerous religious groups, community organizations, and academic associations sought concrete involvement in the struggle to overcome absolute poverty. What became known as the basic needs movement resembled, in certain aspects, the 19th-century movement in Britain and the United States to abolish slavery. A strong link was established between the goal of meeting basic needs and the concept of fundamental human rights, and development assistance began to be viewed more as a matter of justice than charity. While the first signs of this basic needs movement were sporadic and its impetus was almost completely limited to North America, Western Europe, and Japan, by the late–2010s pockets of the movement had spread to South Asia and Latin America.

"During the early years of the 2010s there was an escalating concern among NATO policy makers that the alliance had grown dangerously weak due to the immense public relations success of *glasnost* (openness) and *perestroika* (restructuring), initiated in the late 20th century by the USSR's Mikhail Gorbachev. On two occasions the Bundeskreig of the Federal Republic of Germany came very close to supporting resolutions calling for the withdrawal of West Germany from NATO, believing that such an action would pave the way for the political reunification of Germany.

"The growing doubts about the viability of the NATO alliance, due to the Soviet rapprochement, were accompanied by strong domestic pressures within the NATO countries to limit military expenditures. The combined effect of the anti-nuclear movement and the basic needs movement in Western Europe led to the gradual realization that, short of a return to the cold war era, the alliance needed to reorient its priorities if it was to survive.

"The loss of vision and purpose experienced by the Western alliance was all the more foreboding in light of the impending resource crisis facing the Third World. The ominous pressures of overpopulation, deforestation, dwindling petroleum supplies, macroeconomic instability, and gross economic inequalities promised to unleash a plague of despair and chaos of a magnitude hitherto unknown in human history. While the superconductor revolution had brought about an early solution to the problem of sustained nuclear fusion, this much-touted innovation had little to offer the poor countries of the world, given their uneven electrical grids and the inability of poor communities to utilize electricity for their daily energy needs. The impending loss of cheap oil, anticipated in the mid–2040s, meant that the petroleum-dependent economies of the Third World would experience severe balance-of-payments problems and acute food grain shortages in the coming decades, due to the skyrocketing prices of oil and petroleum-related products, such as fertilizers and PVC pipe.

"By 2016 the generalized fear of an impending global resource crisis and the specter of the breakup of the Western alliance coalesced with the idealism of the basic needs movement, and the Resource Sharing Initiative (RSI) was born. RSI was dubbed as a ''Global Marshall Plan'' that would usher in a new era of global security in an era of scarce resources. Allusions to the postwar Marshall Plan for the reconstruction of Europe and Japan were constantly on the lips of NATO policy makers. It was hoped by politicians throughout the Western alliance that RSI would engender a new sense of *esprit de corps* throughout the alliance.

"Initially the sponsorship for RSI came primarily from the NATO countries (excluding Greece and Turkey), France, Japan, and Saudi Arabia. Each of the sponsoring countries agreed to become charter members of a special intergovernmental agency that became known as the World Development Authority (WDA). The WDA was comprised of two different types of member countries: donor countries and recipient countries. A maximum of 1,000 votes was established under the WDA's charter—500 of which were allocated for the donor countries and 500 for the recipient countries.

"Each member country had at least one vote in the WDA, and the remaining votes were allocated according to two different formulas—one for donor countries and the other for recipient countries. The remaining votes for donor countries were distributed according to the size of their subscription to the WDA in relation to their respective GNPs. The remaining votes for the recipient countries were allocated on the basis of a rather ingenious formula, devised by economists at the World Bank, which became known as the Performance Index (PI). The index measured performance in three areas (basic needs performance, population control policies, and balance-of-payments performance) on a 100-point scale. Recipient countries with higher PIs were allocated more votes than recipient countries with lower PIs.

"The review of performance criteria and the distribution of votes was charged to a special committee that became known as the Council of Eight. One-half of the council was made up of the two donor countries and two recipient countries with the largest number of votes. The other half of the council was comprised of two donor countries and two recipient countries that rotated annually onto the council. The secretary-general of the WDA, who was elected to a five-year term by the membership, chaired all of the council's meetings and was empowered to break a tie, when that became necessary.

"In addition to the review of performance criteria and the allocation of votes, the Council of Eight was charged with the task of allocating RSI's annual budget among the participating recipient countries. The council made its allocation decisions by weighing a variety of factors (including the country's PI, its past use of funds, and special emergencies), submitting their recommendations to the Board of Governors for ratification.

"Recipient countries could access their development accounts by presenting development project/program proposals that were evaluated by the staff of the World Bank. Once approved, the projects would be funded through their account.

Moreover, under a special provision of the WDA charter, nongovernmental organizations could access a country's development account by presenting project proposals and obtaining the country's approval. Additionally the charter permitted a country to access up to one-third of its account for structural adjustment programs, contingent upon the approval of the International Monetary Fund.

"The early years of RSI were tenuous at best. Despite an impressive start by the WDA (by the end of its second year most of the OECD and Arab OPEC countries joined the WDA and donor-country subscriptions averaged 0.5% of their GNPs), enthusiasm for RSI began to wane by 2019 amid reports of corruption and the misuse of funds. If it had not been for the brilliant leadership of Dr. Willys Geffrard of Haiti, the first secretary-general of the WDA, along with the strong public support for the initiative generated by the basic needs movement in the United States, Canada, France, Scandinavian countries, and Japan, the RSI may not have survived its fifth year.

"By the late–2020s it became evident to most observers that the RSI was an unqualified success. The WDA had brought about an unprecedented level of cooperation between MDCs and LDCs, and a host of nongovernmental organizations had become full participants in the development process. Of special significance was the entry of the People's Republic of China as a *donor* country in 2026—the tenth anniversary of the WDA. The event was hailed by the Chinese as a new chapter in the "shining success story of market socialism." Less than a year after China's decision to join the WDA, Yugoslavia announced its intention to join. By 2029, Hungary, Romania, and Poland had become donor members. With the decision of the Soviet Union to join in the spring of 2031, the remaining Warsaw Pact countries followed suit.

"By 2046, 30 years after the inauguration of RSI, the WDA included nearly every country on the planet. While there were still heated debates about economic inequalities and trade reforms, not to mention the continuing problems with terrorism and nuclear proliferation, it was clear that the momentum was in favor of the human race. The crisis had passed."

11.3 THE EVOLUTION OF HUMAN DIGNITY

The belief in the worth and dignity of the individual human being has been a recurring feature of human cultural evolution. Beginning with the Hebraic idea that man was created in the image of God (Genesis 1:26), most religious and secular ideologies have affirmed, in one way or another, the dignity and worth of the individual. Unfortunately, though, concepts of human dignity have typically been infected by either enthnocentrism or anthropocentrism. As a consequence, the worth and dignity of the individual has either been tied to one's tribal affiliation/ethnic heritage or has been predicated upon imperialistic notions about the powers and prerogatives of the human species over other animal species.

The steady, albeit uneven, evolution of the concept of human dignity is a logical extension of the open genetic program of human life. Figure 11.3 rep-

Figure 11.3
The Open Genetic Program and the Formation of Human Dignity

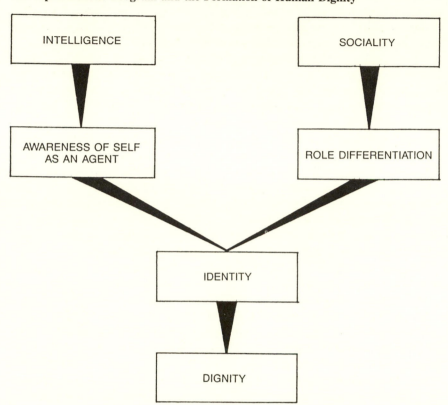

resents one interpretation of the development of human dignity from the open genetic program of human life. The diagram understands dignity as an outcome of a robust sense of identity that proceeds either from the awareness of one's capabilities for agency or from the recognition of one's social role(s). The capabilities conveniently subsumed under the headings of intelligence and sociality have permitted humans to achieve an unprecedented degree of reflective agency in their behaviors and a high level of role differentiation within their communities. Both the awareness of the self as an agent and role differentiation contribute, in varying degrees, to the formation of human identity, which, in turn, facilitates the development of human dignity. Consequently the individual understands him- or herself not only in terms of an organism who is able to formulate and execute behaviors reflectively, but also in terms of the social roles he or she performs in the course of daily existence.

Understandably, particular concepts of human identity (and the notions of dignity associated with them) have often emphasized either the pole of intelli-

gence or sociality, to the exclusion of the other, in the course of their development. As a consequence, human identity has often been conceived in
excessively individualistic or collectivistic terms. On the one hand, concepts of
human identity that are informed primarily by the awareness of the self as an
agent will issue in more individualistic notions of human social behaviors (e.g.,
the social philosophies of the Enlightenment), in which the whole derives its
significance from the part. On the other hand, concepts of human identity that
rely primarily on role-differentiation will generate organic understandings of
human behavior (e.g., Oriental concepts of identity), in which the part finds
significance in its relationship to the whole.

With the industrial revolution and the role plasticity it engendered, concepts
of human identity have been formulated in a decidedly individualistic vein, as
Durkheim (1933) predicted near the turn of the century. The *conscience collective*
of traditional cultures has been replaced by the cult of the individual. Because
industrialization (or modernization) has brought about a wide sphere of choice
and has dramatically altered social roles, it has now become comprehensible to
speak of a nascent world culture that venerates the prerogative of the individual
to formulate his or her own destiny within a moderate sphere of freedom (Dore,
1984). Self-actualization has become a kind of ultimate value that claims a kind
of transcendent, religious aura for itself (Luckmann, 1969).

The concern for the well-being of the individual is evident throughout many
strata of modern social life and represents, in most respects, a very positive
development in human cultural evolution. The priority of intelligence over sociality, discussed in Chapter 2, section 2.4, suggests that concepts of dignity
that are grounded in the recognition of individual agency have a surer foundation
than a notion of dignity based on one's social roles. Moreover, the quest for
self-actualization presumes something of the dignity and worth of the individual,
and, by implication, the dignity of all human beings. Unfortunately, though,
contemporary concepts of self-actualization have devolved into forms of self-
absorption, and individuals tend to define their well-being without reference to
the well-being of others. Consequently we are surrounded with truncated notions
of self-actualization that are characterized by limited scope insofar as the welfare
of others is concerned (see Chapter 5, section 5.4).

The highly individualistic notions of self-actualization in modern life underscore the need for a concept of self-actualization that is meaningfully linked to
some notion of other-actualization. Presumably such a link will be forged in
countless ways as our species proceeds through the K-transition, where the
fortunes of the individual ultimately hinge on the fortunes of the species. Apart
from such substantive connections between the well-being of the individual and
the well-being of others, the concept of self-actualization will become little more
than a legitimation of apathy, and the dignity and worth of the individual will
be forgotten amid the exigencies of narcissistic pursuits. In essence, it is not
possible to truly affirm one's own dignity without affirming the dignity of others,
and the denial of their dignity ultimately entails the denial of one's own.

Certainly the cardinal virtue of the 21st century will be perspective and its two defining characteristics—realism and hope. Without a realistic appraisal of the way things are, as opposed to the way we want them to be, talk of global reforms and institutional change will amount to little more than pipe dreams and empty rhetoric. Yet, without hope we shall lack the energy and creativity to recognize and capture the opportunities for transformation that lie ahead.

In many respects the human community needs to be reinvigorated with a fresh rediscovery of the meaning of faith, defined by the Bible as "the assurance of things hoped for, the conviction of things not seen" (Hebrews 11:1). Somehow, during the darkest days that lie ahead, the human community must keep the faith that our species will rise to the occasion, meet the challenge of globalization, and escape the travail that lies ahead. We must proceed confidently on the assumption that the recognition of the dignity and worth of the individual is irrepressible in the full sweep of human cultural evolution.

The BNM offers the human community an opportunity to affirm its own dignity and to insure a reasonably graceful transition from our lengthy r-culture heritage to a future K-epoch. We face this immense challenge with both the assets and liabilities of our prolonged genetic and cultural heritage as hunter-gatherers. Just as our ancestors looked apprehensively across the hostile and mysterious expanse of the African savanna from their sheltered forest habitat, our eyes strain forward to discern whether the uncertain and foreboding landscape stretched before us will spell our demise or open the way for the flourishing of our species. The events that take place in our lifetimes may determine whether we shall succeed or fail.

NOTE

1. The distinction between r- and K-selection was first developed by MacArthur and Wilson (1967) as a model of density-dependent natural selection in connection with their work on the colonization of islands. Pianka (1970, 1974, p. 90) elaborated the concept by presenting a table of r- and K-selection correlates that became very influential. The controversial aspect of Pianka's elaboration of the r-K continuum was that he linked r-selection to small body size, rapid maturation, a short life span, and productivity; and K-selection was associated with a large body size, slower maturation, a longer life span, and efficiency. Several empirical studies seemed to support aspects of Pianka's correlates (see Gadgil and Solbrig, 1972; McNaughton, 1975); however, some fundamental logical problems with Pianka's extension of the concept have called these r- and K-selection correlates into question (see Boyce, 1984). Consequently most of Pianka's correlates do not appear in Table 11.1.

References

Adelman, Irma, and Morris, Cynthia Taft. (1973). *Economic Growth and Social Equity in Developing Countries*. Stanford, CA: Stanford University Press.

Ahluwalia, Montek S.; Carter, Nicolas G.; and Chenery, Hollis B. (1979). "Growth and poverty in developing countries." *Journal of Development Economics*, 6, 299–341.

Ahluwalia, Montek S., and Chenery, Hollis. (1974). "A model of distribution and growth." In H. Chenery et al., *Redistribution with Growth*. New York: Oxford University Press.

Aiken, William. (1977). "The right to be saved from starvation." In W. Aiken and H. La Follette (Eds.), *World Hunger and Moral Obligation*. Englewood Cliffs, NJ: Prentice-Hall.

Akehurst, Michael. (1984). "Humanitarian intervention." In H. Bull (Ed.), *Intervention in World Politics*. Oxford: Oxford University Press.

Andriole, Stephen J., and Hopple, Gerald W. (1984). *Revolution and Political Instability*. New York: St. Martin's.

Angell, Robert C. (1973). "National support for world order." *Journal of Conflict Resolution*, 17, 429–454.

Archer, Clive. (1983). *International Organizations*. London: George Allen & Unwin.

Arellano, Jose-Pablo. (1985). "Meeting basic needs: The trade-off between the quality and coverage of the programs." *Journal of Development Economics*, 18, 87–99.

Arendt, Hannah. (1958). *The Origins of Totalitarianism*. 2nd ed. Cleveland: World Publishing Co.

Arnold, Steven H. (1982). *Implementing Development Assistance: European Approaches to Basic Needs*. Boulder, CO: Westview.

Arrow, Kenneth J. (1963). *Social Choice and Individual Values*. 2nd ed. New Haven, CT: Yale University Press.

———. (1979). "The trade-off between growth and equity." In H. Greenfield et al. (Eds.), *Theory for Economic Efficiency*. Cambridge, MA: MIT Press.

Ascher, William. (1983). "New development approaches and the adaptability of international agencies: The case of the World Bank." *International Organization*, 37, 415–439.

Austin, James. (1980). *Confronting Urban Malnutrition*. Baltimore: Johns Hopkins University Press.

Axelrod, Robert. (1984). *The Evolution of Cooperation*. New York: Basic Books.

Baldwin, John, and Baldwin, Janice. (1981). *Beyond Sociobiology*. New York: Elsevier.

Ball, Desmond. (1981). *Can Nuclear War Be Controlled?* London: International Institute for Strategic Studies.

Ball, Nicole. (1981). "The military in politics: Who benefits and how." *World Development*, 9, 569–582.

———. (1983). "Defense and development: A critique of the Benoit Study." *Economic Development and Cultural Change*, 31, 507–524.

———. (1984). "Measuring Third World security expenditure: A research note." *World Development*, 12, 157–164.

Balogh, Thomas. (1982). *The Irrelevance of Conventional Economics*. New York: Liveright Publishing Co.

Barash, David P. (1977). *Sociobiology and Behavior*. New York: Elsevier.

Barry, Brian. (1965). *Political Argument*. London: Routledge and Kegan Paul.

Bateson, Patrick. (1982). "Behavioral development and evolutionary processes." In King's College Sociobiology Group (Eds.), *Current Problems in Sociobiology*. Cambridge: Cambridge University Press.

Becker, Lawrence C. (1975). "The neglect of virtue." *Ethics*, 85, 110–122.

Behar, Richard. (1986). "SCF's little secret." *Forbes*, April 21, 106–107.

Beitz, Charles R. (1979). *Political Theory and International Relations*. Princeton, NJ: Princeton University Press.

Belli, Pedro. (1971). "The economic implications of malnutrition." *Economic Development and Cultural Change*, 20, 1–12.

Benoit, Emile. (1973). *Defense and Economic Growth in Developing Countries*. Lexington, MA: Lexington Books.

Berg, Alan. (1981). *Malnourished People: A Policy View*. Washington, DC: World Bank.

Bigelow, Robert. (1975). "The role of competition and cooperation in human evolution." In M. Nettleship et al. (Eds.), *War, Its Causes and Correlates*. The Hague: Mouton.

Blurton-Jones, N. G., and Konner, M. J. (1973). "Sex differences in behavior of London and Bushman children." In R. P. Michael and J. H. Crook (Eds.), *Comparative Ecology and Behavior of Primates*. London: Academic Press.

Boyce, Mark S. (1984). "Restitution of r- and K-selection as a model of density-dependent natural selection." *Annual Review of Ecology and Systematics*, 15, 427–447.

Braybrooke, David. (1987). *Meeting Needs*. Princeton, NJ: Princeton University Press.

Breuer, Georg. (1981). *Sociobiology and the Human Dimension*. Cambridge: Cambridge University Press.

Brodsky, David A., and Rodrik, Dani. (1981). "Indicators of development and data availability: The case of the PQLI." *World Development*, 9, 695–699.

Brody, Baruch. (1975). *Abortion and the Sanctity of Human Life: A Philosophical View*. Cambridge, MA: MIT Press.

Brownlie, Ian. (1984). "The expansion of international society: The consequence for the Law of Nations." In H. Bull and A. Watson (Eds.), *The Expansion of International Society*. Oxford: Oxford University Press.

———. (1979). *Principles of Public International Law*. 3rd ed. Oxford: Oxford University Press.

Bryant, Coralie, and White, Louise. (1982). *Managing Development in the Third World*. Boulder, CO: Westview.

Bueno de Mesquita, Bruce. (1981). *The War Trap*. New Haven, CT: Yale University Press.

———. (1985). "The war trap revisited: A revised expected utility model." *American Political Science Review*, 79, 156–173.

Bull, Hedley. (1984). "The emergence of a universal international society." In H. Bull and A. Watson (Eds.), *The Expansion of International Society*. Oxford: Oxford University Press.

Bundy, McGeorge et al. (1982). "Nuclear weapons and the Atlantic Alliance." *Foreign Affairs*, 60, 752–768.

Burki, Shahid Javed, and ul Haq, Mabub. (1981). "Meeting basic needs: An overview." *World Development*, 9, 167–182.

Burki, Shahid Javed, and Voorhoeve, Joris J. C. (1977). "Global estimates for meeting basic needs: Background paper." Mimeo. Washington, DC: World Bank.

Caliendo, Mary Alice. (1979). *Nutrition and the World Food Crisis*. New York: Macmillan.

Campbell, Donald T. (1979). "Comments on the sociobiology of ethics and moralizing." *Behavioral Science*, 24, 37–45.

Carey, John. (1972). "The international legal order on human rights." In C. Black and R. Falk (Eds.), *The Future of the International Legal Order*. Vol. 4. Princeton, NJ: Princeton University Press.

Carr, Marilyn (Ed.). (1985). *The AT Reader*. New York: Intermediate Technology Development Group of America.

Carter, Gordon. (1977). "The Implications of Basic Services." Address presented to the UNICEF/EADI Workshop on "Basic-needs-oriented Development Strategies and Services," Vienna, December 4–8.

Cassen, Robert. (1976). "Population and development: A survey." *World Development*, 4, 785–830.

Cassen, Robert et al. (1986). *Does Aid Work?* Oxford: Oxford University Press.

Catudal, Honoré M. (1986). *Nuclear Deterrence—Does It Deter?* Atlantic Highlands, NJ: Humanities Press International.

Chambers, Robert. (1981). "Rural poverty unperceived: Problems and remedies." *World Development*, 9, 1–19.

Chenery, Hollis (Ed.). (1974). *Redistribution with Growth*. New York: Oxford University Press.

Chomsky, Noam. (1968). *Language and Mind*. New York: Harcourt, Brace and World.

———. (1976). *Reflections on Language*. New York: Pantheon.

Chossudovsky, Michel. (1986). *Towards Capitalist Restoration: Chinese Socialism After Mao*. New York: St. Martin's.

Churchill, Anthony. (1980). *Shelter*. Poverty and Basic Needs Series. Washington, DC: World Bank.

Coate, Roger A. (1982). *Global Issue Regimes*. New York: Praeger.

Cochrane, Susan H. (1979). *Fertility and Education: What Do We Really Know?* Baltimore: Johns Hopkins University Press.

Cochrane, Susan H.; O'Hara, Donald; and Leslie, Joanne. (1980). "The effects of education on health." World Bank Staff Working Paper, No. 405. Washington, DC: World Bank.

Colclough, Christopher. (1982). "The impact of primary schooling on economic development." *World Development*, 10, 167–185.

Cole, John. (1976). *The Poor of the Earth*. Boulder, CO: Westview.

Collard, David. (1978). *Altruism and Economy: A Study of Non-Selfish Economics*. New York: Oxford University Press.

Commission on International Development. (1969). *Partners in Development*. New York: Praeger.

Coombs, Philip H. (Ed.). (1980). *Meeting the Basic Needs of the Rural Poor*. New York: Pergamon Press.

Coombs, Philip H. et al. (1973). *New Paths to Learning for Rural Children and Youth*. New York: International Council for Educational Development.

Cooter, Robert, and Rappoport, Peter. (1984). "Were the ordinalists wrong about Welfare Economics?" *Journal of Economic Literature*, 22, 507–530.

Corning, Peter A. (1975). "An evolutionary paradigm for the study of human aggression." In M. Nettleship et al. (Eds.), *War, Its Causes and Correlates*. The Hague: Mouton.

Crook, John H. (1980). *The Evolution of Human Consciousness*. Oxford: Clarendon Press.

Czudnowski, Moshe M. (1982). "Political science and psychology: Some problems in communicating between individual-level and system-level paradigms." In W. Bluhm (Ed.), *The Paradigm Problem in Political Science*. Durham, NC: Carolina Academic Press.

Dalgleish, D. Douglas, and Schweikart, Larry. (1984). *Trident*. Carbondale: Southern Illinois University Press.

Daly, Herman. (1977). *Steady-State Economics*. San Francisco: Freeman.

David, Wilfred L. (1985). *The IMF Policy Paradigm*. New York: Praeger.

Dawkins, Richard. (1976). *The Selfish Gene*. New York: Oxford University Press.

———. (1982). *The Extended Phenotype*. Oxford: W. H. Freedman & Co.

Deane, Phyllis. (1978). *The Evolution of Economic Ideas*. Cambridge: Cambridge University Press.

Dell, Sidney. (1982). "Stabilization: The political economy of overkill." *World Development*, 10, 597–612.

Dey, Jennie. (1982). "Development planning in the Gambia: The gap between planners' and farmers' perceptions, expectations and objectives." *World Development*, 10, 377–396.

Di Quattro, Arthur. (1980). "The market and liberal values." *Political Theory*, 8, 183–202.

Dominguez, Jorge I. (1981). "Public opinion on international affairs in less developed countries." In R. Merritt and B. Russett (Eds.), *From National Development to Global Community*. London: George Allen & Unwin.

Dore, Ronald. (1984). "Unity and diversity in world culture." In H. Bull and A. Watson (Eds.), *The Expansion of International Society*. New York: Oxford University Press.

Dubos, Rene. (1968). *So Human an Animal*. New York: Scribners.

Duffy, Michael. (1986). "Public squabbles, private deal." *Time*, July 14, 25.

Dumont, Louis. (1983). *Homo Hierarchicus*. Chicago: University of Chicago Press.

Durkheim, Emile. (1915). *The Elementary Forms of Religious Life*. London: George Allen & Unwin.

———. (1933). *On The Division of Labor in Society*. New York: Macmillan. (Originally published in 1893.)

Duska, Ronald, and Whelan, Mariellen. (1975). *Moral Development*. Paramus, NJ: Paulist Press.

Dworkin, Gerald. (1971). "Paternalism." In R. Wasserstrom (Ed.), *Morality and the Law*. Belmont, CA: Wadsworth.

Dyck, Arthur. (1973). "A unified theory of virtue and obligation." *Journal of Religious Ethics*, 1, 37–52.

Eckstein, Shlomo et al. (1978). "Land reform in Latin America: Bolivia, Chile, Mexico, Peru and Venezuela." World Bank Staff Working Paper No. 275. Washington, DC: World Bank.

Edmonds, D. Keith et al. (1982). "Early embryonic mortality in women." *Fertility and Sterility*, 38, 447–453.

Edwards, Charles S. (1981). *Hugo Grotius, The Miracle of Holland*. Chicago: Nelson-Hall, 1981.

Ehrlich, Paul R. (1971). *The Population Bomb*. 2nd ed. Rivercity, MA: Rivercity Press.

Ekeh, Peter P. (1974). *Social Exchange Theory: The Two Traditions*. Cambridge, MA: Harvard University Press.

Eliade, Mircea. (1954). *The Myth of the Eternal Return*. New York: Pantheon Books.

———. (1959). *The Sacred and the Profane*. New York: Harcourt, Brace & Co.

———. (1961). *Images and Symbols: Studies in Religious Symbolism*. New York: Sheed & Ward.

Ellis, Frank. (1982). "Agricultural price policy in Tanzania." *World Development*, 10, 263–283.

Engels, Friedrich. (1972). "Socialism: Utopian and scientific." In R. Tucker (Ed.), *The Marx-Engels Reader*. New York: W. W. Norton.

Erikson, Erik H. (1968). *Identity, Youth and Crisis*. New York: W. W. Norton.

Estrin, Saul. (1983). *Self-Management: Economic Theory and Yugoslav Practice*. Cambridge: Cambridge University Press.

Etkin, William. (1981). "A biological critique of sociobiological theory." In E. White (Ed.), *Sociobiology and Human Politics*. Lexington, MA: Lexington Books.

Etzioni, Amitai. (1979). "The Kennedy experiment." *Peace Research Review*, 8, 53–89.

Falk, Richard. (1972). "The interplay of Westphalia and Charter conceptions of the international legal order." In C. Black and R. Falk (Eds.), *The Future of the International Legal Order*. Vol. 4. Princeton, NJ: Princeton University Press.

Feinberg, Joel. (1970). *Doing and Deserving*. Princeton, NJ: Princeton University Press.

Finger, Seymour M., and Singh, Gurcharan. (1980). "Self-determination: A United Nations perspective." In Y. Alexander and R. Friedlander (Eds.), *Self-Determination*. Boulder, CO: Westview.

Foot, Philippa. (1979). *Virtues and Vices and Other Essays in Moral Philosophy*. Berkeley: University of California Press.

Fordwor, Kwame D. (1981). "Some unresolved problems of the African Development Bank." *World Development*, 9, 1129–1139.

Forsyth, David J. C.; McBain, Norman S.; and Solomon, Robert F. (1980). "Technical rigidity and appropriate technology in less developed countries." *World Development*, 8, 371–398.

Fotion, N. (1979). "Paternalism." *Ethics*, 89, 191–198.

Fox, M. Louise. (1983). "Income distribution in post–1964 Brazil: New results." *Journal of Economic History*, 43, 261–271.

Franck, Thomas M., and Rodley, Nigel S. (1973). "After Bangladesh: The law of humanitarian intervention by military force." *American Journal of International Law*, 67, 275–305.

Frankena, William. (1973). "The ethics of love conceived as an ethics of virtue." *Journal of Religious Ethics*, 1, 21–36.

Freedman, Daniel G. (1974). *Human Infancy: An Evolutionary Perspective*. Hillsdale, NJ: Lawrence Erlbaum.

Freire, Paulo. (1983). *Pedagogy of the Oppressed*. New York: Continuum.

Freud, Sigmund. (1961). *Civilization and Its Discontents*. New York: W. W. Norton.

Friedlander, Robert. (1980). "Self-determination: A legal-political inquiry." In Y. Alexander and R. Friedlander (Eds.), *Self-Determination*. Boulder, CO: Westview.

Friedman, Edward. (1984). "Three Leninist paths within a socialist conundrum." In D. Solinger (Ed.), *Three Visions of Chinese Socialism*. Boulder, CO: Westview.

Friedman, John. (1979). "Basic needs, agropolitan development, and planning from below." *World Development*, 7, 607–613.

Gabor, Dennis. (1972). *The Mature Society*. London: Secker & Warburg.

Gadgil, Madhav; and Solbrig, Otto T. (1972). "The concept of r- and K-selection: Evidence from wild flowers and some theoretical considerations." *American Naturalist*, 106, 14–31.

Galbraith, John Kenneth. (1978). *The New Industrial State*. 3rd ed. New York: New American Library.

Gallop, Gordon C., Jr. (1983). "Toward a comparative psychology of mind." In R. Mellgren (Ed.), *Animal Cognition and Behavior*. Amsterdam: North Holland Publishing Co.

Galston, William, A. (1980). *Justice and the Human Good*. Chicago: University of Chicago Press.

Gamwell, Franklin. (1984). *Beyond Preferences*. Chicago: University of Chicago Press.

Gardner, R. A., and Gardner, B. T. (1969). "Teaching sign language to a chimpanzee." *Science*, 165, 664–672.

Geertz, Clifford. (1968). *Islam Observed*. Chicago: University of Chicago Press.

———. (1973). "Religion as a cultural system." In *The Interpretation of Cultures*. New York: Basic Books.

Gert, Bernard, and Charles Culver. (1979). "The justification of paternalism." *Ethics*, 89, 199–210.

Gewirth, Alan. (1978). *Reason and Morality*. Chicago: University of Chicago Press.

———. (1979). "Starvation and human rights." In K. Goodpaster and K. Sayre (Eds.), *Ethics and Problems of the 21st Century*. Notre Dame, IN: University of Notre Dame.

Giddens, Anthony. (1979). *Central Problems in Social Theory*. Berkeley: University of California Press.

———. (1981). *A Contemporary Critique of Historical Materialism*. Vol. 1. Berkeley: University of California.

———. (1984). *The Constitution of Society*. Berkeley: University of California Press.

———. (1985). *The Nation-State and Violence*. Berkeley: University of California Press.

Gill, Sam D. (1982). *Beyond "The Primitive": The Religions of Nonliterate Peoples*. Englewood Cliffs, NJ: Prentice-Hall.

Goldstein, Joshua. (1985). "Basic human needs: The Plateau Curve." *World Development*, 13, 595–609.

Gottfried, Kurt; Kendall, Henry W.; and Lee, John M. (1984). " 'No first use' of nuclear weapons." *Scientific American*, 250, (March), 33–41.

Goudzwaard, Bob. (1979). *Capitalism and Progress*. Grand Rapids, MI: Eerdmans.

Goulet, Denis. (1978). *The Cruel Choice: A New Concept in the Theory of Development*. New York: Atheneum.

————. (1983). "Obstacles to world development: An ethical reflection." *World Development*, 11, 609–624.

Gray, Clive, and Marens, Andre. (1983). "The political economy of the 'recurrent cost problem' in the West African Sahel." *World Development*, 11, 101–117.

Green, Reginal H. (1979). "Basic human needs as a strategic focus." In S. Cole and H. Lucas (Eds.), *Models, Planning and Basic Needs*. Oxford: Pergamon Press.

Greene, Thomas H. (1984). *Comparative Revolutionary Movements*. 2nd ed. Englewood Cliffs, NJ: Prentice-Hall.

Griffin, Keith, and Khan, Azizur Rahman. (1978). "Poverty in the Third World: Ugly facts and fancy models." *World Development*, 6, 295–304.

Gurr, T. R., and Bishop, V. F. (1976). "Violent nations, and others." *Journal of Conflict Resolution*, 20, 80–110.

Guyton, Arthur C. (1982). *Human Physiology and Mechanisms of Disease*. 3rd ed. Philadelphia: W. B. Saunders.

Hafez, E. S. E. (1984). "Early embryonic loss: Physiology." In E. Hafez (Ed.), *Spontaneous Abortion*. Lancaster, UK: MTP Press.

Hamilton, W. D. (1964). "The genetical theory of social behavior." *Journal of Theoretical Biology*, 7, 1–52.

Hansen, Roger. (1977). "Major U.S. options on North-South relations: A letter to President Carter." In J. Sewell (Ed.), *The United States and World Development: Agenda 1977*. New York: Praeger.

Harberger, Arnold C. (1984). "Basic needs versus distribution weights in social-cost benefit analysis." *Economic Development and Cultural Change*, 32, 455–474.

Hardin, Garrett. (1977). "Lifeboat ethics: The case against helping the poor." In W. Aiken and H. La Follette (Eds.), *World Hunger and Moral Obligation*. Englewood, NJ: Prentice-Hall.

Harff, Barbara. (1984). *Genocide and Human Rights*. Denver: University of Denver.

Hart, H. L. A. (1961). *The Concept of Law*. Oxford: Oxford University Press.

Healey, Patrick, (1979). "Basic human needs: Methodology and mobilization." HSDRGPID–10/UNUP–62. Tokyo: United Nations University.

Helleiner, Gerald K. (1981). "The Refsnes Seminar: Economic theory and North-South negotiations." *World Development*, 9, 539–555.

Heppenheimer, T. A. (1987). "Signaling subs." *Popular Science*, April, 44–48.

Hertig, A. T. (1967). "The overall problem in man." In K. Benirschke (Ed.), *Comparative Aspects of Reproductive Failure*. New York: Springer-Verlag.

Hicks, Norman. (1979). "Growth vs. basic needs: Is there a tradeoff?" *World Development*, 7, 985–994.

————. (1982). "Sector priorities in meeting basic needs: Some statistical evidence." *World Development*, 10, 489–499.

Hicks, Norman, and Streeten, Paul. (1979). "Indicators of development: The search for a basic needs yardstick." *World Development*, 7, 567–580.

Higgins, Benjamin. (1981). "The disenthronement of basic needs: Twenty questions." In H. Nagamine (Ed.), *Human Needs and Regional Development*. Nagoya, Japan: UNCRD.

Higgins, Rosalyn. (1963). *The Development of International Law Through the Political Organs of the United Nations*. Oxford: Oxford University Press.

Hinds, Stewart W. (1976). "On the relations of medical triage to world famine: A historical survey." In G. Lucas, Jr. and T. Ogletree (Eds.), *Lifeboat Ethics*. New York: Harper & Row.

Hirsh, Fred. (1976). *Social Limits to Growth*. Cambridge, MA: Harvard University Press, 1976.

Horvat, Branko. (1976). *The Yugoslav Economic System*. White Plains, NY: M. E. Sharpe.

The Hunger Project. (1985). *Ending Hunger: An Idea Whose Time Has Come*. New York: Praeger.

Hurni, Bettina S. (1980). *The Lending Policy of the World Bank in the 1970's*. Boulder, CO: Westview.

Husak, Douglas. (1981). "Paternalism and autonomy." *Philosophy and Public Affairs*, 10, 27–46.

Hussain, Athar. (1983). "Economic reforms in Eastern Europe and their relevance to China." In S. Feuchtwang and A. Hussain (Eds.), *The Chinese Economic Reforms*. New York: St. Martins.

Huxley, Julian. (1948). *Man in the Modern World*. New York: Mentor Books.

Inhelder, Barbel, and Piaget, Jean. (1958). *The Growth of Logical Thinking*. New York: Basic Books.

International Labor Office. (1977). *Employment, Growth and Basic Needs*. New York: Praeger Publishers.

Isaac, Glynn LL. (1983). "Aspects of human evolution." In D. S. Bendall (Ed.), *Evolution from Molecules to Man*. Cambridge: Cambridge University Press.

Isenman, Paul. (1980). "Basic needs: The case of Sri Lanka." *World Development*, 8, 237–258.

Jameson, Kenneth, and Wilber, Charles. (1981). "Socialism and development." *World Development*, 9, 803–811.

Jayawardena, Lal. (1974). "Sri Lanka." In H. Chenery et al., *Redistribution with Growth*. New York: Oxford University Press.

Jevons, Stanley. (1911). *Theory of Political Economy*. 4th ed. London: Macmillan.

Jones, Derek C. (1980). "Producer co-operatives in industrialised Western economies." *British Journal of Industrial Relations*, 18, 141–154.

Josephson, Wendy L. and Colwill, Nina Lee. (1978). "Males, females, and aggression." In Hilary M. Lips and Nina Lee Colwill (Eds.), *The Psychology of Sex Differences*. Englewood Cliffs, NJ: Prentice-Hall.

de Kadt, Emanuel. (1982). "Community participation for health: The case of Latin America." *World Development*, 10, 573–584.

Kalbermatten, John M.; Julius, DeAnne S.; and Gunnerson, Charles. (1980). *Appropriate Technology for Water Supply and Sanitation*. Washington, DC: World Bank.

Kalbermatten, John M. et al. (1982). *Appropriate Sanitation Alternatives*. Baltimore: Johns Hopkins University Press.

Karadawi, Ahmed. (1983). "Constraints on assistance to refugees." *World Development*, 11, 537–547.

Katouzian, Homa. (1980). *Ideology and Method in Economics*. New York: New York University Press.

Keare, Douglas H., and Parris, Scott. (1982). "Evaluation of shelter programs for the urban poor." World Bank Staff Working Papers, No. 547. Washington, DC: World Bank.

Kelman, Steven, (1981). "Regulation and paternalism." *Public Policy*, 29, 219–254.

Keohane, Robert O., and Nye, Joseph S., Jr. (1972). *Transnational Relations and World Politics*. Cambridge, MA: Harvard University Press.

Khatkhate, Deena. (1982). "Anatomy of financial retardation in a less developed country: The case of Sri Lanka, 1951–1978." *World Development*, 10, 829–840.

Kimura, Doreen. (1979). "Neuromotor mechanisms in the evolution of human communication." In H. Steklis and M. Raleigh, *Neurobiology of Social Communication in Primates*. New York: Academic Press.

King, Russell. (1977). *Land Reform: A World Survey*. London: G. Bell and Sons.

Klein, Robert A. (1974). *Sovereign Equality Among States: The History of an Idea*. Toronto: University of Toronto Press.

Kleinig, John. (1984). *Paternalism*. Totowa, NJ: Rowman & Allanheld.

Knudsen, Odin K. (1981). "Economics of supplemental feeding of malnourished children: Leakages, costs and benefits." World Bank Staff Working Paper, No. 451. Washington, DC: World Bank.

Kohlberg, Lawrence. (1973). "Continuities in childhood and adult moral development revisited." In P. Baltes and K. Schaie (Eds.), *Life-Span Developmental Psychology*. New York: Academic Press.

Kohlberg, Lawrence, and Gilligan, Carol. (1971). "The adolescent as a philosopher." *Daedalus*, 100, 1051–1086.

Kohr, Leopold. (1973). *Development without Aid*. New York: Schocken.

Kornai, János. (1975). "Models and policy: The dialogue between model builder and planner." In Charles R. Blitzer et al. (Eds.), *Economy-Wide Models and Development Planning*. London: Oxford University Press.

———. (1979). "Appraisal of project appraisal." In Michael J. Boskin (Ed.), *Economics and Human Welfare*. New York: Academic Press.

———. (1980). "The dilemmas of a socialist economy: The Hungarian experience." *Cambridge Journal of Economics*, 4, 147–157.

———. (1983). *Growth, Shortage and Efficiency: A Macrodynamic Model of The Socialist Economy*. Berkeley: University of California Press.

Krasner, Stephen. (1983). "Power structures and regional development banks." *International Organization*, 35, 303–328.

Kuhn, Thomas S. (1970). *The Structure of Scientific Revolutions*. 2nd ed. Chicago: University of Chicago Press.

Kuper, Leo. (1981). *Genocide*. New Haven, CT: Yale University Press.

Lal, Deepak. (1976). "Distribution and development: A review article," *World Development*, 4, 725–738.

Lange, Oskar, and Taylor, Fred M. (1938). *On the Economic Theory of Socialism*. New York: McGraw-Hill.

Lasch, Christopher. (1979). *The Culture of Narcissism*. New York: Warner Books.

Lasswell, Harold. (1972). "Future systems of identity in the world community." In C. Black and R. Falk (Eds.), *The Future of the International Legal Order*. Vol. 4. Princeton, NJ: Princeton University Press.

Laughlin, Charles D., and d'Aquili, Eugene G. (1974). *Biogenetic Structuralism*. New York: Columbia University Press.

Lauritsen, Jørgen G. (1976). "Aetiology of spontaneous abortion." *Acta Obstetricia et Gynecologica Scandinavica*, Supplement 52, 1–29.

Lavell, Kit. (1981). "The flying black ponies." In *Everything We Had: An Oral History of the Vietnam War* . . . New York: Random House.

Leakey, Richard E., and Lewin, Roger. (1977). *Origins*. New York: E. P. Dutton.

———. (1978). *People of the Lake*. New York: Doubleday.

Lechtig, Aaron et al. (1975). "Maternal nutrition and fetal growth in developing countries." *American Journal of Diseases of Children*. 129, 553–561.

Lee, Steven. (1981). "On the justification of paternalism." *Social Theory and Practice*, 7, 193–203.

Leipziger, Danny M. (1981a). "The basic human needs approach and North-South relations." In Edwin P. Reubens (Ed.), *The Challenge of the New International Economic Order*. Boulder, CO: Westview.

———. (1981b). "Policy issues and the Basic Needs Approach." In D. M. Leipziger (Ed.), *Basic Needs and Development*. Cambridge, MA: Oelgeschlager, Gunn and Hain.

Leiss, William. (1976). *The Limits to Satisfaction*. Toronto: University of Toronto Press.

Lerner, Abba P. (1946). *The Economics of Control*. New York: Macmillan.

Levi-Strauss, Claude. (1955). "The structural study of myth." *Journal of American Folklore*, 68, 428–444.

Levitsky, Jacob. (1986). "World Bank lending to small enterprises: A review." Industry and Finance Series, Vol. 16. Washington, DC: World Bank.

Lewis, David K. (1969). *Convention: A Philosophical Study*. Cambridge, MA: Harvard University Press.

Lewis, Maureen A. (1981). "Sectoral aspects of a basic human needs approach: The linkages among population, nutrition, and health." In D. Leipziger (Ed.), *Basic Needs and Development*. Cambridge, MA: Oelgeschlager, Gunn and Hain.

Lim, David. (1983). "Government recurrent expenditure and economic growth in less developed countries." *World Development*, 11, 377–380.

Lisk, Franklyn. (1985). "The role of popular participation in basic needs-oriented development planning." In F. Lisk (Ed.), *Popular Participation in Planning for Basic Needs*. New York: St. Martin's.

Little, I. D. M. (1957). *A Critique of Welfare Economics*. 2nd ed. Oxford: Clarendon Press.

———. (1982). *Economic Development*. New York: Basic Books.

Liu, Pak-wai, and Wong, Yue-chim. (1981). "Human capital and inequality in Singapore." *Economic Development and Cultural Change*, 29, 275–293.

Livingston, Dennis. (1972). "Science, technology, and international law: Present trends and future developments." In C. Black and R. Falk (Eds.), *The Future of the International Legal Order*. Vol. 4. Princeton, NJ: Princeton University Press.

Lockett, Martin. (1983). "Enterprise management—Moves towards democracy?:" In S. Feuchtwang and A. Hussain (Eds.), *The Chinese Economic Reforms*. New York: St. Martin's.

Lockheed, Marlaine E.; Jamison, Dean T.; and Lau, Lawrence, J. (1980). "Farmer education and farm efficiency: A survey." *Economic Development and Cultural Change*, 29, 37–76.

Lorenz, Konrad Z. (1966). *On Aggression*. New York: Harcourt, Brace and World.

————. (1981). *The Foundations of Ethology*. New York: Springer-Verlag.

Luard, Evan. (1984). "Collective Intervention." In H. Bull (Ed.), *Intervention in World Politics*. Oxford: Oxford University Press.

Luce, R. Duncan, and Raiffa, Howard. (1957). *Games and Decisions*. New York: John Wiley.

Luckmann, Thomas. (1969). *The Invisible Religion*. New York: Macmillan.

Lumsden, Charles J., and Wilson, Edward O. (1981). *Genes, Mind and Culture*. Cambridge, MA: Harvard University Press.

————. (1983). *Promethean Fire: Reflections on the Origin of the Mind*. Cambridge, MA: Harvard University Press.

Lyons, David. (1976). "Ethical relativism and the problem of incoherence." *Ethics*, 86, 107–121.

Mabogunje, A. L.; Hardoy, J. E.; and Misra, R. P. (1978). *Shelter Provision in Developing Countries*. Chichester, UK: John Wiley.

MacArthur, Robert, and Wilson, Edward. (1967). *The Theory of Island Biogeography*. Princeton, NJ: Princeton University Press.

Maccoby, Eleanor, and Jacklin, Carol. (1974). *The Psychology of Sex Differences*. Stanford, CA: Stanford University Press.

MacIntyre, Alasdair. (1981). *After Virtue: A Study in Moral Theory*. London: Duckworth Press.

Malenbaum, Wilfred. (1982). "Modern economic growth in India and China: The comparison revisited, 1950–1980." *Economic Development and Cultural Change*, 31, 45–84.

Mansbach, Richard W.; Ferguson, Yale E.; and Lampert, Donald E. (1976). *The Web of World Politics*. Englewood Cliffs, NJ: Prentice-Hall.

Marshall, John C. (1980). "On the biology of language acquisition." In D. Caplan (Ed.), *Biological Studies of Mental Processes*. Cambridge, MA: MIT Press.

Marx, Karl. (1964). *Economic and Philosophical Manuscripts of 1844*. New York: International Publishers.

Maslow, Abraham H. (1948). " 'Higher' and 'lower' needs." *The Journal of Psychology*, 25, 433–436.

————. (1970). *Motivation and Personality*. 2nd ed. New York: Harper and Row.

Mata, Leonardo J. et al. (1975). "Survival and physical growth in infancy and early childhood." *American Journal of Diseases of Children*, 129, 561–566.

Mauss, Marcell. (1967). *The Gift: Forms and Functions of Exchange in Archaic Societies*. New York: W. W. Norton.

Maynard Smith, John. (1972). *On Evolution*. Edinburgh: Edinburgh University Press.

————. (1974). "The theory of games and the evolution of animal conflicts." *Journal of Theoretical Biology*, 47, 209–221.

————. (1982). *Evolution and the Theory of Games*. Cambridge: Cambridge University Press.

————. (1983). 'Game theory and the evolution of cooperation." In D. S. Bendall (Ed.), *Evolution from Molecules to Men*. Cambridge: Cambridge University Press.

Mayr, Ernst. (1970). *Population, Species and Evolution*. Cambridge, MA: Harvard University Press.

————. (1976). *Evolution and the Diversity of Life*. Cambridge, MA: Harvard University Press.

———. (1988). *Toward a New Philosophy of Biology*. Cambridge, MA: Harvard University Press.

McCamant, John F. (1981). "A critique of present measures of 'human rights development' and an alternative." In V. Nanda et al. (Eds.), *Global Human Rights*. Boulder, CO: Westview.

McGranahan, Donald; Richard, Claude; and Pizarro, Eduardo. (1981). "Development Statistics and Correlations." *World Development*, 9, 389–397.

McHale, John, and McHale, Magda Cordell. (1978). *Basic Human Needs*. New Brunswick, NJ: Transaction Books.

McNamara, Robert S. (1979). "Address to the board of governors [World Bank]." Belgrade, October 2, pp. 9–10.

McNaughton, S. J. (1975). "r- and K-Selection in Typha." *American Naturalist*, 109, 251–261.

McRobie, George. (1981). *Small is Possible*. New York: Harper and Row.

Medawar, Peter B. (1959). *The Future of Man*. New York: Mentor Books.

de Melo, Martha. (1981). "Modeling the effects of alternative approaches to basic human needs: Case study of Sri Lanka." In D. M. Leipziger (Ed.), *Basic Needs and Development*. Cambridge, MA: Oelgeschlager, Gunn and Hain.

Meulders, M. (1983). "Praxia and language." In M. Monnier (Ed.), *Psycho-Neurobiology*. Amsterdam: Elsevier.

Milgram, Stanley. (1974). *Obedience to Authority*. New York: Harper and Row.

Mill, John Stuart. (1965). *Principles of Political Economy*. New York: Augustus M. Kelly.

Miller, David. (1976). *Social Justice*. Oxford: Oxford University Press.

Miller, J. F. et al. (1980). "Fetal loss after implantation: A prospective study." *Lancet*, 2, 554–556.

Mirrless, James A. (1975). "A pure theory of underdeveloped economies." In L. Reynolds (Ed.), *Agriculture in Development Theory*. New Haven, CT: Yale University Press.

Mishan, E. J. (1975). *Cost-Benefit Analysis: An Informal Introduction*. 2nd ed. London: George Allen and Unwin.

Molyneux, Maxine. (1981). "Women's emancipation under socialism: A model for the Third World?" *World Development*, 9, 1019–1037.

Moore, G. E. (1903). *Principia Ethica*. Cambridge: Cambridge University Press.

Morawetz, David. (1977). *Twenty-Five Years of Economic Development, 1950–1975*. Baltimore: Johns Hopkins University Press.

———. (1978). "Basic needs policies and population growth." *World Development*, 6, 1251–1259.

———. (1980). "Economic lessons from some small socialist developing countries." *World Development*, 8, 337–369.

Morris, Morris David. (1979). *Measuring the Condition of World's Poor: The Physical Quality of Life Index*. New York: Pergamon Press.

Muñoz, Heraldo (Ed.). (1981). *From Dependency to Development*. Boulder, CO: Westview.

Mussen, Paul H., and Eisenberg-Berg, Nancy. (1977). *Roots of Caring, Sharing and Helping*. San Francisco: Freeman.

Myrdal, Gunnar. (1953). *The Political Element in the Development of Economic Theory*. London: Routledge & Kegan Paul.

————. (1970). *The Challenge of World Poverty*. New York: Pantheon Books.

Nagamine, Haruo. (1981). "Studying the basic needs at the micro-area level." In H. Nagamine (Ed.), *Human Needs and Regional Development*. Nagoya, Japan: UNCRD.

Nair, P. R. G. (1979). "Role of primary education in socio-economic change." In M. A. Oommen (Ed.), *Kerala Economy Since Independence*. New Delhi: Oxford and IBH Publishing Co.

National Academy of Sciences. Committee on Resources and Man. (1969). *Resources and Man*. San Francisco: Freeman.

Navari, Corneli. (1982). "Diplomatic structure and idiom." In J. Mayall (Ed.), *The Community of States*. London: George Allen & Unwin.

Neill, Robin F. (1978). "The ethical foundations of economics." *Philosophy in Context*, 7, 86–95.

Nelson, A. D. (1978). "Ethical relativism and the study of political values." *Canadian Journal of Political Science*, 11, 3–31.

Nielsen, Kai. (1966). "Ethical relativism and the facts of cultural relativity." *Social Research*, 33, 531–551.

Noor, Abdun. (1981). "Education and basic human needs." World Bank Staff Working Paper, No. 450. Washington, DC: World Bank.

Norbye, Ole David Koht. (1974). "Adequate health services for poor countries." *World Development*, 2, 13–17.

Nove, Alec. (1983). *The Economics of Feasible Socialism*. London: George Allen & Unwin.

Nozick, Robert. (1974). *Anarchy, State and Utopia*. New York: Basic Books.

Oakeshott, Robert. (1978). *The Case for Worker Coops*. London: Routledge & Kegan Paul.

Okun, Arthur M. (1975). *Equality and Efficiency: The Big Tradeoff*. Washington, DC: The Brookings Institute.

Osgood, Charles E. (1962), *An Alternative to War or Surrender*. Urbana: University of Illinois Press.

Paddock, William, and Paddock, Paul. (1967). *Famine—1975!* Boston: Little, Brown.

Page, John M., Jr., and Steel, William F. (1984). "Small enterprise development: Economic issues from African experience." World Bank Technical Paper, No. 26. Washington, DC: World Bank.

Panikar, P. G. K., and Soman, C. R. (1984). *Health Status of Kerala*. Trivandrum: Centre for Development Studies.

Parsons, Jacquelynne E. (Ed.). (1980). *The Psychobiology of Sex Differences and Sex Roles*. New York: McGraw-Hill.

Partan, Daniel G. (1985). "Increasing the effectiveness of the International Court." In R. Falk, F. Kratochwil, and S. Mendlovitz (Eds.), *International Law: A Contemporary Perspective*. Boulder, CO: Westview.

Pašić, Najdan; Grozdanić, Stanislav; and Radević, Milorad. (1982). *Workers' Management in Yugoslavia: Recent Developments and Trends*. Geneva: International Labor Office.

Patterson, Francine. (1978). "Conversations with a gorilla." *National Geographic*, 154, 438–465.

Paust, Jordan. (1980). "Self-determination: A definitional focus." In Y. Alexander and R. Friedlander (Eds.), *Self-Determination*. Boulder, CO: Westview.

Perkins, Dwight. (1978). "Meeting basic needs in the People's Republic of China." *World Development*, 6, 561–566.

Perkins, Dwight, and Yusuf, Shahid. (1984). *Rural Development in China*. Baltimore: Johns Hopkins University Press.

Piaget, Jean. (1954). *The Construction of Reality in the Child*. New York: Basic Books.

Pianka, Eric. (1970). "On r- and K-Selection". *American Naturalist*, 104, 592–597.

———. (1974). *Evolutionary Ecology*. New York: Harper and Row.

Pilisuk, Marc. (1984). "Experimenting with the arms race." *The Journal of Conflict Resolution*, 28, 296–315.

Pinera, Sebastian, and Selowsky, Marcelo. (1981) "The optimal ability-education mix and the misallocation of resources within education: Magnitude for developing countries." *Journal of Development Economics*, 8, 111–131.

Pomerance, Michla. (1982). *Self-Determination in Law and Practice*. The Hague: Martinus Nijhoff.

Premack, Ann James, and Premack, David. (1972). "Teaching language to an ape." *Scientific American*, 277, No. 4, 92–99.

Prosterman, Roy L., and Riedinger, Jeffrey M. (1987). *Land Reform and Democratic Development*. Baltimore: Johns Hopkins University Press.

Prout, Christopher. (1985). *Market Socialism in Yugoslavia*. Oxford: Oxford University Press.

Pugh, George Edgin. (1977). *The Biological Origin of Human Values*. New York: Basic Books.

Quibria, M. G. (1982). "An analytical defense of basic needs: The optimal savings perspective." *World Development*, 10, 285–291.

Rajeev, P. V. (1983). *Economic Development and Unemployment: Relevance of the Kerala Model*. New Delhi: Asian Publication Services.

Rapoport, Anatol; Guyer, Melvin; and Gordon, David. (1976). *The 2 X 2 Game*. Ann Arbor: University of Michigan Press.

Rati, Ram, and Schultz, Theodore W. (1979). "Life span, health, savings, and productivity." *Economic Development and Cultural Change*, 27, 399–421.

Rawls, John. (1971). *A Theory of Justice*. Cambridge, MA: Harvard University Press.

Raz, Joseph. (1975). "Permissions and supererogation." *American Philosophical Quarterly*, 12, 161–168.

Reinis, Stanislav, and Goldman, Jerome. (1980). *The Development of the Brain*. Springfield, IL: Charles C. Thomas.

Reutlinger, Shlomo, and Selowsky, Marcelo. (1976). *Malnutrition and Poverty: Magnitude and Policy Options*. Baltimore: Johns Hopkins University Press.

Ricci, David M. (1984). *The Tragedy of Political Science*. New Haven, CT: Yale University Press.

Richards, P. J. (1981). "Comment on Isenman, 'Basic needs: The case of Sri Lanka'." *World Development*, 9, 215–216.

Ricoeur, Paul. (1967). *Symbolism of Evil*. New York: Harper & Row.

Robbins, Lionel. (1932). *An Essay on the Nature and Significance of Economic Science*. London: Macmillan.

Roberts, C. J., and Lowe, C. R. (1975). "Where have all the conceptions gone?" *Lancet*, 1, 498–499.

Rondinelli, Dennis A. (1976). "International assistance and development project administration: The impact of imperious rationality." *International Organization*, 30, 573–605

Ronen, Joshua. (1983). "Some insights into the entrepreneurial process." In J. Ronen (Ed.), *Entrepreneurship*. Lexington, MA: Lexington Books.

Rolfe, Barbara E. (1982). "Detection of fetal wastage." *Fertility and Sterility*, 37, 655–660.

Rose, Stephen. (1973). *The Conscious Brain*. New York: Alfred A. Knopf.

Rosenberg, Irwin, H.; Solomons, Noel W.; and Levin, Douglas M. (1976). "Interaction of infection and nutrition: Some practical concerns." *Ecology of Food and Nutrition*, 4, 203–206.

Rothstein, Robert. (1979). *Global Bargaining: UNCTAD and the Quest for a New International Order*. Princeton, NJ: Princeton University Press.

Rozakis, Christos L. (1976). *The Concept of Jus Cogens in the Law of Treaties*. Amsterdam: North-Holland.

Ruse, Michael. (1985). *Sociobiology: Sense or Nonsense?* 2nd ed. Dordrecht, Holland: D. Reidel.

Sacks, Stephen. (1983). *Self-Management and Efficiency: Large Corporations in Yugoslavia*. London: George Allen & Unwin.

Sahlins, Marshall. (1972). *Stone Age Economics*. Chicago: Aldine-Atherton.

———. (1977). *The Use an Abuse of Biology*. Ann Arbor: University of Michigan Press.

Salmen, Lawrence F. (1987). *Listen to the People*. New York: Oxford University Press.

Sankaranarayanan, K. C., and Karunakaran, V. (1985). *Kerala Economy*. New Delhi: Oxford and IBH Publishing Co.

Sartorius, Rolf, ed. (1983). *Paternalism*. Minneapolis: University of Minnesota Press.

Saunders, Robert J., and Warford, Jeremy J. (1976). *Village Water Supply*. Baltimore: Johns Hopkins University Press.

Schelling, Thomas S. (1963). *The Strategy of Conflict*. Oxford: Oxford University Press.

Schelling, Thomas S., and Halperin, Morton H. (1985). *Strategy and Arms Control*. New York: Pergamon.

Schenck, David, Jr. (1976). "Recasting the 'ethics of virtue/ethics of duty' debate." *Journal of Religious Ethics*, 4, 269–286.

Schrenk, Martin; Ardalan, Cyrus; and El Tatawy, Nawal. (1979). *Yugoslavia: Self-Management Socialism and the Challenges of Development*. Baltimore: Johns Hopkins University Press.

Schuh, G. Edward. (1979). "Approaches to 'basic needs' and to 'equity' that distort incentives in agriculture." In T. W. Schultz (Ed.), *Distortions of Agricultural Incentives*. Bloomington: Indiana University Press.

Schultz, Theodore W. (1980). "Investment in entrepreneurial ability." *Scandinavian Journal of Economics*, 82, 437–448.

Schumacher, E. F. (1973). *Small is Beautiful*. New York: Harper & Row.

Schumpeter, Joseph A. (1939). *Business Cycles*. New York: Mc-Graw Hill.

———. (1965). "Economic theory and entrepreneurial history." In H. Aitken (Ed.), *Explorations in Enterprise*. Cambridge, MA: Harvard University Press.

Scoble, Harry M., and Wiseberg, Laurie S. (1981). "Problems of Comparative Research on Human Rights." In V. Nanda et al. (Eds.), *Global Human Rights*. Boulder, CO: Westview.

Scrimshaw, Nevin S.; Taylor, Carl E. and Gordon, John E. (1968). *Interactions of Nutrition and Infection*. Geneva: World Health Organization.

248   References

Sebenius, James K. (1984). *Negotiating the Law of the Sea*. Cambridge, MA: Harvard University Press.

Seers, Dudley. (1977). "Life expectancy as an integrating concept in social and demographic analysis and planning." *Review of Income and Wealth*, No. 3, 195–203.

Self, Peter. (1975). *Econocrats and the Policy Process*. Boulder, CO: Westview.

Selowsky, Marcelo. (1979a). "The economic dimensions of malnutrition in young children." World Bank Staff Working Paper, No. 294. Washington, DC: World Bank.

———. (1979b). "Target group oriented food programs: Cost effectiveness comparisons." *American Journal of Agricultural Economics*, 61, 991–993.

———. (1981). "Nutrition, health and education: The economic significance of complementarities at early age." *Journal of Development Economics*, 9, 331–346.

Sen, Amartya K. (1960). *Choice of Techniques*. Clifton, NJ: Augustas M. Kelly.

———. (1977). "Rational fools: A critique of the behavioral foundations of economic theory." *Philosophy and Public Affairs*, 6, 317–344.

Sheehan, Glen, and Hopkins, Mike. (1979). *Basic Needs Performance*. Geneva: International Labor Office.

Shepard, Thomas H., and Fantel, Alan G. (1979). "Embryonic and early fetal loss." *Clinics in Perinatology*, 6, 219–243.

Shepherd, Gordon M. (1983). *Neurobiology*. New York: Oxford University Press.

Shue, Henry. (1980). *Basic Rights*. Princeton, NJ: Princeton University Press.

Shure, Gerald; Meeker, Robert; and Hansford, Earle. (1965). "The effectiveness of pacifist strategies in bargaining games." *The Journal of Conflict Resolution*, 9, 106–117.

Silber, Jacques. (1983). "ELL (The Equivalent Length of Life) or another attempt at measuring development." *World Development*, 11, 21–29.

Simon, Julian L. (1977). *The Economics of Population Growth*. Princeton, NJ: Princeton University Press.

Sinclair, Ian. (1984). *The Vienna Convention on the Law of Treaties*, 2nd ed. Manchester, U.K.: Manchester University.

Singer, Hans. (1977). *Technologies for Basic Needs*. Geneva: International Labor Office.

Singer, Peter. (1977a). "Famine, affluence, and morality." In W. Aiken and H. La Follette (Eds.), *World Hunger and Moral Obligation*. Englewood Cliffs, NJ: Prentice-Hall.

———. (1977b). "Reconsidering the Famine Relief Argument." In P. Brown and H. Shue (Eds.), *Food Policy*. New York: The Free Press.

———. (1981). *The Expanding Circle: Ethics and Sociobiology*. New York: Farrar, Straus, & Giroux.

Sipes, Richard G. (1975). "War, combative sports, and aggression." In M. Nettleship et al. (Eds.), *War, Its Causes and Correlates*. The Hague: Mouton.

Skjelsback, Kjell. (1971). "The growth of international nongovernmental organizations in the twentieth century." *International Organization*, 25, 422–442.

Spragens, Thomas A. (1973). *The Dilemma of Contemporary Political Theory*. New York: Dunellen.

Srinivasan, T. N. (1981). "Malnutrition: Some measurement and policy issues." *Journal of Development Economics*, 8, 3–19.

Stenhouse, David. (1974). *The Evolution of Intelligence*. London: George Allen & Unwin.

Stewart, Frances. (1985). *Basic Needs in Developing Countries*. Baltimore: Johns Hopkins University Press.

Stone, Julius. (1984). *Visions of World Order*. Baltimore: Johns Hopkins University Press.

Streeten, Paul. (1967). "The use and abuses of models in development planning." In K. Martin and J. Knapp (Eds.), *The Teaching of Development Economics*. Chicago: Aldine.

————. (1979). "Basic needs: Premises and promises." *Journal of Policy Modeling*, 1, 136–146.

————. (1982). "Approaches to a New International Economic Order." *World Development*, 10, 1–17.

Streeten, Paul, and Burki, Shahid Javed. (1978). "Basic needs: Some issues." *World Development*, 6, 411–421.

Streeten, Paul et al. (1981). *First Things First: Meeting Basic Needs in Developing Countries*. New York: Oxford University Press.

Sukhatme, P. V. (1970). "Incidence of protein deficiency in relation to different diets in India." *British Journal of Nutrition*, 24, 447–487.

Sullivan, Michael. (1982). "Transitionalism, power politics, and the realities of the present system." In R. Maghroori and B. Ramberg (Eds.), *Globalism Versus Realism*. Boulder, CO: Westview.

Sztucki, Jerzy. (1974). *Jus Cogens and the Vienna Convention on the Law of Treaties*. Vienna: Springer-Verlag.

Taylor, Phillip. (1984). *Nonstate Actors in International Politics*. Boulder, CO: Westview.

Tendler, Judith. (1975). *Inside Foreign Aid*. Baltimore: Johns Hopkins University Press.

Thirlway, H. W. A. (1985). *Non-Appearance Before the International Court of Justice*. Cambridge: Cambridge University Press.

Thomas, Henk, and Logan, Chris. (1982). *Mondragon: An Economic Analysis*. London: George Allen & Unwin.

Thurow, Lester C. (1984). *Dangerous Currents: The State of Economics*. New York: Vintage Books.

Tinbergen, Niko. (1973). *The Animal in Its World*. Vol. 2. Cambridge, MA: Harvard University Press.

Trigg, Roger. (1983). *The Shaping of Man: The Philosophical Aspects of Sociobiology*. New York: Schocken Books.

Trivers, Robert L. (1980). "The Evolution of reciprocal altruism." In J. Hunt (Ed.), *Selected Readings in Sociobiology*. New York: McGraw Hill.

Turnbull, Colin M. (1972). *The Mountain People*. New York: Simon and Schuster.

————. (1983). *The Human Cycle*. New York: Simon and Schuster.

Tyson, Laura D'Andrea. (1980). *The Yugoslav Economic System and Its Performance in the 1970s*. Berkeley: University of California Press.

U.N. Research Institute for Social Development. (1974). "Report on a unified approach to development analysis and planning." E/CN.5/510. New York: United Nations.

U.S. Agency for International Development. (1976). *A Basic Human Needs Strategy of Development*. Washington, DC: U.S. Government Printing Office.

U.S. Agency for International Development, Development Coordination Committee. (1980). "Evolution of the Basic Human Needs Concept." Washington, DC: USAID.

U.S. Council on Environmental Quality and Department of State. (1980). *The Global 2000 Report to the President*. Vol. 1. Washington, DC: U.S. Government Printing Office.

U.S. Presidential Commission on World Hunger. (1980). *Overcoming World Hunger: The Challenge Ahead*. Washington, DC: U.S. Government Printing Office.

Urmson, J. O. (1958). "Saints and heroes." In A. I. Melden (Ed.), *Essays in Moral Philosophy*. Seattle: University of Washington Press.

Uytenbogaardt, W. (1973). "De Grondstoffenverdeling in de wereld als mogelijke oorzaak van konflikten." [The distribution of raw materials in the world as a possible source of conflicts]. *Transactie*, February.

Vanek, Jaroslav (Ed.). (1975). *Self-Management: Economic Liberation of Man*. Harmondsworth, UK: Penguin.

Van Ness, Peter, and Raichur, Satish. (1983). "Dilemmas of socialist development: An analysis of strategic lines in China, 1949–1981." In *Bulletin of Concerned Asian Scholars* (Eds.), *China From Mao to Deng*. Armonk, NY: M. E. Sharpe.

Vattel, Emmerich de. (1863). *The Law of Nations*. Philadelphia: T. and J. W. Johnson. (Originally published in 1758).

Vogel, Robert C., and Burkett, Paul. (1986). "Mobilizing small-scale savings: approaches, costs, and benefits." Industry and Finance Series, Vol. 15. Washington, DC: World Bank.

Vu, My T. (1985). *World Population Projections 1985*. Baltimore: Johns Hopkins University Press.

Walker, Stephen G. (1979). "New nations and an old model: The applicability of the garrison state theory to the Third World." In S. Simon (Ed.), *The Military and Security in the Third World*. Boulder, CO: Westview.

Walzer, Michael. (1980). "The moral standing of states." *Philosophy and Public Affairs*, 9, 209–229.

Weber, Max. (1946). "Religious rejections of the world and their directions." In H. H. Gerth and C. W. Mills (Eds.), *From Max Weber*. New York: Oxford University Press.

————. (1963). *Sociology of Religion*. Trans. by E. Fischoff. Boston: Beacon Press.

Weigel, Van. (1986). "The Basic Needs Approach: Overcoming the poverty of *Homo oeconomicus*." *World Development*, 14, 1423–1434.

Weintraub, Sidney. (1979). "The New International Economic Order: The beneficiaries." *World Development*, 7, 247–258.

Westermarck, Edward. (1906). *The Origin and Development of Moral Ideas*. 2 vols. New York: Macmillan.

White, Gordon. (1983). "Revolutionary socialist development in the Third World: An overview." In G. White et al. (Eds.), *Revolutionary Socialist Development in the Third World*. Sussex, UK: Wheatsheaf Books.

Wijemanne, E. L., and Earl Wanigasekera. (1980). "Needs—their perception and expression: The Sri Lanka experience." Mimeo. HSDRGPID–21/UNUP–132. Tokyo: United Nations University.

Williams, George C. (1966). *Adaptation and Natural Selection*. Princeton, NJ: Princeton University Press.

Wilson, Brian. (1973). *Magic and the Millennium*. New York: Harper & Row.

Wilson, Edward O. (1975). *Sociobiology: The New Synthesis*. Cambridge, MA: Harvard University Press.

———. (1978). *On Human Nature*. Cambridge, MA: Harvard University Press.

Winick, Myron. (1976). *Malnutrition and Brain Development*. New York: Oxford University Press.

Wolin, Sheldon S. (1969). "Political theory as a vocation." *American Political Science Review*, December, 1062–1082.

Wong, David. (1984). *Moral Relativity*. Berkeley: University of California Press.

World Bank. (1975a). *The Assault on World Poverty*. Baltimore: Johns Hopkins University Press.

———. (1975b). *Land Reform*. Sector Policy Paper. Washington, DC: World Bank.

———. (1978). *Employment and Development of Small Enterprises*. Sector Policy Paper. Washington, DC: World Bank.

———. (1980a). *Water Supply and Waste Disposal*. Poverty and Basic Needs Series. Washington, DC: World Bank.

———. (1980b). *World Development Report, 1980*. New York: Oxford University Press.

———. (1982). *World Development Report, 1982*. New York: Oxford University Press.

———. (1983). *China: Socialist Economic Development*. Vol. 3. Washington, DC: World Bank.

———. (1984). *World Development Report, 1984*. New York: Oxford University Press.

———. (1985). *China: Long-Term Development Issues and Options*. Baltimore: Johns Hopkins University Press.

———. (1986). *World Development Report, 1986*. New York: Oxford University Press.

———. (1987). *World Development Report, 1987*. New York: Oxford University Press.

Worsley, Peter. (1957). *The Trumpet Shall Sound: A Study of the "Cargo" Cults in Melanesia*. London: Macgibbon & Kee.

Young, Clarence W. (1975). "An evolutionary theory of the causes of war." In M. Nettleship et al. (Eds.), *War, Its Causes and Correlates*. The Hague: Mouton.

Young, Mary, and Prost, Andre. (1985). "Child Health in China." World Bank Staff Working Paper, No. 767. Washington, DC: World Bank.

Young, Oran. (1982). "Interdependencies in world politics." In R. Maghroori and B. Ramberg (Eds.), *Globalism Versus Realism*. Boulder, CO: Westview.

Zachariah, K. C. (1984). "The anomaly of the fertility decline in India's Kerala State." World Bank Staff Working Paper, No. 700. Washington, DC: World Bank.

Index

Abortion: and birth defects, 140, 144 n.4; brain-life criterion, 139, 144 nn.2, 3; Gewirth on, 86 n.4; high incidence of spontaneous, 138–39; and phenotypic thresholds, 138–40; and Principle of Comparable Harm, 140; and the quality of life, 58 n.13; and rape/incest, 140

Absolute poverty: magnitude and characteristics, 3–4, 19 n.2; public awareness of, 4–5

Access threshold, 41

Adelman, Irma, 88, 119 n.1

African Development Bank, 90

Aggression: and basic defense needs, 45; dominance, 66–67; scope and intensity among humans, 61, 63–68; sexual, 67–68; territorial, 64–66, 86 n.2; territorial and humanitarian intervention, 205–6; territorial/dominance and economic systems, 63, 181, 185; types of, 64

Agricultural price policies: and Basic Needs Approach, 92; in China, 98, 100; in Tanzania, 92

Ahluwalia, Montek, 105, 119 nn.1, 2

Altruism: contagion thesis, 69; kin selection, 69; maladaptive aspects of, 61–62, 68; reciprocal, 69; species, 62, 221; supererogatory acts, 69, 85, 130–31 n.3

Amnesty International, 49, 203

Anthropocentrism, 62–63, 80, 177, 226, 229

Appropriate technology, 31, 89–90, 106–7, 115

Argentina, 41, 44

Argument from Personal Integrity, 84–85

Aristotle, 18, 27, 74

Arrow, Kenneth, 166, 185

Asian Development Bank, 90

ASNCP (Alternative Submarine National Command Post), 157–58

Australiopithecus, 13

Ball, Desmond, 152–53

Ball, Nicole, 42, 44

Bangladesh, 3, 141–42, 196

Barefoot doctors, 31, 39, 99

Barry, Brian, 23, 57 n.1

Basic education, 45–46

Basic needs (BN): basic education/literacy, 45–48, 58 n.11; and contraceptive technologies, 47–48, 137–40; employment, 49–50; external rank-ordering and weighting, 55–56; first- and second-order goods, 29; interclass rankings, 29–30; interclass weights, 53–55; intraclass rankings, 51–55; leisure/recreation, 50; minimum nutrition, 35, 37; municipal protection/national defense,

About the Author

VAN B. WEIGEL received a Ph.D. in Ethics and Society from the University of Chicago and holds a Master of Divinity degree from Eastern Baptist Theological Seminary. His doctoral dissertation explored the ethical dimensions of the Basic Needs Approach to economic development, and the preliminary findings of his research were published in *World Development*. Dr. Weigel is currently Assistant Professor of Economic Development at Eastern College in St. Davids, Pennsylvania, and he also serves as the field education director for the school's MBA/MS Programs in Economic Development.

Dr. Weigel is the founder and Executive Director of Basic Needs International, a nonprofit organization that sponsors participatory seminars on global development and assists colleges and universities in "globalizing" their educational curricula. More information about Basic Needs International and its development education programs may be obtained by writing: Basic Needs International, P.O. Box 36, Wayne, PA 19087.